FEMALE ENTERPRISE IN THE NEW ECONOMY

D0730315

The rise of women's self-employment and small business ownership has received a great deal of attention in North America and industrialized countries around the world. In *Female Enterprise in the New Economy*, Karen D. Hughes examines whether an increasingly entrepreneurial economy offers women better opportunities for economic success, or instead increases their risk of poverty and economic insecurity.

Drawing on original data from interviews, statistical research, and other sources, Hughes explores the reasons why women are starting businesses in record numbers. She looks at the type of work that entrepreneurial women are pursuing, the satisfaction they derive from their work, and the economic risks and rewards they face. Placing this study in the context of broader debates on economic restructuring, the emergence of a 'risk society,' and growing economic polarization, Hughes illustrates the diversity within women's self-employment and small business ownership, and the need for policies to better address the particular needs of this sector of the workforce.

Tackling a range of issues and theoretical assumptions, *Female Enterprise in the New Economy* will be of interest to a wide audience in a number of disciplines, including sociology, organizational studies, entrepreneurship studies, public policy, political economy, and women's studies.

KAREN D. HUGHES is an associate professor in the Faculty of Arts and in the School of Business at the University of Alberta.

KAREN D. HUGHES

Female Enterprise in the New Economy

UNIVERSITY OF TORONTO PRESS
Toronto Buffalo London

© University of Toronto Press Incorporated 2005
Toronto Buffalo London
Printed in Canada

ISBN 13: 978-0-8020-8917-5 (cloth)
ISBN 10: 0-8020-8917-8 (cloth)
ISBN 13: 978-0-8020-8672-3 (paper)
ISBN 10: 0-8020-8672-1 (paper)

Printed on acid-free paper

Library and Archives Canada Cataloguing in Publication

Hughes, Karen D., 1960–
Female enterprise in the new economy / Karen D. Hughes.

Includes bibliographical references and index.
ISBN 0-8020-8917-8 (bound).   ISBN 0-8020-8672-1 (pbk.)

1. Women-owned business enterprises – Canada.   2. Self-employed
women – Canada.   3. Businesswomen – Canada.   4. Entrepreneurship –
Canada.   5. Small business – Canada.   I. Title.

HD6072.C2F43 2005   338'.04'0820971   C2005-903698-2

This book has been published with the help of a grant from the Canadian
Federation for the Humanities and Social Sciences, through the Aid to
Scholarly Publications Programme, using funds provided by the Social
Sciences and Humanities Research Council of Canada.

University of Toronto Press acknowledges the financial assistance to its
publishing program of the Canada Council and the Ontario Arts Council.

University of Toronto Press acknowledges the financial support for its
publishing activities of the Government of Canada through the Book
Publishing Industry Development Program (BPIDP).

For my parents, George and Doreen Hughes
And for Barry and Sam
With love and thanks

Contents

Figures and Tables

Figures

Tables

Acknowledgments

I have always been interested in small business and entrepreneurship. But it was not until the late 1990s, when I received a grant from the Social Sciences and Humanities Research Council, that I was in a position to study the issue. By then Canada was in the midst of a 'self-employment boom,' and women were very much at its centre. In many ways the timing of this project was opportune, allowing me to observe first hand a significant economic transition as it unfolded in the Canadian economy and the lives of Canadian women.

For supporting this research, I am extremely grateful to the Social Sciences and Humanities Research Council, who funded this project both through their Standard Grants Program and through the Thérèse Casgrain Fellowship, which I held in 2001–02. Special thanks also to the board of the Thérèse Casgrain Foundation for their interest in this research, and for their ongoing commitment to funding research on women and social change in Canada. Completing this project would not have been possible without support from the University of Alberta, who provided start-up and release-time grants from the Central Research Fund and the Faculty of Arts' Support for the Advancement of Scholarship. I greatly appreciate this support.

Writing this book has been both a pleasure and challenge, the process lightened by the generosity of many people. My most immediate debt is to the women who agreed to be interviewed for this book. Despite hectic work and family lives, they opened their offices and workplaces, offering rich insights into the joys and rewards of their work, as well as the hardships and risks. I appreciate their candour, thoughtfulness, and interest in this project, and for sharing one of their most valuable resources – their time.

Carrying out this research would not have been possible without the first rate assistance of Tricia Bell and Deana Hall-Hoffarth, who helped recruit participants, carry out interviews, compile data, and review final transcripts. I greatly appreciate their contribution and hard work at so many important stages. I also want to thank those who helped recruit women into the study, in particular Jill Hilderman at Alberta Women's Enterprise Initiative Association (AWEIA), Jean Crozier, Sonia Bitar of Changing Together, and Linda Nider at Connecting Women. Finally my thanks to Liz Jobagy and Joanne McKinnon for their skilled administrative support, and to Nickela Anderson for her assistance as this manuscript neared completion.

Over the years the ideas in this book have taken shape through conference presentations, work in progress, and in the course of general conversation. I am enormously grateful to my colleague Graham Lowe for his valuable comments and encouragement on earlier drafts of this manuscript, and for his generous mentoring and collaboration over the years. I also wish to thank many others who have invited presentations, commented on papers, encouraged my work, and challenged my thinking, in particular Tricia Bell, Bob Blackburn, Sarmite Bulte, Jennifer Cliff, Dallas Cullen, Benoit Delage, Andrea Doucet, Judy Fudge, Harvey Krahn, Judith Maxwell, Kathryn McMullen, Susan McDaniel, Kiran Mirchandani, Gregor Murray, Barbara Orser, Gillian Ranson, Barry Scholnick, Susan Smith, Leah Vosko, Dave Wallace, and Nancy Zukewich. My thanks also to Grant Schellenberg, formerly of Canadian Policy Research Networks (CPRN), for his help with the job quality data used in Chapter 4 from the CPRN-Ekos *Changing Employment Relationships Survey*, and to Judith Maxwell and Ron Saunders for making these data available. At the University of Toronto Press, I want to thank Virgil Duff, Anne Laughlin, Diane Mew, and the anonymous reviewers, for their helpful comments and feedback on this manuscript. Thanks also to Noeline Bridge for so carefully preparing the index.

Though most of the material in this book is original and has not been previously published, I have drawn selectively on some of my earlier writing on this topic. Some sections of Chapter 3 update and extend material found in 'Pushed or Pulled? Women's Entry into Self-Employment and Small Business Ownership,' *Gender, Work and Organization* 10, 4 (2003). Parts of Chapter 6 draw from 'Rethinking Policy for the "New Economy": The Case of Self-Employed Women,' *Saskatchewan Law*

Review 67, 2 (2004), and a 2001 HRDC working paper entitled 'Self-Employment, Skill Development and Training in Canada.'

Finally, I am enormously grateful to my wonderful family and friends for providing support, perspective, and welcome diversion as this project has taken shape. To my parents, George and Doreen, I owe a very special thanks for the love and support, and gifts of education and opportunity, they have so generously given me. I also want to thank our amazing friends at the University (UITC) daycare, especially Mary Badu-Acheaupong, Kim Gravel, Kelly Hanrahan, Shannon Marquette, and Rebecca Solis-Damas, without whom this book could not have been written. To my partner Barry, who encouraged this book in so many ways, and my son Sam, who entered this world while it was being written, I am deeply grateful. Their joyful presence and support makes all things possible.

FEMALE ENTERPRISE IN THE NEW ECONOMY

1 Introduction

There's risk in everything. You know? You're an employee today, there's a risk that you're not going to be an employee tomorrow.

(Reta, Interview B02)

I do everything from cooking to cleaning to shopping ... I am a 'one woman show.'

(Janice, Interview C18)

It's very, very stressful. You have to be up for the stress ... You have to take the risk. Otherwise you'll never reap the benefits.

(Susan, Interview A01)

I was going down the elevator and this man ... said 'So dearie, is the boss letting you go early today? And I laughed and I said, 'I am the boss.'

(Celine, Interview B12)

At first glance it is hard to see what connects these individuals, to see what sets them out as markers of the 'new' economy. They are diverse workers in diverse worksites – residential, commercial, suburban, inner city. Some are 'business moms,' juggling the demands of family and business from cramped offices or kitchen tables of busy suburban homes. Others are 'one woman shows,' running bustling cafés and restaurants around the city. Growing numbers are 'bosses,' working in manufacturing plants or the gleaming towers of the downtown core. Others fill tiny strip-mall shops that dot the city's landscape, jostling for customers alongside Wal-Mart, Starbucks, and other giants of today's global economy. Looking across these workplaces, it is hard at first to see the connections, to see what they might share. But the thread running through them is the people working within them. They are all women, all business owners, all self-employed.

Together these women, and thousands of others like them, make up one of the surprise stories of the twenty-first-century economy in Canada: the dramatic rise of self-employment and small business ownership (SE/SBO).[1] After declining for much of the twentieth century, self-employment has witnessed a renaissance in many industrialized countries and, in Canada, this trend has been especially dramatic (Hughes 2003b; OECD 2000a; Tal 2000). Since the mid-1970s, self-employment has accounted for one-quarter of all job growth in Canada, and its importance has accelerated over time. In the early to mid-1990s, when economic downturn and extensive public and private sector restructuring brought job growth to a near halt, nearly three-quarters of all new jobs in the economy were created through self-employment. Even after the economy rebounded towards the end of the decade, self-employment still accounted for 58% of all job growth in the 1990s, compared to just 18% in the 1980s (Picot and Heisz 2000). Canada entered the twenty-first century with nearly one in every six people self-employed, accounting for 2.4 million Canadians (Statistics Canada, CANSIM II Series 2522952). Of these, more than eight hundred thousand were women. Most were solo workers, but a growing number had employees. Together they contributed an estimated $18 billion to the Canadian economy (Canada 2003).

Rising self-employment and small business ownership marks not just a significant material change in the employment relationships and structure of the Canadian labour market, but also an important cultural shift in individual and public ways of thinking about employment and work. Indeed, over the past two decades, public policy and debate in Canada and many other countries have increasingly promoted the merits of entrepreneurship and an 'enterprise culture' – celebrating the ideals of individual initiative and self-reliance, and emphasizing self-employment as a solution to the problem of high and persistent unemployment that has plagued many industrialized countries. Against this largely positive view, however, has also emerged a more critical perspective – one that sees self-employment not as a solution to, but as a result of, deeply rooted economic and political change. Viewed from this perspective, self-employment and small business ownership is 'risky business': a form of precarious work that individu-

Figure 1.1
Percentage of Self-Employed Women and Men, Canada, 1976–2003

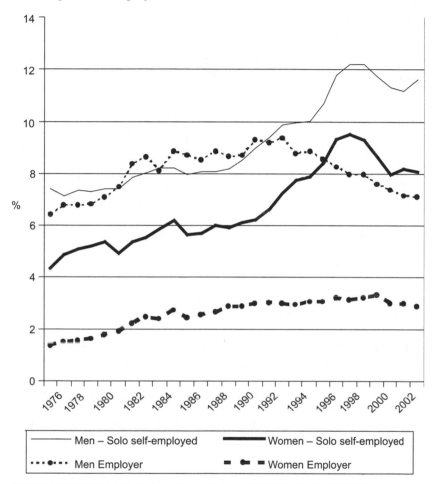

Source: Statistics Canada, *Labour Force Survey*, CANSIM II Series 2522952

als have increasingly been forced into as once secure, full-time jobs in the Canadian economy have declined.[2]

Taken together, these contrasting views spark many critical questions about the growing role of self-employment and small business ownership in the Canadian labour market, and its implications for workers, the economy, and our society. At one level are basic empirical questions about the extent of change, and the nature of this work compared to more traditional forms of employment. But beyond these lie broader questions about the implications for individuals, their working lives, and the economy and society as a whole. Embedded within all these issues are particularly important questions about the gendered dimensions of such change. In many industrialized countries, such as Canada, the United States, and Britain, women have made particularly notable gains within the overall expansion of self-employment and small business.[3] Indeed, as Figure 1.2 shows, Canada is a leader in this regard (see also OECD 2000e; OECD 1997).

Commentators have questioned whether women are pursuing this as an emancipatory route to bypass gender segregation within paid employment, or whether women have been increasingly pushed into marginalized forms of self-employment as economic restructuring has eroded the availability of more secure forms of paid work. To date, we do not know the answers to these questions in Canada as we lack detailed information on women's self-employment and small business ownership, and a fully gendered analysis that is placed in the context of economic restructuring and change.

This book takes up the issue of women's self-employment and small business ownership in Canada, examining recent trends and considering the economic, personal, and policy consequences of this type of work for women. It draws on two primary sources of empirical data: national-level survey and labour-market data such as the *Labour Force Survey* and the *Survey of Self-Employment in Canada*; and an in-depth study of sixty-one women engaged in small and micro-businesses. Working between these two sources, as well as existing academic research and policy discussions, I explore a number of questions that are central to understanding the growing importance of this type of work in the Canadian economy: Why are women entering self-employment and small business ownership in such numbers? What forces motivate or propel them into such work? What is the nature of their work, their job quality, and job satisfaction? How do they fare financially? What risks do they face?

Beyond exploring the meaning of self-employment and small business ownership for women themselves, I also consider some of the broader academic and policy questions raised by this work. In particular, what insights do these women's experience offer to debates over economic restructuring and the emergence of the 'new' economy?

Figure 1.2
Women's Share of Self-Employment (%), Selected Industrialized Countries, 2001

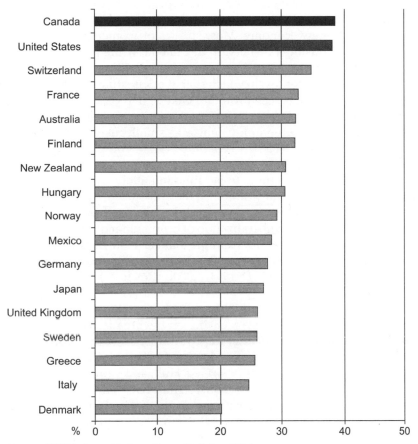

Source: OECD, Annual Labour Force Statistics, 2001

What policy needs and gaps emerge with growing numbers of self-employed workers and small business owners in the Canadian economy, and how can they be best addressed? In posing these questions, I hope to offer a detailed portrait of 'female enterprise in the new economy' – assessing its risks and rewards, its potential and pitfalls, and the extent to which it conforms or departs from conventional ideas about business and the entrepreneurial economy.

Economic Restructuring and the 'New' Canadian Economy

In taking up these themes, I deliberately place this study against the backdrop of debates over economic restructuring, and the shift from the so-called old to new economy. Most studies of women's self-employment and small business ownership in Canada, while providing valuable insights on a range of issues, pay scant attention to the broader social and economic context in which such work is situated. Yet Canada, like other countries, has seen profound change in recent years – change that has reshaped available employment and, some would argue, the level and nature of self-employment and small business ownership itself. While the notion of a new economy is an ongoing point of debate (see, for example, OECD 2000b), most commentators agree that economies have been, and continue to be, fundamentally transformed by a complex set of factors. Central amongst these are globalized trading and production, new technologies, emerging knowledge-based industries, and the deregulation and liberalization of economic activity both within and between countries (see, for example, Bakker 1996; Beck 1995; Betcherman and Lowe 1997; Duffy et al. 1997; ECC 1991; Florida 2002; Harvey 1990; Leadbeater 2000; OECD 1994, 2000b; Reich 2001; Sassen 2002; Wood 1989).

Many terms have been used to describe this qualitative shift in economic and social life. Analysts focusing on the broader economy have posited a shift from an industrial to post-industrial society (Bell 1973), Fordist to post- (or neo) Fordist production (Aglietta 1979; Jessop 1990), old to new capitalism (Sennett 1998; Gee, Hull, and Lankshear 1996), or managed to entrepreneurial economy (Audretsch and Thurik 2001). Those concerned with firm behaviour argue that a shift has occurred from bureaucratic to flexible firms (Atkinson 1984) or to flexible specialization (Piore and Sabel 1984), with workforces now divided between insiders and outsiders (Kalleberg 2003). For individuals, the change is said to involve a shift from traditional employment relationships and careers, to boundaryless careers (Arthur and Rousseau 1996), portfolio careers (Cohen and Mallon 1999; Handy 1994), free agent status (Pink 2001), non-standard or contingent work (ECC 1990; Krahn 1991, 1995; Kalleberg 2000), vulnerable work (Saunders 2003), or precarious work arrangements (Vosko et al. 2003).

While there are important differences between many of these ideas, at the centre of each is the belief that a fundamental shift has occurred in contemporary economic and social life – one where work organization is far more flexible and contingent, and individuals are increasingly detached from what have been called traditional or standard employment relationships (Fudge et al. 2002a; Lowe and Schellenberg 2001; Vosko 2000). Significantly, at the same time that these changes have unfolded, women's employment patterns have also dramatically changed. The intersection of these trends raises important questions about the gendered nature of economic restructuring in industrialized countries – in particular, the extent to which women have been benefi-ciaries within newly expanding occupations and industries, or have instead seen economic opportunities erode through downsizing, deskilling, and the casualization of work.

To date, research on restructuring in Canada has not explored the full range of consequences for women, tending either to ignore gender in the analysis of broad trends (for example, Beck 1995; Osberg et al. 1995) or to focus on selected issues in relation to women. In feminist scholar-ship, for example, there has been excellent analysis of broad economic trends (Armstrong 1996, 1997; Connelly 1996; Zeytinoglu and Muteshi 2000), as well as specific issues such as part-time work, temporary work, downsizing, and free trade (for example, see Bakker 1996; Duffy and Pupo 1992; Luxton and Corman 2001; Vosko 2000). But many other areas deserving attention remain unexplored. Self-employment and small business ownership is a key issue in restructuring economies, vastly under-researched relative to its growing role (Aldrich 1999: 8). By examining self-employment and small business ownership – an area that has been widely touted as a key site of opportunity for women in the new economy – this study seeks to contribute to current academic research, policy development, and public understanding. In particular, it addresses three broad issues: debates over good jobs / bad jobs, eco-nomic polarization, and job quality; risk, insecurity, and opportunity in the new economy; and public policy and the creation of an enterprise culture. In the following sections I discuss each of these in turn.

Good Jobs, Bad Jobs: Economic Polarization and Job Quality

The first of these concerns the extent to which we are seeing economic polarization in Canadian society, and whether and how self-employ-ment and small business ownership is contributing to this process. It has been well over a decade since the Economic Council of Canada (1990) first coined the phrase 'good jobs, bad jobs.' Before and since that time, many studies in Canada, and elsewhere, have explored whether and how the economic landscape is being divided into jobs that, on the one hand, offer good income and benefits, security, training, and advancement, and those, on the other, that are low-paying and insecure.[4] Evidence to date suggests that polarization is occurring for a number of reasons: a declining manufacturing sector, rapid growth in lower-tier services, and the increased use of numerical flexibility in both the public and private sectors where temporary, part-time, and contract jobs have become more common (Betcherman and Lowe 1997; Lowe 2000; Peters 1999; Saunders 2003).

Injecting a gendered analysis into this debate, Armstrong (1996) has argued that restructuring has in fact created more 'women's work' in the Canadian economy – jobs that are low paid and insecure – and that work is becoming more feminized, as more women (and men) concentrate at lower ends of the labour market (see also Connelly 1996; Standing 1989; Vosko 2002). Likewise Sassen (2002) points to a polarized job structure in global cities in the north that is strongly marked by gender, class, and race divisions. In her view, dominant narratives of globalization gloss over this, focusing on professional, knowledge workers while ignoring the low-paid, insecure, service work typically done by poorly educated, working class, and immigrant women.

In the debate over good and bad jobs, self-employment has often been identified as one type of non-standard or contingent work – along with part-time, part-year, temporary, and multiple job-holding (Krahn 1995). Often the assumption that flows from this classification is that own account self-employment – where individuals work alone with no employees – typically constitutes a bad job. Certainly there is some academic and anecdotal evidence of this, especially with regards to home-based self-employment (for example, Jurik 1998). But, as other analysts have noted, there is reason to be cautious about drawing one-size-fits-all conclusions about the self-employed (Baines and Wheelock 1998; Kalleberg 2000; Kalleberg et al. 2000; Krahn and Lowe 2002: 87; Mirchandani 1999; Vosko and Zukewich 2003). Surveying existing studies, Mirchandani notes a tendency to essentialize female entrepreneurs, ignoring differences between them. In one of the most rigorous examinations to date, Kalleberg et al. found considerable diversity among self-employed workers in the United States, noting that many had 'jobs that were not all that "bad"' (2000: 273). Though less likely to have fringe benefits, for example, many self-employed workers in the study earned higher wages than regular full-time workers and showed little preference for a standard job (270–3). In Canada, Vosko et al. (2003: 24) also suggest that greater attention needs to be paid to 'variations within self-employment' and the different dimensions that make up job quality.

Such diversity has led analysts increasingly to question a simple divide between good and bad, or standard and non-standard jobs, as well as an automatic conflation of work arrangements (for example, non-standard arrangements such as part-time, self-employment, and so on) and job quality (income, security, content, challenge). Writing about this, Cranford et al. critique the 'persistence of a dichotomy – standard versus non-standard – that fails to paint an accurate portrait of precarious work' (2003: 7–8). Their research attempts to develop an empirical based, multi-dimensional understanding. As to problems of conflation, it is clear we need much more detailed information about the quality of jobs under different types of work arrangements. As Kalleberg et al. argue 'only by measuring job quality independently can we determine whether and what kinds of non-standard employment raise workers' risk of bad jobs' (2000: 259).

Towards these ends, this study attempts to deepen our knowledge about the job quality and conditions experienced by self-employed workers and small business owners in Canada. As the analysis will show, self-employed women constitute a highly diverse group, about which it is very difficult to generalize. This does not mean self-employment is not caught up in processes of polarization, but the nature of its contribution to these processes may be quite different from what is commonly assumed. Moreover, as with other types of non-standard work arrangements, it may be difficult to classify self-employment as good or bad in the way these terms are commonly understood. As later chapters show, women's self-employment and small business ownership often contains an intermingling of 'good' and 'bad' job features, making it difficult to fit it into conventional categories. Indeed, a key contribution of this study is to provide a comprehensive, and finely grained, measure of job quality – focusing not just on important traditional indicators such as income and job security, but equally important softer job features, such as opportunities for skill development, challenge, and control (see Lowe and Schellenberg 2001; Lowe 2000).

Risk, Insecurity, and Opportunity in the New Economy

Closely linked to the emergence of polarization and good and bad jobs, is another key feature of the new economy – the transferring of greater risk and insecurity onto the individual (Beck 1992: 2000; Burchell et al. 2002; Doogan 2001; Osterman 1996; Perrons 2003; Saunders 2003; Sennett 1998). This comes not just from changing employment practices, but from changing discourses on the role of the government and the rise of the neo-liberal state – what McDaniel (1997) has called the rise of 'skinny government.' Describing this in his influential 1992 book *Risk Society*, Ulrich Beck posits a transition from a modern society to a risk society, where individuals are increasingly free of traditional work and life trajectories. Less continuous attachment to an employer and workplace over the course of one's lifetime, and growing flexibility in organizing work and leisure time are central features. While positive benefits potentially flow from such change, they also exact a heavy price. For Beck, rising economic insecurity and the erosion of steady employment are two key costs that accompany this transition (see also Burchell et al. 2002; Jacoby 2001; Littler and Innes 2003).

Writing later in *The Brave New World of Work*, Beck places these changes in comparative context, arguing that we are seeing the 'Brazilianization of the West.' As he states:

> Equally remarkable is the new similarity in how paid work itself is shaping up in the so-called first world and the so-called third world; the spread of temporary and insecure employment, discontinuity and loose informality into Western societies that have hitherto been the bastions of full employment. The social structure in the heartlands of the West is thus coming to resemble the patchwork quilt of the South, characterized by diversity, unclarity and insecurity in people's work and life. (Beck 2000: 1)

For Beck, self-employment is a key part of this trend towards growing insecurity, risk, and informality. As he notes: 'More and more individuals are encouraged to perform as "Me & Co.", selling themselves on the marketplace' (3)

Other writers also identify growing risk and insecurity as a key feature of current economies. For instance, Appelbaum (2001) speaks about the 'new insecurity' and Richard Sennett (1998) about the risks of 'new capitalism'. For Sennett what is new is that risk is 'no longer meant to be the province only of venture capitalists or extraordinarily adventurous individuals. Risk is to become a daily necessity shouldered by the masses' (80). While such arguments overlook the risk and precariousness workers have faced historically in labour markets (Kalleberg et al. 2000; Bradbury 1993), it does highlight concerns expressed by many over a perceived breakdown in postwar labour market arrangements and institutions that have shielded workers, or at least absorbed and socialized some of the risks (see Jacoby 2001; Osterman 1999 for useful discussions). Equally important as the growing incidence of risk is the question of how new risks and insecurities are distributed in society. In Beck's risk society, for instance, risks affect some more than others, so that 'social risk positions spring up' (1992: 23). While risk is distributed unevenly, further entrenching existing lines of social inequality (for example, class and gender), it is also more pervasive, expanding and widening its circle. Growing risk, coupled with a retrenched welfare state and an eroded safety net in many countries, thus affects growing numbers of people, with inequalities reinforced and redefined through 'the individualization of social risks' (Beck 1992: 100).

Nowhere can this be more clearly seen than in the growing ranks of small business owners and the self-employed, where individuals often take significant risks in investing their time, skills, and financial resources with no guarantee of a 'fair' return. Yet while risks may be unwanted or imposed on some individuals, others may actively take risks and create change in their working lives in order to learn new skills and improve their economic prospects in the long run. In her book *Crossing the Great Divide: Worker Risk and Opportunity in the New Economy*, Vicki Smith argues that many analysts of the new economy emphasize the downside of risk and the dangers facing workers, ignoring the intertwining of risk with opportunity and the potential for good as well as bad. In her view, the new economy may well bring greater risk, but individuals may also pursue risk deliberately in order to better their economic prospects and circumstances. In so doing, they demonstrate their agency, acting as 'creative agents negotiating through the often disadvantaging structures within which they find themselves' (Smith 2001: 13).

In making this claim, Smith's intent is not to minimize the dangers of risk and insecurity. On the contrary, her argument is that we need to subject them to greater scrutiny, to think about them in more complex ways (167–70). As she notes:

> Individual-level risk ranges from mild to intense, and the depth and extent of risks taken by individuals are inextricably shaped by the institutional context within which they are taken. Reasons for undertaking and shouldering risk are similarly variegated; some people may choose to accept risk and shoulder greater burdens because they feel they have no choice, others because they feel they have nothing to lose but quite possibly something to gain. (168)

If risk is indeed a growing feature of economic life, then understanding how individuals perceive, experience, and negotiate risk is critical for making sense of the new economy. Indeed, as I will show in this book, self-employment may often be highly risky for the women who engage in it, but it is relative to their own past biography and to the changing economic, personal, and family circumstances they face. When there has been no economic security in the past, for example, or where there is growing turbulence and instability in the labour market, self-employment may not feel like a 'bad move', and for some women it may not be. For others, however, shouldering risk may prove both stressful and difficult, leading them to wish for the security of a 'proper job.' Still other women view risk as simply a trade-off for the benefits that come with working for themselves – whether that be greater independence, work-family balance, or the opportunity to create meaningful work.

Creating an Enterprise Culture

A final issue this study speaks to is the creation of an enterprise culture. This notion first emerged in the British context around the political project and priorities of Thatcherism (Burrows 1991; McRobbie 1997). Since then it has been folded into economic and political reforms in many countries, such as Canada, that have followed a neo-liberal agenda, reasserting the role of free enterprise and the primacy of markets, individuals, and competition, while also dismantling or 'hollowing out' the welfare state (Brodie 1996; Bakker 1996; Cossman and Fudge 2002). Writing about the enterprise culture, Du Gay and Salaman notes that it is one in which 'personal responsibility, boldness, and a willingness to take risks in the pursuit of goals – are regarded as human virtues and promoted as such' (1992: 628).[5] In capturing the imagination of governments and policy-makers, the enterprise culture has, they argue, 'reconceptualized and remodelled almost everything in its path' (622). In this way, the enterprising self has become the 'driving identity of the new economy' (Du Gay 1996).

While such arguments are specific to the British context, and need to be viewed critically, there are some indications that Canadians have become increasingly entrepreneurial in outlook (Swift 2001). In recent years there has been a flurry of books and newspaper articles promoting and celebrating self-employment and small business ownership, especially for women. Titles such as Yaccato's *Raising Your Business: A Canadian Women's Guide to Entrepreneurship* (1998) and Robertson's *Taking Care of Business: Stories of Women Entrepreneurs* (1997) are but a few examples.[6] Small business owners and entrepreneurs also enjoy high public esteem. At the height of the self-employment boom in the late 1990s, an Angus Reid poll found that they were the most highly respected of a group of fourteen professions in Canada that included traditionally well-respected figures such as doctors, police officers, teachers, and judges. Around the same time, another poll found that nearly half of Canadians, not already self-employed, expressed interest in running their own business some day (Angus Reid 1998a; 1998b).

While international comparisons are not well developed, current evidence suggests that Canada ranks relatively high in terms of entrepreneurial motivation (Reynolds 1999; Peterson 1999) or what has been called 'latent entrepreneurship' (Blanchflower et al. 2001). Drawing on the International Social Survey Program (ISSP), Blanchflower et al. found that a majority of Canadians (57.5%) would prefer to be self-employed, putting them in the top third of twenty-seven countries in terms of latent entrepreneurship. In the Global Entrepreneurship Monitor, an ambitious project tracking trends in self-employment and small business internationally (Reynolds 1999; 2002), Canada ranked third behind the United States and Israel on an entrepreneurial motivation index,[7] as well as third in terms of entrepreneurial start-up activity.

Of course, all of these arguments suggest that change has taken place largely at an ideological or discursive level, reflecting changing ideas and attitudes towards SE/SBO and individual responsibility. Left out of such arguments are the extent to which rising interest in self-employment and small business ownership, or a perceived increase in risk-taking on the part of the population, is a result of material changes in the economic and political landscape. Downsizing, restructuring, and changing hiring practices – in particular, the growing use of contract workers – may all play a key role in shaping an enterprise culture, forcing or encouraging workers into such work. Equally important are changing family and household work strategies and constraints. In addition, some analysts suggest factors such as changing tax regimes in Canada have made self-employment more attractive in recent years (Schuetze 2002).

Taking a cue from these discussions, one of the questions I examine in this study is the extent to which Canada is being reshaped into an enterprise culture. By this I refer not only to the motivations and plans of individual women who are creating and running their own businesses, but also to the changing economic climate and the role of federal and provincial governments in supporting and actively promoting self-employment, small business, and entrepreneurship. Looking at the short- and long-term contribution women are making to the economy through their current activities, and their future plans, provides a number of insights into the way in which an enterprise culture is taking shape in Canada. So, too, does an examination of government policy and programs, shedding light on how the development of a more entrepreneurial economy is being encouraged or hindered.

Women's Self-Employment and Small Business Ownership (SE/SBO)

Beyond these broader debates over restructuring, polarization, enterprise and risk, this study also contributes more directly to the growing literature on women's self-employment and business ownership. This literature comes from a range of disciplines – business, economics, sociology, political science, women's studies – and addresses a variety of national contexts. To date, many different questions have been addressed (for example, financing, business approach), not all of which can be examined here (for useful reviews of this rapidly expanding literature, see Carr 2000; Cliff and Cash 2004; Moore 1999; Mirchandani 1999). Given my interest in understanding the growth and engendering of self-employment and small business in restructuring economies, I focus on three sets of questions that are especially significant:

- What factors are encouraging women to enter self-employment and small business ownership in such dramatic numbers?
- What is the nature of their daily work and their job satisfaction? What do they find meaningful? How do they feel about their short- and long-term economic security?
- How well does government policy mesh with the needs of self-employed women, both in terms of training, support, and broader labour market policy?

Understanding the Growth of SE/SBO in Canada

There has been a great deal of debate over what is driving the growth of self-employment and small business ownership, both as a general trend within the labour market and one that appears to have gender specific dimensions. As with other types of non-standard work, there are differing views as to whether it is workers' personal choices or employers' desires to create more flexible firms that have fuelled the growth of such work (ECC 1991: 82–3; European Foundation 2000; Lin et al. 1999a; 1999b; Manser and Picot 1999a, 1999b; Smeaton 2003; Statistics Canada 1997; Steinmetz and Wright 1989). Whereas the former view places the emphasis on individual choice, suggesting workers have been voluntarily 'pulled' into better opportunities within a growing enterprise culture, the latter contends workers have been 'pushed' out of secure, paid employment into marginalized jobs. Existing evidence on this issue suggests that both push and pull factors are involved, though to differing degrees.

In the United States, for instance, research suggests that while some workers can be considered involuntarily self-employed, they constitute only a small minority of the self-employed.[8] Similarly, in Canada, the *1995 Survey of Work Arrangements* found just 12% of self-employed workers lacked other work alternatives, with this being higher for own-account workers (15.4%) than those who were employers (6.9%) (Statistics Canada 1997: 35). Longitudinal analysis by Lin et al. (1999b) also argues there is little evidence that push factors have been the dominant factor in rising self-employment levels in Canada, suggesting instead the influence of both push and pull. More recent evidence from the *2000 Survey of Self-Employment in Canada*, however, suggests higher figures (21.8%), though the report based on this survey emphasizes that the majority of the self-employed (78.2%) have chosen this work voluntarily (HRDC 2002).

Notwithstanding this evidence, several small-scale studies of women's self-employment note the importance of push factors, in particular the growing insecurity and marginality within much of women's work. They have also underlined the role played by other factors, such as growing education, skills and autonomy on the part of women; attempts to escape gender barriers and segregation with the labour market; and workers' desire to balance family work and paid work (see, for example, Arai 2000; Carr 1996, 2000; Clark and James 1992; Green and Cohen 1995; Jurik 1998; McManus 1994; Reed, 2001).

Among the questions I examine in this study are not just what factors are motivating women to become self-employed, but how well existing research has captured motivations, whether they be push or pull. As will become clearer in Chapter 3, the circumstances and desires that underlie individual actions are complex, fluid, and often difficult to measure. Existing approaches in Canada, and other industrialized countries, do not appear to have always fully captured the forces encouraging or pushing women into self-employment and small business ownership, and in this respect may have underestimated the role of push factors such as economic restructuring in the process.

The Nature of Women's Work, Economic Security, and Job Satisfaction

Beyond the factors fuelling its growth, a second critical question concerns the nature and quality of work that self-employment and small business ownership provides – a question linked not only to debates over economic restructuring and polarization but also to long-standing questions about gender segregation and women's marginalization in the labour market. While some analysts believe that self-employment offers a good strategy for increasing female economic autonomy, and in fact escaping traditional gender barriers and inequality at work, others challenge this view, arguing that self-employment, like paid employment, is deeply segregated by gender.

In examining the nature of women's work and economic security in the United States and Britain, for example, researchers have noted that strong links exist between women's previous employment field and the type of self-employment they enter, ensuring that traditional patterns of gender segregation are replicated. Generally speaking, self-employed women cluster within 'female' areas, such as retail, hospitality, and personal services (Clark and James 1992; Carr 1996, 2000; Loscocco and Robinson 1991; Green and Cohen 1995). These 'peripheral economic niches' are expanding, but highly competitive, industries that are unattractive to men, being female-dominated and having much lower than average earnings than male sectors. Even when women do work in the same industrial sectors as men, some studies suggest they tend to run smaller, and less profitable, enterprises (Johnson and Storey 1993; Marlow and Strange 1994). Women also face additional disadvantages such as lack of access to capital and contacts, and greater responsibilities for domestic work and childcare. Geographic location may also play a role (Bird and Sapp 2004; Du Plessis 2004).

In considering the possible reasons for the segregated nature of self-employment, several authors suggest that women are far more likely than men to pursue self-employment as a way to balance work and family demands, and that it is these types of considerations, rather than higher earnings or advancement opportunities, that lead them into specific areas. Under these circumstances, some researchers question the potential of self-employment to offer new choices or new forms of freedom for women. Instead, self-employment may simply entrench women's labour market disadvantage, allowing them to cope with the competing demands of paid and family work, while continuing to accept responsibility for both (Marlow and Strange 1994; Green and Cohen 1995).

In Canada, recent analysis of labour force and survey data sheds some light on issues of job quality and economic security, but only at a very general level (see, in particular, HRDC 2002; Hughes 1999; Statistics Canada 1997). Still, several findings are relevant here. For example, though women are now entering a more diverse array of industrial sectors than in the past, there is still significant concentration in traditional areas – such as trade, food/accommodation and other services – especially for those working alone. Moreover, despite growing numbers of female employers, self-employed women are still far less likely than men to employ others. In 2001, for example, just one-quarter of employers were women (Statistics Canada CANSIM II, table 282-0012). Self-employed women are also far more likely to work part-time than their male peers, especially when they work alone. Finally, earnings for self-employed workers are more polarized than for paid workers, and the wage gap between women and men is more pronounced.[9] However, as many published figures do not control for critical determinants of income, such as hours, education, and experience, there is a need for more detailed analysis – an issue I take up in Chapter 5.

Beyond questions of pay and economic security are important but less explored issues of job satisfaction. In Canada, just a handful of studies address this subject, either directly or as part of broader exploration of workplace trends (CFIB 1999, 2000, 2002; CPRN 2001; Duxbury and Higgins 1999; Hughes, Lowe and Schellenberg 2003; Lowe and Schellenberg 2001). Studies focusing specifically on small business owners and the self-employed suggest that their job satisfaction is higher than that of paid employees – in fact, the smaller the business, the greater satisfaction appears to be. Specific areas of high satisfaction include trust, communication, flexibility, and work relationships, as well as schedule, work content, workload, respect, and involvement in decision making.

To date, we have little detail on gender differences in job quality and satisfaction, with the exception of the *2000 Survey of Self-Employment* which asks men and women what they like most and least about their work (HRDC 2002). Existing research also relies solely on survey techniques, providing valuable baseline information but insufficient detail to help us understand why self-employed workers and small business owners derive such satisfaction from their work. In an effort to deepen our knowledge both about job quality and satisfaction in this type of work, this study examines in detail what women find satisfying and dissatisfying, drawing on original interviews and unpublished data from national surveys. By focusing on a range of issues such as the nature of women's day-to-day work, opportunities for creativity, responsibility, independence, job security, income, work-family balance, and personal fulfilment, the analysis sheds needed light on debates over job quality, good and bad jobs, and the trade-offs women make in their daily working lives.

Policy Issues

In addition to clarifying the implications of self-employment and small business ownership for individual workers, it is also important to consider the appropriate role of government in regulating and supporting this form of work. In the 1980s and the 1990s, federal and provincial governments in Canada moved away from past approaches of direct intervention and job creation to address high unemployment, choosing instead to promote the merits of an enterprise culture. Guided by the belief that small business and self-employment offered the greatest potential to regenerate the Canadian economy, governments opted for a role as facilitators rather than creators of job growth. As such they have actively championed self-employment, placing heavy emphasis on policies and programs aimed at encouraging small-scale enterprise (Arai 1997: 367; Fudge 1996: 59; Peterson 1999, 2001).

Federal policy documents in the last decade – such as *Building a More Innovative Economy* (1994a) and *Growing Small Business* (1994b) – reflect this policy emphasis, outlining numerous initiatives for building a more dynamic and entrepreneurial economy. Examples of some of the initiatives proposed or taken at the federal level include: increased lending ceilings under the Small Business Loans Act; expansion of Canada Business Service Centres to provide single-window access to government information for entrepreneurs; changing government procurement policies to increase the value of purchases from small business; and new or revised financing programs to promote the growth of small business. To assist self-employed workers, the federal government also produces a *Guide to Government Services and Support for Small Business* outlining a range of programs. Self-employment initiatives have also been tied into existing programs such as employment insurance through self-employment assistance (SEA) – a program that offers financial support, orientation, and coaching to unemployed Canadians wishing to pursue self-employment.[10]

For women, additional programs aim at encouraging self-employment and business ownership, as is the case for other targeted groups such as young Canadians, the disabled, and Aboriginals. For example, Western Economic Diversification Canada provides federal funding for the Alberta Women's Enterprise Initiative Association – an organization providing information, coaching, and mentoring to women entrepreneurs. Perhaps the most important initiative in recent years has been the Prime Minister's Task Force on Women Entrepreneurs, chaired by MP Sarmite Bulte, which tabled its report on October 2003, following consultations with hundreds of women in twenty-one Canadian cities (Canada 2003: 93–111). Among its key recommendations were the need to better coordinate the design and delivery of programs aimed at women entrepreneurs; to improve women's access to capital, business skill training, mentoring and networking programs, government contracts, and export programs; and to extend employment insurance and other social safety-net benefits to self-employed women.

Given the active promotion of self-employment by both federal and provincial governments in recent years, any discussion of SE/SBO must consider its success as a job creation strategy. While there is clear evidence that self-employment has generated significant numbers of jobs, the question is not purely one of numbers; job quality and longevity remain crucial considerations. In the United States, several commentators have questioned the value of government supported initiatives encouraging women into self-employment, which typically offers much lower paying, less secure, work than paid employment (Clark and James 1992; Ehlers and Main 1998; for an alternative view, see Raheim and Bolden 1995). Similar questions need to be addressed in the Canadian context, in order to assess the relative merits and shortcomings of a SE/SBO strategy.

In exploring policy issues, this study focuses on several key issues. One of the most central concerns job quality, which includes not only the type of work (occupation, industry, full-time/part-time), but also its intrinsic (challenge, autonomy) and extrinsic (income, benefits) rewards. On this dimension, self-employment raises some unique considerations. In terms of income, for example, self-employment may offer excellent earning opportunities for some workers, but it also generates greater income extremes than does paid employment. In addition, many self-employed workers are not included in government programs,[11] such as employment insurance, disability, parental benefits/leave, leaving them vulnerable in cases of illness, pregnancy, or business failure. Beyond issues of job quality and income security are questions concerning training and education, and whether the self-employed have adequate opportunities and resources for skill development. Work-family considerations are also central, given ongoing debate in Canada over this issue and the fact that many women appear to use self-employment as a way to combine paid work and childcare (Connelly 1992; Hall-Hoffarth 2003).

Book Outline

To briefly recap, there are an enormous range of issues emerging from the rapid growth of women's self-employment and small business ownership. In the chapters that follow, I take up what I consider to be some of the most central questions about this growing form of work. These include:

– What factors are encouraging women to enter self-employment and small business ownerships? What are the pathways they follow into this type of work?
– What is the job quality of the work they do? How satisfied are they with their work?
– What are the implications of rising self-employment for women's economic lives – for their income, benefits, retirement, and long-term economic security?
– What type of contribution have they made to the economy? What are their plans for growth?
– How is and should the federal and provincial governments be responding to this segment of the labour force?

As a first step in the analysis, I introduce the data sources that inform this study in Chapter 2. These include existing labour force data from national surveys, such as the *Labour Force Survey* and special surveys such as the 2000 *Survey of Self-Employment in Canada* (*SSE*), and the 2000 CPRN-Ekos *Changing Employment Relationships Survey* (*CER*). They also include data from in-depth interviews with sixty-one self-employed women in Alberta working in a range of businesses. In introducing these women, I explore their personal and business backgrounds. I also address definitional issues around self-employment, small business ownership, and entrepreneurship, in order to clarify my use of these terms.

In Chapter 3, I examine the pathways women take into self-employment, looking at the relevance of their education, past work experience, and family background to their business, and exploring their reasons for becoming self-employed. This analysis sheds light on a significant debate that has developed over whether women have been pulled or attracted into self-employment and small business ownership by the promise of a greater independence, income, and autonomy, or whether they have instead been pushed or forced into their own businesses by a lack of economic choice.

In Chapters 4 and 5, I undertake a detailed look at the daily work done by women business owners, examining their hours, working patterns, job quality, and the satisfaction they receive from their jobs. Their accounts shed light on the debate over good and bad jobs and how well or poorly small business ownership is able to fulfill the aspirations of working women. I also explore the diversity in women's experiences based on their reasons for becoming self-employed, as well as socio-demographic and business factors.

I turn in Chapter 6 to consider key policy questions, asking how well federal and provincial policy matches the present-day realities of the self-employed. I identify two main areas where current government policy needs to be reconsidered. The first concerns the significant attention and resources devoted to high-end business growth (for example, exporting, financing) that may be appropriate for some, but certainly not all, women business owners. This policy mismatch is made clear by examining the growth aspirations of women in the study, as well as their training needs. A second issue that emerges concerns the relative neglect of social protection for self-employed workers through their exclusion from core government programs designed to provide some minimal level of security to workers (e.g., unemployment insurance, maternity leave, Canada pension). While this policy mismatch affects both women and men, there are also important gender differences as well. I focus on several issues of special importance for self-employed women, suggesting how federal and provincial governments can better respond to this growing segment of the workforce

In concluding, Chapter 7 provides a broad summary of the key findings of the study, drawing out it academic implications and suggesting important avenues for future research.

2 Researching Women in the Entrepreneurial Economy

Writing about the practice of social research, Sandra Harding (1987) observes that the questions we ask are as determinant of the knowledge we produce as the actual answers we uncover. So, too, are the decisions we make in the process of doing social research – from deciding how to gather information to choosing participants to determining how data are to be analysed and presented. For this reason, Harding argues, it is crucial that the research process be placed 'on the same critical plane' as the subject itself, so that the researcher's assumptions, decisions, and tools can be held up to scrutiny. Providing this type of transparency allows readers to understand how the research has been carried out and how specific assumptions and decisions have come to shape it. All of this acknowledges the social nature of knowledge production, and the way in which knowledge is shaped by the researcher's own social location and background – an argument that is now well established within the sociological tradition (DeVault 1999; Reinharz 1992; see Mauthner and Doucet 2003 for a valuable overview of the 'reflexive turn' in the social sciences as well as the limits to reflexivity).

In exploring the subject of self-employment and small business ownership, I approach it as a sociologist of work who is interested in broad transformations within the economy, structured patterns of inequality, and the linkages between economic and social life. I also take a gendered perspective that asks how women in particular have been affected by changing economic and social circumstances (Reinharz 1992). In focusing on women, I recognize the diversity embraced within this category, and have sought to the extent possible to explore differences, as well as similarities, in women's experience, as they are shaped by different aspects of their social location (for example, class, motherhood, race, age, and so on).

Unlike some researchers, however, who believe in a strict alignment of gender-based research and qualitative methods, I have made use of both quantitative and qualitative modes of inquiry, being convinced, as others have argued, that together they provide powerful insights (Bryman 1988; Jayaratne 1983; Reinharz 1990). Indeed, in the context of this study, it is interesting to note that the prime minister's Task Force on Women Entrepreneurs underlined the value of using qualitative and quantitative data in 'constant parallel' to inform policy (Canada 2003: 131). Working between these sources, I have been guided by some of the ideas of Marjorie DeVault's, in particular her notion of excavation. As she states:

> The term 'excavation' – used to point to a research goal – is meant to capture this process of uncovering and articulating what has been hidden or unacknowledged and the sense of discovery that accompanies that process. It refers to a kind of investigation that begins with what can be seen and heard but holds in mind a sense that there is more to find – like the archaeologist's knowledge that any bone or fragment of pottery, for instance, points toward a complete organism or object. Investigation of this sort is a matter of uncovering evidentiary artifacts, studying them with respect, and working to understand how they illuminate and extend what is already known. (1999: 55–6)

While DeVault uses this approach for interpreting interview material, focusing particularly on language and meaning, she notes that excavation characterizes many other research approaches, from survey research, ethnography to policy analysis (57). In this study, I use her notion of excavation to bridge different sources of qualitative and quantitative data, working not in a compartmentalized way, but in cross referential fashion. Through this process, quantitative findings are used to help situate qualitative findings within the broader context, while qualitative findings provide rich insights and illumination into what quantitative data can only suggest.

Data Sources

In examining women's self-employment and small business ownership, I draw on two main sources of empirical evidence. One is labour force statistics and survey findings from Statistics Canada that allow me to sketch a broad picture of the changing contours of the Canadian economy and the place of self-employment and small business ownership within it. Three surveys I make particular use of are the ongoing *Labour Force Survey*, the *2000 Survey of Self-Employment in Canada*, and the 2000 CPRN-Ekos *Changing Employment Relationships Survey*. Methodological details for these surveys are provided in Table 2.1.

While the first two of these surveys – the *Labour Force Survey* and the *Survey of Self-Employment* – are useful for sketching out broad trends within the entrepreneurial economy, they are limited in the depth of information they provide. Indeed, a key challenge facing researchers interested in the SE/SBO sector stems from limitations of existing data – a point emphasized by the prime minister's Task Force on Women Entrepreneurs and other international forums such as the second OECD Conference on Women Entrepreneurs (OECD 2000e: 5). The *Labour Force Survey*, for instance, provides information about the self-employed, broadly defined, but says little about the nature of their business. Conversely, existing data gathered on businesses in Canada and many other countries are rarely gender based. For this reason the *2000 Survey of Self-Employment in Canada* (HRDC 2002) provides much-needed data on a range of issues. While it does not examine some issues (such as job quality) as fully as we might desire, it does provide a solid quantitative starting point for this study.

To take the analysis further, a third and very valuable source of survey data used is the 2000 CPRN-Ekos *Changing Employment Relationships Survey*. This survey provides a significant amount of detail on the issue of job quality, for both paid employees and the self-employed, allowing us to develop a richer and more comprehensive picture of job quality than we have to date, and to make comparisons between paid employees and the self-employed. The findings from these data, previously unpublished, are presented in Chapter 4.

Survey data allow us to identify general trends in women's SE/ SBO but it provides less scope to understand the meaning of this activity. For this reason, the second source of evidence, and the source that informs much of this book, comes from in-depth interviews with sixty-one women who are self-employed or own their own business. Their personal and business histories provide a valuable window for understanding what it means to be self-employed at the start of a new century in Canada. Not only do their stories bring aggregate trends and statistics to life, they provide a greater depth of information than is available through existing survey data, allowing us to examine how women move into self-employment, how they spend their working days, what they find satisfying, dissatisfying,

TABLE 2.1
Sources of Survey Data

Statistics Canada, *Labour Force Survey (LFS)*
This household survey provides representative data on major labour market trends such as labour force participation, occupation, industry, hours worked, unemployment rates. Using a 'class of worker' or 'status in employment' variable, it is possible to obtain information on the self-employed. The *LFS* distinguishes between five types of self-employed workers: (1) working owners of incorporated businesses with paid help; (2) working owners of incorporated businesses without paid help; (3) working owners of unincorporated businesses or other self-employed with paid help; (4) working owners of unincorporated businesses or other self-employed without paid help; and (5) unpaid family members. The *LFS* has run in various forms since 1945. Currently the sample size is 54,000 households. The sample is drawn to provide reliable estimates at the national, provincial, and local levels. For further details, see the *Guide to the Labour Force Survey* (Statistics Canada 2003).

Statistics Canada, *Survey of Self-Employment in Canada (SSE)*
This survey was conducted by Statistics Canada in April 2000 on behalf of Human Resources Development Canada. The objective of the survey was to provide in-depth information on a range of issues relevant to the self-employed, such as work-related training, working arrangements, financial security and benefits, and reasons for becoming self-employed. The survey was administered as a supplement to a sub-sample of participants in the monthly *Labour Force Survey (LFS)*. The survey included self-employed workers working alone (own account self-employed) and those who employed others (employer self-employed). The *SSE* had a response rate of 60.62% and a final sample of 4,015. The final sample used in this study is based on 3,840 observations (for those individuals who agreed to release their data to HRDC). The estimates reported have been weighted to ensure they are representative of the population. Further details on the methodology of the *SSE* are available from the Microdata User Guide (Statistics Canada and Human Resources Development Canada, 2000).

CPRN-Ekos, *Changing Employment Relationships Survey (CERS)*
This telephone survey was conducted by Ekos and Associates on behalf of Canadian Policy Research Networks (CPRN) in February and March 2000. Based on a household sampling frame, the final sample included 2,500 currently employed Canadians aged eighteen years and old. The sample was weighted and is representative of the general population, with a margin of error of plus or minus 2 percent, nineteen times out of twenty. In addition to standard socio-demographic information, the survey gathered a wide range of information on individual labour market and workplace experiences, especially in relation to issues of trust, commitment, communications, influence, and the legal aspects of employment relationships. A particularly valuable part of the survey comes from the detailed data collected on intrinsic and extrinsic aspects of job quality. For further details on the methodology of this survey, see Lowe and Schellenberg (2001).

---

challenging or rewarding, and what plans they have for their businesses in the long term.

Study Details

The women interviewed for this study own a range of businesses in Edmonton, Alberta. Some are solo, home-based practices. Others operate from a commercial location and employ others. In most cases, their businesses serve a local market, though for some activities extend across the province, country, or into other national markets. I chose to study women in Alberta for two reasons. First, it is a region and labour market with which I am very familiar. Second, the province is an ideal site for studying women's self-employment in the context of the economic restructuring. Alberta is very much an entrepreneurial province. It has one of the highest provincial rates of self-employment in the country (HRDC 2002; Statistics Canada, CANSIM II, Table 282–0012), and has made significant efforts to encourage small business start-ups and to attract small businesses from other regions (Economic Development Edmonton 2000: 56). In the 1990s – the 'downsizing decade' (Littler and Innes 2003) – the provincial economy underwent extensive public and private sector economic restructuring, as a result of cutbacks under both provincial and federal governments (Hughes, Lowe, and McKinnon 1996; Peters 1999). Many individuals who were laid off and downsized through this period were encouraged to set up small businesses and become self-employed through a variety of retraining and assistance programs. A key program was the Self-Employment Assistance (SEA) program run through employment insurance, which provides training to help unemployed Canadians set up a business.

Identifying and Recruiting Participants for the Study

The women in the study included several who were forced into their own business by economic circumstances, and many more who had become self-employed because of their own desires and ambitions. However, the sample was not chosen along these dimensions. Because I was interested in comparing women in diverse SE/SBO situations, the sample was drawn purposively in order to include roughly equal numbers of women who were solo self-employed (those working alone) and employers (those employing others). A second interest was in getting a mixture of participants who had businesses in areas that were traditional and non-traditional for women.

While the type of business was the main criterion in selecting the sample, I also wanted to ensure diversity in the socio-demographic backgrounds of the owners. Participants were therefore recruited through a number of different channels: word of mouth, as well as formal contacts through several different self-employment, community, and professional organizations. In order to broaden the networks I was accessing, I tried to contact as wide a group of organizations as possible.[1] Some were specifically focused on self-employment and small business, others were professional associations, others were general community groups for women. The organizations included the Alberta Women's Enterprise Initiative Association (AWEIA), Alberta Registered Nurses in Independent Practice (ARNIP), Changing Together: A Centre for Immigrant Women; Connecting Women, Edmonton Community Loan Fund, Women Business Owners of Canada (WBOC), and Women's Economic and Business Solutions (WEBS).

Data Collection

Interviews were carried out in the summer and fall of 1999 by myself and two research assistants, Tricia Bell and Deana Hall-Hoffarth. All of the interviews were done in person, and in most cases lasted between one to one and a half hours. Before interviewing the sixty-one women, I drew up a semi-structured interview schedule covering the issues I wanted to discuss. The draft schedule was used in pilot interviews, and then revised slightly based on input from interviewees (Rubin and Rubin 1995). The final interview covered a range of topics and was used to ensure that we discussed a common set of issues with all of the women (see Appendix 1 for the interview schedule).

In particular, I was interested to know about the women's work and educational background, the pathways they took into self-employment, their reasons for becoming self-employed, the nature of their businesses, and their day-to-day work. I also wanted to learn more about job quality and their experience of running their own business. How satisfied were they with their independence? Their income? Their hours? How much did they enjoy the work they were doing? Recognizing the social context in which women's entrepreneurship operates, I also wanted to learn more about the sources of support they had and drew upon (for example, family, colleagues, organizations), the types of challenges they faced in their business, and how they defined their own success. Finally, given both policy and academic debates over small business and economic growth, I was also interested to know more about the plans women had, and the extent to which they planned to grow and expand their businesses.

In addition to the interview questions, the women also filled in a short form at the start of each interview that provided basic demographic and other information (see Appendix 2). This ensured we had common information for each woman on key variables and allowed us to collect basic information quickly – an important consideration given the time constraints facing many of these women. Women responded to a set of questions on the self-completion sheet concerning their reasons for becoming self-employed, and also discussed these issues in greater detail during the course of the interview. This process provided rich data, as well as unexpected insights on substantive issues and methodology, that I discuss in later chapters.

All of the interviews were taped with the women's consent, and were then transcribed, resulting in approximately fifteen hundred pages of material. Following transcription, each interviewer reviewed the tape and transcript, and made any necessary changes. We also sent copies of the final transcripts to the participants for their information, and made any additional changes or corrections they identified. Because the interviews were typically conducted at the women's place of business – which could be a home office, a restaurant, a store, a commercial office, or a manufacturing plant – we also made field notes on their work surroundings, as well as other relevant information about the interview that might aid us in later analysis.

Data Analysis and Presentation

In analysing the interview data, I used the qualitative software programs NUD*IST (Non-numerical UnStructured Data*Indexing Searching and Theorizing QSR N4) and N-VIVO (see Richard and Richards 1995 for an overview), as well as the statistical software SPSS. The quantitative data, such as Statistics Canada's *Labour Force Survey,* the *Survey of Self-Employment in Canada,* and historical labour force data from *CANSIM II* – were analysed using SPSS and Excel.

In analysing the interviews, I have used a thematic form of content analysis developed with colleagues in previous projects (see Neufeld et al. 2002). Data from interviews related to a common idea were assigned preliminary codes. As similarities and differences amongst the preliminary codes became clear, these sensitizing concepts (Blumer 1954) were defined more specifically and used in the coding and analysis. To develop an audit trail, I kept notes, memos, and a research diary to track coding decisions and questions for further investigation (Morse 1995; Morse and Field 1995). In addition, analytic procedures such as the generation of matrices helped to identify general patterns in the data and establish linkages between key concepts.

Coding the data in this way allowed me to identify consistent, systematic patterns, and to explore areas of similarity and difference between women. It also allowed me to identify and extract representative quotes from the interviews that nicely illustrated key themes and findings. These quotes are included throughout this volume, with interview numbers indicating the source of the data (for example, Interview A01). Because we promised confidentiality to the women who were interviewed, where names appear, as in the epigraphs that start each chapter, I have used pseudonyms. In contextualizing quotes, I have not always been able to provide the level of detail I would like, for fear of identifying participants. Typically I use one or two descriptors that seem most relevant – for example, whether they are a solo worker or employer, or the general business area they work in.

It should be noted that while confidentiality was promised to all women, many were happy for others to know they had participated in the study. Appendix 3 therefore lists the names of the women who participated in the study, with the exception of those who explicitly asked not to be included on this list. It also includes the names of other organizations and individuals who helped recruit women to the study.

Introducing the Women

While the interview study does not provide a representative sample of Canadian women, it does contain a diverse group of women and work situations. Roughly half of the women worked alone in their business and were 'solo self-employed'. The rest were 'employers,' many having just one or two employees, though some had many more. In terms of their socio-demographic background, roughly one-third of the women were under forty-five years of age, about half were forty-five to fifty-four, with the remainder being fifty-five years and older (see Table 2.2). Two-thirds were married or cohabiting, and nearly 90 percent had children, with two being the average number. In some cases, women had young children and were raising their children while also running their business. In other cases, the children were school aged or already adults themselves. Compared to the self-employed population in

TABLE 2.2
Socio-Demographic Background,* Alberta Study

	Solo workers (%)	Employers (%)	All respondents (%)
Age			
25–34	6.3	3.4	4.9
35–44	25.0	27.6	26.2
45–54	53.1	44.8	49.2
55–64	15.6	20.7	18.0
64+	0	3.4	1.6
Education			
Grades 10–12 non-graduate	0	3.4	1.6
High school graduate	3.1	6.9	4.9
Some post-secondary	9.4	10.3	9.8
Trade certificate or diploma	12.5	20.7	16.4
College diploma	18.8	10.3	14.8
University degree (bachelor)	34.4	24.1	29.5
University degree (professional)	6.3	6.9	6.6
University degree (master)	15.6	13.8	14.8
University degree (doctoral)	0	3.4	1.6
Marital Status			
Single	9.4	13.8	11.5
Married / cohabiting	68.8	65.5	67.2
Separated / divorced / widowed	21.9	20.7	21.3
Children			
Yes	87.5	89.7	88.5
Country of Birth			
Canada	65.6	72.4	68.9
Other	34.4	27.6	31.1
Equity Groups			
Visible minority	25.8	27.6	26.7
Aboriginal	0	3.4	1.7
Disabled	0	0	0
None of these	74.2	69.0	71.7
Total (n)	32	29	61

*The number of respondents varies from 60 to 61.

Canada generally, the women in this study were very well educated, with over half having a university degree of some kind (bachelor, graduate, professional). In line with the large number of self-employed who are immigrants in Canada, nearly one-third of the women were immigrants, and just over one-quarter were visible minorities. On average, immigrant and visible minority women were somewhat better educated, being slightly more likely to have university education than the rest of the sample.

While there were no striking socio-demographic differences between women who were solo self-employed and employers, there were important contrasts in terms of the businesses[2] they own (see Table 2.3). One was the length of time they had been in business. Solo self-employed women had much younger businesses, compared to employers – over two-thirds of solo self-employed women had been operating for less than five years, compared to over one-third of employers. But in terms of the way they started their business, there was little difference between the two groups. In both cases, more than four-fifths of the women had created their own business as an original start up, while the remainder had purchased a going concern, either an existing business or a franchise.[3] None of the women became self-employed through a family business, though several had come to employ or involve their own family members in their business. Few were 'co-prenuers' (Marshall 1999), however, with most running their businesses independently from family members. Perhaps the greatest difference between the groups was in the location, and legal status, of the business. Three-quarters of solo self-employed women were based at home, and only one in five had an incorporated business. In contrast, 90% of the women who were employers had a workplace away from home, and over three-quarters were in an incorporated business. There were also important differences between the two groups in the hours that they worked. While one-third of solo self-employed women worked part-time (less than thirty hours per week), there were no employers who did so. In fact, what is striking about employers is the extremely long hours they worked – on average nearly fifty-nine hours a week. Solo self-employed women working full-time also worked extremely long hours by national standards – about fifty hours a week – with this falling to nineteen hours a week for solo women working part-time.

In terms of the types of businesses, the women were involved in a wide range of areas, as Table 2.4 shows. Over one-quarter provided some type of business service, such as accounting or consulting. Nearly 20% were in health and social services (for example, health consulting, therapies, counselling) and close to 20% were in other services (dress-making, hair stylist, travel services). Over 15% were involved in some type of retail trade (gift stores, food stores) and a small number were involved in various types of manufacturing (home products,

TABLE 2.3
Business Background,* Alberta Study

	Solo workers (%)	Employers (%)	All respondents (%)
Years in Business			
1–5	71.0	37.9	55.0
6–10	25.8	27.6	26.7
11–15	0	13.8	6.7
16+	3.2	20.7	11.7
Average years	4.8 years	10.5 years	7.5 years
Current business			
New business start-up	83.9	82.8	83.3
Purchased business	0	17.2	8.3
Family business	0	0	0
Other	16.1	0	8.3
Incorporated			
Yes	22.6	75.9	48.3
No	77.4	24.1	51.7
Work status			
Part-time (< 30 hours/week)	34.4	0	18.0
Full-time (> 30 hours/week)	65.6	100.0	82.0
Weekly hours			
Avg hours for full-time	50.1 hours	58.4 hours	54.8 hours
Avg hours for part-time	18.6 hours	n/a	18.6 hours
Overall average hours	39.0 hours	58.5 hours	48.0 hours
Home-based business			
Yes	75.0	10.3	44.3
No	25.0	89.7	55.7
With employees			
Yes	0.0	100.0	49.2
No	100.0	0.0	50.8
Total (n)	32	29	61

*The number of respondents varies from 57 to 61.

clothing, commercial products). There were similarities and difference in business area, depending on whether women were solo self-employed or employers. While business services and other services were very important areas for both groups, solo workers were somewhat more likely to operate in health and social service areas, whereas

TABLE 2.4
Type of Business, Alberta Study

Industry	Solo workers (%)	Employers (%)	All respondents (%)
Manufacturing	3.1	10.3	6.6
Construction	3.1	0	1.6
Wholesale trade	0	3.4	1.6
Retail trade	9.4	24.1	16.4
Finance & insurance	3.1	0	1.6
Real estate	3.1	0	1.6
Government services	3.1	0	1.6
Business services	28.1	27.6	27.9
Education	3.1	0	1.6
Health/social services	21.9	13.8	18.0
Accomodation/food/beverage	3.1	3.4	3.3
Other services	18.8	17.2	18.0
Total (n)	32	29	61

employers tended towards businesses in retail trade. This was particularly true for visible minority women, who were slightly more likely to be employers, but also more likely to be overrepresented in retail trade and other services. As we would expect, manufacturing was also more important for employers than for solo women working alone.

Generally speaking, then, the profile of these two groups differs not so much in terms of their socio-demographic background, but in terms of the nature of their businesses. Overall, solo self-employed women tended to be mid-life and older, ranging from their mid thirties to their early sixties. Most had children and were married or cohabiting. Compared to the general population, they were well educated. Many were Canadian-born but about one-third were immigrants and one-quarter were visible minorities. In terms of their businesses, most had become self-employed in the past five years, and had a business that was unincorporated, and home-based. While the majority worked full-time, about one-third worked part-time. Typically they provide business and personal services, as well as health care and social services, to a range of individuals and companies.

Employers shared many of the same socio-demographic characteristics as the solo women, although they were slightly older and slightly less likely to have finished high school or have a university degree.

Their marital, family, and immigrant statuses were similar to solo women, although they were slightly more likely to be visible minorities. Where they differed from solo self-employed women, however, was in terms of their businesses. Most employers had been in business for more than five years, and one-third had been in business for more than a decade. Only a minority worked at home, most had an incorporated business, and all of them worked full-time, typically averaging almost sixty hours each week.

Terminology: Self-Employed, Small Business Owners, and Entrepreneurs

In the next chapter I explore the pathways these women took into their businesses, attempting to shed light on the question of why Canadian women have entered self-employment and small business ownership at such a dramatic rate in recent years. But before turning to these issues, I want to comment briefly on the terminology used in this book.

As I noted in the introduction in Chapter 1, there has been a great deal of debate over how best to describe individuals who work for themselves. 'Small business owners,' 'entrepreneurs' or 'microentrepreneurs,' 'independent contractors,' 'free agents,' and 'self-employed workers' are all terms that are used, even though they can mean quite different things. Writing about this in Britain, Angela Dale (1991) observes that some commentators, in their enthusiasm to embrace an enterprise culture, have conflated often widely diverging work situations, arguing they all contribute to an emerging entrepreneurial economy. In Canada, Rein Peterson makes a similar observation in the Canadian report for the *Global Entrepreneurship Monitor* (*GEM*), noting the need to distinguish between 'growth oriented' entrepreneurship, 'lifestyle' entrepreneurs, and other small business activity aimed simply at self-sufficiency (1999: 24). Others in Canada have noted the importance of ensuring that the self-employed are truly independent workers, and not 'disguised employees' or 'dependent contractors' (Lowe 2002; Lowe and Schellenberg 2001).[4] Given this complexity, it has become standard practice for researchers to preface their analysis with comments about the difficulties in making clear distinctions between those who are self-employed, small business owners, and entrepreneurs (for example see Aronson 1991; Dale 1991; Dennis 1996; Gauthier and Roy 1997; Lavoie 1988; Allen and Truman 1992, 1993b; Simpson 1991; Steinmetz and Wright 1989; Taylor 1997; Yeager 1999).

Yet, despite these efforts to clarify terms, there continues to be much debate around definitional issues.

Surveying the literature reveals a range of definitions in use, depending on whether they are made for legal, tax, economic, socio-logical or statistical reasons. In Canada, for example, the self-employed are defined in different ways for statistical, taxation, and legal pur-poses (see Gauthier and Roy 1997; Fudge et al. 2002). In the *Labour Force Survey*, for instance, individuals are asked to identify themselves as 'self-employed'. Further distinctions are then made depending on whether individuals work alone (own account self-employment) or employ others (employer), and whether they are involved in an incor-porated and unincorporated business (see Table 2.1 in this chapter). In contrast, the definition of self-employment for tax purposes is based on tests around four key factors: control over work, ownership of tools, chance of profit/loss, and integration (Revenue Canada 1998). In the legal arena, control over work has traditionally been used as the key criterion for determining whether or not an employment contract exists, thus distinguishing between employees and the self-employed (Fudge et al. 2002; Fudge 2003). A recent Supreme Court decision, however, acknowledges that additional factors may be important, such as whether a worker provides his or her own equipment, hires help, is responsible for management and investment, or faces financial risk or opportunity to profit. Even where there is agreement on the definitions and criteria used to identify independent workers, variations may exist in the thresholds used. For instance, distinctions between the self-employed and small business owners are often made in terms of the size of business (number of employees, revenue levels), but across countries cut-offs and thresholds vary (OECD 2000c, 2000d).[5]

From a gendered perspective, analysts also note how male bias is embedded within many existing definitions, so that standard defini-tions reflect men's, rather than women's, activities (Allen and Truman 1992, 1993b; Bruni et al. 2004; Lavoie 1988; Simpson 1988; Stevenson 1986, 1990; Yeager 1999). This is most apparent in relation to the term 'entrepreneur' and 'business owner' which commonly pinpoint inno-vation, risk-taking, legal status, and size as key criteria. Given this, women are often not considered to be entrepreneurs or business own-ers because their businesses are small, unincorporated, and without staff – even if these women have created a business, assumed financial, administrative, and social risks and responsibilities for it, and partici-pate in its day-to-day affairs (Lavoie 1988; Stevenson 1986, 1990).

Debates over terminology are not confined to the academic area, as this study shows, but play out in policy and public debates and discussions. Throughout the interviews for this book, for example, questions about language and terminology surfaced again and again. Early in the study, as we were busy trying to recruit women to participate, one interviewee strongly recommended we use the term business owners rather than self-employed, explaining that 'most women would be dearly insulted to be considered self-employed' (Interview A05). Along the same lines, the recently released report from the Prime Minister's Task Force on Women Entrepreneurs recommends that government no longer use the term 'non-standard work' when discussing women entrepreneurs, arguing that the term 'non-standard work' perpetuates the notion that 'the self-employed are second-class individuals, and many women entrepreneurs throughout Canada already feel that they are not taken seriously by government departments and agencies or by financial institutions' (Canada 2003).

In light of these comments, it is interesting to note that many participants in the study referred to themselves as business owners and entrepreneurs, even though their work situations would not meet some of the standard definitions of those terms. In this respect, their use of such terms suggests an awareness of discursive issues, and an intentional effort to establish legitimacy and assert a specific identity by claiming the label entrepreneur. Yet other women did not use these labels and one woman – an employer in a very successful and rapidly expanding business – had strong views about making distinctions in this regard. Raising this issue on her own at the end of the interview she said:

> I have to tell you as a woman, I don't find a woman working, or a man for that matter, working out of his basement or his home, I don't view that as a 'business,' which might be arrogance on my part. But I think that it has to be, there has to be a greater definition. When we talk about women going into business, is a woman really in business if she's at home sewing ballet dresses for six-year-old kids? Is that a 'business'? In my own mind I haven't got that yet. So when I read that self-employment has been the most dynamic sector of the Canadian economy ... what does that mean? ... I would say that women are in business, or men are in business for that matter, if their companies are performing at 'x level' where they are creating employment. Because a lot of this, it bothers me, these home-based business things. You know I don't see their value long-term and I think that's where a lot of women are stuck. (Interview B02)

At the heart of her comments is a distinction between what she sees as 'real businesses' and 'other endeavours (such as hobby businesses, lifestyle businesses), following conventional ideas about business owners and entrepreneurs. Expanding on this at a later point she says:

> Typically home-based businesses don't employ a lot of people and it's just another way of using the room I think and making a hobby or making a business out of hobby and, and ... that saddens me. Why aren't women in manufacturing? Why aren't they running big corporations that you know that have come from their own passion and from their own idea? I'd like to see more of that, I'd love to see more of that, where women were getting involved in more *meaningful, real businesses*. (Interview B02, emphasis added)

Her comments reflect a certain perspective on what constitutes a real business, and who is a business owner or entrepreneur.

This view would be echoed by analysts and commentators who adhere to traditional definitions of entrepreneurship, and who question whether we are truly seeing the emergence of an entrepreneurial economy – given that so much growth has occurred amongst the solo self-employed. For them, self-employment does not equal business ownership or entrepreneurship. Certainly it involves being one's own boss and pursuing some type of business activity. But it is not marked by the same innovation and risk-taking traditionally associated with entrepreneurship, where individuals take a new product or service and build a large and successful company around that. But many other women in the study would disagree, identifying themselves as business owner or entrepreneur, even if they are working alone at home in an endeavour that is unincorporated and very small in scale.

In raising this issue, my intent is not to resolve definitional debates at this point, but instead to highlight the differences of opinion and the difficulties surrounding terminology in this field. Indeed, one of the contributions of the book is to show what the face of self-employment and small business ownership in Canada looks like at the present time. Despite the underlying implications in disputes around terminology – that many women's businesses are not real businesses – it remains the case that both self-employment and small business ownership form a key part of the emerging new economy. As such, it requires serious attention in all of its diversity. Moreover, as noted organizational sociologist Howard Aldrich has argued, academic research has vastly under-researched small businesses and organizations relative to large corporations, despite the fact that most organizations are 'small and short-lived, coming and going on a much shorter time scale than the humans who create and run them' (1999: 8). This orientation has left a significant gap in our understanding of work and organizations and, I would add, to our current understanding of women's work in particular. It is this gap that the current study seeks to fill.

With respect to terminology and definitions in the following chapters, I typically use the term self-employed and small business owners (and the acronym SE/SBO) to refer to the women in the study, and more occasionally the term independent worker or entrepreneur. In discussing specific individuals I try to provide further detail on their work situation and status, noting, for example, whether they are an employer or solo worker, in an incorporated or unincorporated business, or in a home or non-home based location.

3 Women's Paths into Self-Employment and Small Business

I guess I've been an entrepreneur all my life. My father had his own business. I think it's something to do with that too. Just seeing, you know, the sense of independence. It's a wonderful thing to control your own destiny and to make things happen.

(Susan, Interview A01)

Job loss, that was the reason I opened my business ... I had thought about having a business earlier. I just knew it was very hard, particularly in my profession. That's why I didn't do that until the last moment, until I was really forced.

(Nadia, Interview B04)

Asked why they became self-employed, Susan and Nadia tell two very different stories. For Susan, the founder of a small, quickly growing, manufacturing business, the decision to become self-employed was a natural, something she had always wanted to do. An entrepreneurial father, a first marriage to a small business owner, instilled a desire to 'make things happen,' to set out on her own. When her marriage ended, taking with it a successful family business, she took a paid job for a time and then made the plunge on her own. 'It's an amazing thing' she says laughing and looking around with obvious pride in her thriving business. 'It gives you a real sense of power.'

Just a few city blocks away, Nadia could not be further removed in her experience of the entrepreneurial economy. Forced into self-employment when her employer's firm suddenly folded, she is a reluctant entrepreneur, struggling financially, often frustrated and discouraged by her situation. Despite having a professional degree, and a well-paying job behind her that was 'half the work, twice the salary,' she finds herself in unexpected territory. 'Here I am,' she says sounding bewildered, 'highly qualified, highly educated in the field and I am lower than the low, you know, poorer than the poor.'

Prompting these two women's stories is one of the key questions raised by rising self-employment and small business ownership: what factors are fuelling its growth? Have workers been 'pulled' into self-employment by a growing entrepreneurial culture, and a desire for independence and autonomy? Or have they been 'pushed' in to such work, as restructuring and downsizing has eroded the availability of once secure jobs in the public and private sectors? Those interested in women's self-employment have added explicitly gendered questions to this debate. Are women entering self-employment as an 'emancipatory route' to bypass barriers and discrimination in paid employment? Or do they represent the classic case of marginalized workers, forced into self-employment as a 'job of last resort'?

To date, existing research has not adequately answered these questions. In many countries, survey and labour force analysis suggest only very general trends (in Canada, see, for example, Statistics Canada 1997; HRDC 2002), while research on women and restructuring has paid little attention to women's growing involvement in self-employment and small business (see, for example, Bakker 1996; Brodie 1996; O'Connor et al. 1999). Thus, as commentators have observed (Arai 1997; Myles and Turegun 1994), explanations for the resurgence in self-employment remain under-developed, tending to be based more on theoretical propositions than on empirical evidence. In addition to having a limited understanding of the specific factors shaping women's dramatic entrance into self-employment, we also know little in Canada about the particular paths women take into self-employment and the relationship between their work, education, and family histories and the businesses they eventually establish.

With an eye towards filling this gap, this chapter examines the pathways the women in this study took into self-employment and the factors encouraging them to start up their own business. Several key questions are addressed: How do women's past work experience, or education, relate to the business they have? How many had past experiences of self-employment before starting their current business, either through a family business (for example, parents or a partner who were small business owners) or an earlier small business of their own? What were the most important factors encouraging them to become self-employed? Was their decision shaped primarily by the pull of an entrepreneurial desire and ambition? By the push of economic necessity, such as job loss or a lack of other work opportunities? By responsibilities for family and children? Or by a combination of different factors? Looking at the women's experiences reveals important insights about the interplay between individual autonomy and economic constraints, and suggests a need to broaden the push-pull debate from the way in which it has been traditionally conceived.

Before turning to discuss this analysis, it is helpful to look at what existing research has to say about the factors fuelling self-employment, both in Canada and other countries. I address this in the next section and then turn to consider how the push-pull debate could be more usefully reframed. Moving from this foundation, I then turn to examine the Alberta women's experiences, looking at their education, work histories, and their reasons for entering the SE/SBO sector.

What Fuels Self-Employment and Small Business Ownership?

There are strong differences of opinion over whether self-employment is the product of a growing enterprise culture or the inevitable result of globalizing, restructuring economies. Those advancing the first perspective – the pull view – see self-employment as largely shaped by individual choice and agency, with workers voluntarily seeking out greater independence and opportunity in an expanding enterprise culture. At the other end of the spectrum – the push view – self-employment is viewed as the outcome of downsizing, restructuring, and the growing use of flexible employment practices that have pushed once secure employees out into marginal forms of work. To date several approaches have been taken to this question: aggregate analysis at the macro-level, surveys of self-employed individuals, and smaller qualitative studies and overviews of existing research. Each approach offers distinct insights and conclusions. Moreover, while some studies focus specifically on women, or gendered self-employment patterns, other studies focus on general employment trends without paying detailed attention to gender issues.

In terms of aggregate macro-level analysis, researchers have examined whether rising self-employment is a response to cyclical or structural unemployment (for useful overviews, see Arai 1997; Aronson 1991; Lin et al. 1999b; Moore and Mueller 2002). Yet despite a considerable amount of research, evidence to date has been inconclusive and in many cases contradictory (Meagher 1992: 128). Those supporting a push hypothesis have pointed to a strong positive relationship between rising self-employment and unemployment rates in Canada and several other countries from the 1950s to late 1980s (Bogenhold and Staber 1991). More recent research in Canada, however, does not support this view. Extensive analysis by Arai and Lin et al. at the national level found no evidence that push factors are the dominant factor in rising self-employment levels in Canada,[1] despite widespread public beliefs that persistently high unemployment in Canada in the 1990s triggered an unemployment push. The only evidence of some connection is in analysis disaggregated by region and gender. For instance, Chambers (1998)[2] found self-employment was an important response to restructuring and downsizing in Alberta from the mid-1980s to late 1990s. Kuhn and Schuetze (2001) also find a link between unemployment and self-employment for Canadian men from 1982 to 1995, suggesting the push hypothesis is gender specific. More recently, Moore and Mueller (2002) suggest that while there is no connection between unemployment rates and self-employment, other factors such as involuntary layoff and prolonged joblessness appears to be important.

Within survey research, available evidence suggests that the vast majority of individuals have been pulled into self-employment by a desire for independence, with limited economic opportunities and barriers in the labour market being important for only a minority of the self-employed. In Canada, the 1995 Survey of Work Arrangements (SWA) asked respondents about their main reason for becoming self-employed (Statistics Canada 1997: 35–6). The top three reasons were a desire for independence (41.8% of responses), involvement in a family business (17.1%), and a lack of other available work (12.0%).[3] While a lack of available work was the third most important reason for both women (13.3%) and men (11.3%),[4] it was relevant only for a minority of workers – leading many to conclude that 'push' factors were not significant to rising self-employment in the 1990s. Further analysis of the 1995 SWA by Arai (2000) points to other constraints, with the presence and number of children significantly increasing the likelihood of women being self-employed (see also Taniguchi 2002 in the United States).

In Canada, more recent findings from the 2000 *Survey of the Self-Employment* also suggest that a minority of the self-employed in Canada (21.8%) have been pushed into their own business, with the majority citing entrepreneurial values such as independence, control, and challenge when asked about their main reason for becoming self-employed (HRDC 2002: 26–7). Internationally, the 2002 *Global Entrepreneurship Monitor*, suggests just 1% of the Canadian labour force are 'necessity entrepreneurs,' but they also caution that the experts surveyed in each country seem poorly informed about 'necessity based' or 'forced' entrepreneurs (Reynolds et al. 2002: 7, 17).

Similar conclusions emerge in the United States, where Bureau of Labor Statistics (Dennis 1996) and surveys of women business owners (Carr 2000; Buttner and Moore 1997) indicate that a minority of the self-employed have been forced into such work. For example, Buttner and Moore found that push factors were not as important as pull factors and, where relevant, were related to gender barriers rather than job loss or restructuring. Similarly, a 1998 survey by Catalyst and the National Foundation for Women Business Owners found the vast majority of women were self-employed in order to fulfill entrepreneurial desires, with just a minority citing downsizing and gender barriers (Carr 2000: 212–13). In the United Kingdom, however, recent work by Smeaton (2003) suggests 'push factors' have taken on growing importance since the 1980s, due to 'contracting out' and redundancy in certain sectors.

Finally, small-scale, qualitative studies and overviews of existing research on self-employed women suggest a diverse range of findings, reflecting the particular local or national economy and the specific profile of participants. For the most part, small-scale studies of self-employed women in Canada suggest that push factors have not been central (Belcourt 1988; Lavoie 1988), but this has not been a key focus of studies and there has been little exploration of this issue in the 1990s, which was a period of significant economic change. For example, Lavoie's review of studies from the 1980s indicates that the most common reasons cited by women for entering into self-employed were the desire to make greater use of their abilities, to be financially independent, and to take on a challenge (1988: 30). In none of the studies was job loss or the difficulty of finding employment a major motivating factor. Belcourt's study of thirty-six successful self-employed women also found that independence, money, and the chance to test an idea were primary motivators. However, she notes that past labour market experiences of discrimination and displacement were also relevant for half of the women. More recent research by Fenwick (2002) suggests that a combination of push and pull factors motivate most women into self-employment, and that these factors are complex, integrated, and sometimes conflicting. Of note, nearly two-thirds of the women in her study left former jobs 'unhappily' for a range of reasons, such as ethical conflicts, lack of recognition and creative opportunity, or a desire for greater freedom and control.

Beyond Canada, other small-scale studies offer diverse findings. In the United States, Jurik's 1998 study of forty-six self-employed home workers in New England and the Sun Belt states found that only a minority (20%) were forced into self-employment due to family or economic constraints.[5] Reed's 2001 study of New Jersey women also finds just a few cases of economic push. In contrast, in Britain, several small-scale studies done in the 1990s suggest that many women have become self-employed due to economic necessity. For example, Granger et al.'s 1995 study of freelance workers in book publishing in the Greater London area (mostly women) indicates redundancy was a primary reason for becoming self-employed in nearly half the cases. Similarly, Baines and Wheelock's 1998 study of micro-businesses in north and southeast England found that harsh economic conditions were a primary reason for women becoming self-employed. While MacDonald (1996) comes to similar conclusions in his study of Teeside, Green and Cohen's (1995) study in Sheffield found that family reasons were important, as were the inflexibility and barriers within organizations.

Taken together, existing research on this issue suggest a number of conclusions. At the aggregate level, analysis for the Canadian economy as a whole indicates that self-employment has not been fuelled in any significant way by economic restructuring and necessity – at least not when measured by unemployment rates and employment levels. However, at a disaggregate level, analysis suggest that push factors may be relevant in specific provincial economies, such as Alberta, or for certain groups of workers, such as men. It also suggests that involuntary layoff and long-term joblessness are important. In terms of survey research, available evidence suggests that the vast majority of individuals have been pulled into self-employment by a desire for independence, with limited economic opportunities and barriers in the labour market being important for only a minority of the self-employed. But small-scale qualitative studies and overviews suggest a broader range of findings, reflecting the local or national economy and the specific profile of participants (for example, occupation, industry, socio-economic status). For the most part, qualitative studies in Canada suggest that push factors have not been important in the 1980s, but this has not been a key focus and there has been little exploration of this issue in the 1990s, a period of significant economic change.

Rethinking the Push-Pull Debate

Making sense of these findings is difficult, and further complicated by some of the limitations of existing research and approaches. Within aggregate and survey analysis, for example, push factors have been very narrowly construed, focusing primarily on the quantity of jobs, as measured by unemployment rates or self-reported job loss. These approaches do not capture other types of factors, such as eroding working conditions and job quality, that may nudge individuals into working for themselves. This is an important oversight given the stress, insecurity, and increased workloads experienced by many workers in downsized organizations in recent years (Duxbury and Higgins 2001; Lowe 2000; Luxton and Corman 2001; Thorne 2000; Wallace 1998), and evidence of eroding trust and commitment towards employers. For example, in large-scale studies of Canadian workers in 1991 and 2001, Duxbury and Higgins found evidence of increased hours and stress, and lower job satisfaction and organizational commitment. Equally important are household constraints, such as childrearing responsibilities and a lack of daycare options, which may force some individuals, particularly women, to become self-employed (Arai 2000; Green and Cohen, 1995; Smeaton 2003; Taniguchi 2002; Vosko and Zukewich 2003).

Similarly, while survey evidence suggests that the vast majority of individuals are pulled rather than pushed into self-employment, this interpretation is open to debate. As Statistics Canada itself notes in discussing the Survey of Work Arrangements, many reasons given for entering self-employment 'do not clearly indicate whether the individual was pushed or pulled' (1997: 35) 'A desire for independence,' for example, may reflect a positive attraction to self-employment (a pull) or a rejection of a lack of independence in prior work (a push). Similarly, 'work-family balance' may be a voluntary choice (a pull), or a forced option (a push) due to a lack of affordable quality daycare. Surveys thus have difficulty capturing the meaning and complexity of the factors involved, and ensuring uniform interpretation of similar reasons between respondents (Stevenson 1990; Belcourt 1988).

A final, and particularly significant, limitation of much research is the tendency to dichotomize individual choices in order to determine who was pushed and who was pulled (for example, by asking for the *main* reason for becoming self-employed). Yet decisions may not always be neatly delineated between push and pull, instead involving elements of both. It may be, then, as Granger et al. (1995: 501) have argued that the twofold typology of entrepreneurial pull and unemployment push is better viewed as a continuum along which 'many combinations of opportunities and constraints' exist. Getting at these motivations may require going beyond existing approaches, as Stevenson has observed:

To understand a person's motivation for starting a business, a checklist of possible motivating factors cannot capture the complexity of the decision process ... Only an interview can allow full expression of the interrelationships between the many variables that can impact on one person's ultimate decision to start a business. In my research, it has become obvious that 'to be my own boss' or 'to be independent' are very simplistic expressions of a set of complex motivational factors. We are still at the exploratory stage in terms of developing theories of entrepreneurship and as such more qualitative, face to face, and in depth interview methods are appropriate. (1990: 442)

Taking into account these critiques, the analysis in the following sections explores the reasons why women in the Alberta study took the path into self-employment and small business. Drawing on survey responses and in-depth interviews, I examine how personal desires and motivation, as well as economic restructuring and constraint, shaped women's decisions to become self-employed. Given the small sample, the intent is not to provide a general account about the importance of push and pull factors for all Canadian women, but instead to deepen our understanding of the nature and consequences of such factors, and the extent to which they have been adequately captured in existing research (Devault 1999). The analysis also provides important insights into the routes women take into self-employment, and the links between their past work experience and education, and the businesses they establish.

Women's Education and Work Histories

A question I begin with concerns the educational and work-related pathways women follow into self-employment. As Chapter 2 illustrated, the women in this study were well educated, with all but one having completed at least high school. One in ten had taken some post-secondary courses, nearly one-third had a trade certificate or a college diploma, and over half had some type of university degree. Diversity, rather than similarity, marks the educational pathways taken by women, and the timing and order in which it took place. Some did post-secondary education or training right after high school, before taking a paid job. Others moved right into the workplace after completing high school, upgrading their education as they worked, either at their own initiative or with encouragement from their employer. Several women raised their families first, in some cases picking up courses while they cared for their children, in others waiting until their children were grown. Others juggled courses, employment, and raising children all at once, while a few gained their education just before, or in the midst of, setting up their business.

In addition to their educational background, most of the women also had previous work experience in other jobs prior to setting up their own business. In some cases, this work was directly related to the business they had started but in others there was no obvious connection. In this respect, some women were 'intentional entrepreneurs' who has used the organization they had previously worked in as an incubator to gain skills, make contacts, and test out ideas for the business venture they hoped to eventually launch (Moore and Buttner 1997). By contrast, other women had taken a quantum leap, moving in an entirely new direction. In some cases, women were forced or necessity entrepreneurs, who made the move because of job loss or a lack of available jobs. In other cases, it was entirely a personal choice: women were excited by a business idea, or simply wanted to do something completely new.

To get a sense of the how women's education and work experience related to their businesses, we began our interviews by asking them to outline their work, education, and family histories, and explain the pathways they had taken into their business. As Table 3.1 shows, the vast majority of women had an educational and work background that was directly or at least somewhat related to their business.[6] Nearly half of the women had an educational background that was directly relevant to their business, and one-fifth had a background that was somewhat relevant. For work experience, the pattern was somewhat the same, with over 40 percent of women having worked in an area that had direct relevance to the business, and over one-quarter having experience in an area that was somewhat related. Yet almost one-third of women had educational credentials that were not at all relevant to their business. And over one-quarter of the women had previously worked in jobs with no specific relevance to the business they were now operating.

To what extent did employers and solo self-employed women differ in this regard? On the one hand we might expect the educational and work histories of many solo self-employed women to be more relevant to their businesses if, as some argue, they have been contracted out by previous employers, and are now working for them as 'disguised

TABLE 3.1
Relevance of Education and Work Experience to Business, Alberta
Study

	Solo workers (%)	Employers (%)	All respondents (%)
Educational history			
Directly relevant	54.8	41.4	48.3
Somewhat relevant	22.6	17.2	20.0
Not at all relevant	22.6	41.4	31.7
Work history			
Directly relevant	43.8	44.8	44.3
Somewhat relevant	34.4	20.7	27.9
Not at all relevant	21.9	34.5	27.9
Total (n)	32	29	61

employees.' In this case there would be a tight fit between past work experience and their current business. On the other hand, if solo self-employed women are more likely to be forced into self-employment by a lack of economic choice, there may be weaker connections between current businesses and past work and educational histories. Having been laid off, or unable to find work, have they had to abandon their previous work in order to pursue an entirely new area?

Addressing this question, Table 3.1 shows that the vast majority of solo self-employed women in fact had education and work experience that was directly or somewhat relevant to their business. Instead, it was employers who were less likely to be running a business connected to their past education and work experience. For example, more than 40% of employers had an educational background that was not relevant to their business, and over one-third had work experience that was not relevant. This compared to just under one-quarter of all solo self-employed.

Women's Past Experience with Business Ownership

Beyond their education and work experience, another important question is whether women had past experience in running a business – whether a business of their own, or the business of a family member,

TABLE 3.2
Past Experience in Own (Previous) or Family Business, Alberta Study

	Solo workers (%)	Employers (%)	All respondents (%)
Women with past experience in:			
Own business	31.3	13.8	23.0
Family business	3.1	6.9	4.9
Own and family business	15.6	6.9	11.5
None	50.0	72.4	60.7
Total (n)	32	29	61

such as a parent or spouse? As Table 3.2 shows, just under one-quarter of women had been self-employed in the past, working in a business different from the one they were operating at the time of the study. Another three women had worked in or been involved with a family-owned business, and seven had gained work experience both through their own past business and a family business.

There are some interesting similarities and differences in past business experience between solo self-employed women and employers, though not in the direction we would necessarily expect. For example, while we might assume that employers come from a family tradition of small business ownership, there was relatively little difference between employers and solo self-employed women in this regard. Overall, 18.7% of solo self-employed women had experience either in a family business, or a combination of their own and a family business, compared to 13.8% of employers. Where differences are more apparent is in the number of women who had run another business in the past. Nearly one-half of solo self-employed women had previously been involved in their own business, compared to just 20.7% of employers. In terms of the solo women, two had been in a partnership with their spouses, while another three had owned successful businesses before moving into completely new endeavours as their interests had changed. Several other solo women had been self-employed briefly in the past, doing limited contract work and commission sales. Finally, three solo women had been self-employed while raising their families, though their business was not a main focus but rather a way to 'make ends meet' and 'keep a hand in the workplace.' Illustrating the tendency to minimize such endeavours, one woman indicated she had never been self-employed in the past, but then realized she had, as she explained how she had quit her job as a hair stylist to cut hair at home for five years after her last child was born. Laughing about her initial response she explained that she had never thought of herself as being self-employed, or as having a business: 'I never thought of that ... It was just sort of like, okay, buy the bread and the milk today, that kind of thing ... so yeah I did that until [my daughter] was ... ready to go to kindergarten' (A09). This experience of 'accidental' or 'necessity entrepreneurship' nevertheless provided her with valuable skills and experience that proved helpful in later pursuing her current business in a more 'intentional' way. Her comments are interesting as well in light of discussions in Chapter 2, because they reflect the ways in which some women may not identify themselves as business owners, self-employed, or entrepreneurs.

Reasons for Becoming Self-Employed

Given their backgrounds and experience, why did these women become self-employed? What factors encouraged them to start their own businesses? Looking first at how women ranked the importance of various factors in starting their own businesses, Table 3.3 shows the results of self-completion items.[7] On the face of it, the findings concur with existing survey research in Canada, suggesting that economic constraints have been 'very important' for only a minority of women. In terms of the responses that reflect push factors, 17.5% of women indicated 'a lack of job opportunities' as a very important reason for becoming self-employed, and 12.7% indicated job loss was very important. Only 3.8% cited contracting out by a past employer. In terms of job loss, important differences exist between solo self-employed and employers – in fact, all but one of the women citing job loss was solo self-employed. Importantly, if we look only at those women who became self-employed during the 1990s (that is, those self-employed less than ten years), the importance of push factors rises slightly. For this group, nearly 20% cited no other job opportunities as very important, and 15.6% cited job loss as very important. Contracting out was very important for just 4.8% (results not reported in table).

In addition to clear-cut push factors, women were also asked about a range of other reasons, drawing on some items from the *Survey of Work Arrangements* as well as other surveys.[8] As with the findings from that survey, the results here suggest that several factors were central for the

TABLE 3.3
Reasons for Starting a Business, Alberta Study (% for whom factor was 'very important')*

	Solo self-employed	Employers	All respondents
Challenging work	93.8	74.1	84.7
Positive work environment	84.4	75.0	80.0
Desire for independence	81.3	77.8	79.7
Desire for meaningful work	78.1	66.7	72.9
Flexible schedule	75.0	50.0	63.3
Having responsibility	65.6	44.4	55.9
Work and family balance	50.0	44.4	47.5
Ability to work from home	41.9	28.0	35.7
Better income	28.1	35.7	31.7
No other job opportunities	16.1	19.2	17.5
Job loss	19.4	4.2	12.7
Contracting out by past employer	3.7	4.0	3.8
Family business	3.7	4.2	3.9
Total (n)	32	29	61

*Respondents indicated the importance of each item on a three-point scale, with 1 = very important, 2 = somewhat important, and 3 = not at all important. Response rate varies from 52 to 61.

majority of women. For example, challenging work was the most important reason for becoming self-employed. Closely behind that was a positive work environment (80.0%), a desire for independence (79.7%), and a desire for meaningful work (72.9%). Each of these are critical ingredients to job quality as discussed in Chapter 1, and highlight the importance of softer, non-monetary aspects of work, in addition to more commonly recognized aspects such as income and security.

While these top four features – challenge, positive work environment, independence, and meaningful work – really stand out, there were additional reasons that were important for many women. These include a flexible schedule, and a desire to have responsibility. In addition, just under half of women cited work and family balance as a very important reason for becoming self-employed, and one-third the ability to work from home. Both of these highlight the ongoing importance of work-family responsibilities in shaping women's work – though, even here, differences should be noted. For example, work-family related reasons were less important for visible minority women, who were more motivated by meaningful work, as well as for younger women. Interestingly the opportunity for better income was very important for less than one-third of women, with this being higher for employers than for solo workers.

Understanding Pull Factors

In terms of the most important factors attracting women to self-employment, it is useful to probe more deeply into these reasons, excavating the meaning women attached to them. In the following sections I explore pull factors in more detail.

Challenge

Challenging work, while cited by the vast majority of women, actually meant a number of different things. For many women, it meant having work that was *technically, creatively,* and *substantively complex* – in short, a job where they could use their skills and abilities to solve problems and meet client needs. For example, women in a range of businesses, from manufacturing to accounting, talked enthusiastically about the satisfaction they got from solving technical problems or working with clients to meet their needs. As one woman in the health care field explained: 'I consider myself a problem-solver. It's just my way of dealing with things. If there's not a problem to be solved, I'd just as soon not be there' (Interview C12).

Another woman with a successful business designing clothing and apparel felt the same: 'When I come up with a solution, that makes me really happy! I think it's probably the strongest thing that I do and of course I can do it on my own terms' (Interview C06). The same was true for the owner/manager of a media production company: 'For me, that's the challenge ... to get into it and figure out what I'm doing for them. It just comes to me, "Oh, this, this, this, they need this ..." It just comes to me and I love it' (Interview C04).

Challenging work was not just about *complexity* however. For many women, it was also about having *variety* in their daily work – a mix of tasks that kept their job fresh and exciting. Several women talked happily about being kept 'on my toes', having to 'wear many hats during a day' and not knowing 'from month to month what I will be doing' (Interview B07, C10, A14). Discussing this, one woman who operates a young, holistic health practice said: 'I don't like routine. I'm a person that likes to do many things at one time ... I like that, it makes me thrive, so, challenging work is definitely up there' (Interview B03).

For some women, challenging work was also about having opportunities to *learn* and *acquire new skills*. Several emphasized that having a small business gave them no shortage of learning opportunities, whereas in large organizations they had found that 'challenges are limited' (Interview B14). Running a business also gave them much more freedom to choose to take on work that they found interesting and new. Speaking to this, an owner/manager of two very successful retail stores explained how she could build challenges into the job: 'There's always room for growth, you know? You can make decisions; you don't have to wade through all the channels to get approval or anything like that' (Interview B07).

Another women with a successful consultancy concurred:

Challenging work, there's always, working for a large organization, it's very, very, difficult to tailor-make your position in a large company. So with this kind of work, you can change. I can change. If all of a sudden I don't want to develop marketing strategies anymore then I won't do that anymore. I'll pick something else up that maybe I'll enjoy even more. So I can actually change my position and change my company as I go along. (Interview B10)

A final feature of challenge that some women mentioned was the actual work of *building a successful business* – attending not just to the product or service they were providing, but to a wide range of functions such as accounting, marketing, managing employees, and business strategy. For some women, challenge came primarily in starting up the business and getting a new initiative off the ground. This was true for one woman in a very non-traditional area in manufacturing: 'I'm one of these guys that likes being a pioneer. I just like challenging the system, I like pushing the limits, I like opening new doors' (Interview B19). Others found a great deal of satisfaction in working to ensure the success of the business, and in the ongoing 'challenge of making a living' (Interview B12). Doing the work for themselves, rather than for an employer, made it especially challenging, as the comments of this owner/operator of a small, thriving restaurant make clear:

I just feel if you're doing something for yourself it's more of a challenge, you put more into it than if you're working for somebody else. You want to succeed, right? Whereas, if you're working for somebody else, what do you care if they succeed or not? ... I just feel it's a challenge to get in there and do it and see if you can really succeed or not. (Interview C02)

In discussing their interest in challenging work, a small number of women also talked about where the need for challenge came from. Some women, such as this woman working the arts and cultural field, saw it as a *personality trait*: 'I love to be challenged. And having responsibility, I'm very responsible. These are innate traits' (Interview B24).

Other women felt the need for challenge was due to the *lack of opportunities* for challenge and skill development in most workplaces. One woman, who ran a flourishing financial planning business, remarked:

I am the kind of person who thrives on challenges. The more challenging it is, the better off I am. I feel much better rewarded. That's why even when I was an employee as an accountant, I revamped the whole accounting system. I started putting this and that, so challenge to me is very important. If I work for a larger organization I believe challenges are limited in the organization. Within the team you cannot go above and beyond. (Interview B14)

Her comments are in line with much analysis of women's work in Canada and other countries which suggests that many jobs available to women are routine and lack opportunities for challenge, growth, and promotion (Armstrong and Armstrong 1994; Kemp 1994; Reskin and Padavic 2002; Walby 1997).

Positive Work Environment

Close behind challenging work was a positive work environment, which 80.0% of women indicated as very important in their decision to become self-employed. Here one theme predominated – *women's ability to control their working environment.* This took several forms, from the way work was done, to the staff or clients one worked with, to the workplace culture itself. For some women, both solo self-employed and employers, a positive working environment was strongly linked to the ability to choose their colleagues or clients. Said one owner/ employer of a three-year-old health services business: 'Positive work environment is the best thing about being self employed. You create whatever environment you want. If somebody is rocking the boat or whatever, you just say, "Sorry, shape up or ship out"' (Interview C19).

Another woman, who worked in a solo home-based business and spent a large portion of her time advising and interacting with clients, said: 'There are drawbacks to working at home, because it's always there ... But it certainly is self-determining, in that you generate your own surroundings. You can decide who you will work with and who you won't. So for me that's part of the positive' (Interview A04).

For many women, a positive work environment also meant *the absence of a supervisor or boss* who could dictate how work was done or clients were dealt with. Many women clearly enjoyed bringing their own personal style to their workplace, and allowing that to shape the way their business functioned. Here there was clearly an interest in moving away from a corporate environment, to create something that more personal, more humane. Said one solo owner of a design company who was very people-oriented:

> A positive work environment is incredibly important, especially when you're in the creative field ... I enjoy my work and I like having fun with people ... I like the fact that I can take as much time as I want with a client now versus someone telling me I better be back in an hour. (Interview C08)

Another woman working with a successful business consultancy observed: 'I think that by going into business for yourself ... you can make your environment whatever you want it to be. There's no one else that's dictating the structure to you' (Interview B10).

Not surprisingly, one place where solo business owners and employers differed was in the specific working relationships they were concerned about. Solo women spoke much more about the ability to *choose clients,* or *to develop partnerships* with other small business owners. For example, one woman who ran a counselling practice and shared office space and support with several other solo practitioners highlighted the importance of these partnerships:

> We have picked each other because we are all independent. We respect each other's spaces and if there's a problem we deal with it and it's over. There's no angry stress. I'm dealing with people who are competent, it's good. (Interview C03)

Employers, in turn, were more concerned about *creating a positive work-*

place not just for themselves but for their staff and co-workers. Many discussed working hard to make the workplace an enjoyable place to be and to avoid the 'stress,' 'bitching and bickering,' 'gossiping,' and 'office politics' they had had to deal with in previous jobs. One woman, who had left a poor work environment in the public sector to open up a small, thriving food business, remarked:

> It's really very important to me to create a work environment that I would call life-giving. And that's not, that's not an easy thing to do. And what does that mean? Well, it means things like people are happy to be here and enjoying themselves and learning and growing and doing something that feels useful. (Interview C01)

In speaking about the importance of a positive work environment, many women set their comments in the context of past jobs where they had encountered bad working situations, either because of unhelpful colleagues, a bad boss, or poor workplace morale. Comments such as these were typical:

> When you're employed you have no choice. You have to work with people who are lazy, or who doesn't want to do the work. You pick up the slack you know, and it's frustrating. (Interview A06)

> I'm not the only one who has experienced that with her ... She's caused at least four people that I know to quit the business. (Interview A18).

> People sit around and they gossip and they do all kinds of inappropriate things ... gossiping about staff and about the problems and they get all caught up in really stupid little things. (Interview B12)

These comments are in line with other research that shows that a positive workplace – where individuals have helpful and friendly colleagues, enjoy good communication, and are treated with respect – is one of the job features that Canadian workers value most (Lowe and Schellenberg 2001; Hughes, Lowe and Schellenberg 2003: 12). They also coincide with research by Melvin Kohn and others that suggest a link between opportunities for self-direction at work and positive psychological functioning (Kohn and Schooler 1983; Kohn 1990; Lowe and Krahn 2002: 453–4). Equally important, they highlight how the desire for a positive work environment can act both as an attraction into self-employment, as well as a powerful push out of an unsatisfactory situation.

Meaningful Work

Another important motivator for many women in setting up their own business was a desire to have *meaningful work*. Nearly three-quarters of the women in the study indicated that meaningful work had been very important in deciding to start their own business, with solo entrepreneurs (78.1%) being more concerned about this than employers (66.7%).

For some women, meaningful work was defined as work that was linked to a broader life purpose – for example, *making a difference in the world, helping others,* or *contributing to the community.* One woman working in a creative field spoke at length about this:

> A lot of people would say, why would you be interested in doing that? Why on earth? Well, you can make a difference. You can make things better, you can bring some interesting, innovative ideas, some open-mindedness to the table. There's nothing I like better than somebody who's interested in doing, not something different, but something meaningful. (Interview C11)

Helping others was also an important theme in discussions about meaningful work. Talking about this, the owner of an events production business said:

> It has to have meaning for me personally but it also has to have meaning for the people I'm doing the work with. Like the [women in the program I mentioned], that program was life-changing for them. And it was very fulfilling for me to know that I made a difference for somebody. (Interview B20)

In a couple of cases, women had begun their own businesses because they felt they would be in a better position to help others than they had been when working for an employer. Said one woman working in the counselling field: 'I saw that a lot of people really needed help and they weren't getting it ... and I really felt that was something I could do working more independently' (Interview B12). Another woman had left a partnership in a consultancy to set up a solo practice so that she could to return to the work she enjoyed, helping clients directly:

> I got removed, taken further and further away from the work, which was the direct contact with clients. And that was an element of frustration in my old position that I welcome the opportunity to undo ... because that's really where the satisfaction in the work comes from, being able to help and being able to deal with individuals, deal with the individual owners and help them with their decision-making. (Interview C10)

Discussions of meaningful work also encompassed, in some cases, a *critique of the work* that was generally available in our society. Based on their own past work experience, several women felt there was 'more to life' than working in a job for someone else. One young woman who had worked very hard to establish her six-year-old photography business said: 'What's the point of doing something that doesn't have any ... you know, if it doesn't have the passion or meaning for you? It's like working at a retail job. It's like, what's the point?' (Interview C14).

Another woman who had left a professional job in order to open a small bakery echoed these comments: 'I just think that life's just too short to be wasting it. And lots of people are just wasting their lives' (Interview C01). These comments are reminiscent of some of the woman in Fenwick's 2002 study who articulated 'post-corporate' values and a desire for work that provided ethical integrity, quality of life, and meaningful relationships.

Beyond these core themes, the search for meaningful work was also, in a small number of cases, motivated by personal or family illnesses or crises that had sparked major changes in women's lifestyles and attitudes. These events, not surprisingly, encouraged these women to pursue work that was more personally satisfying. For example, one woman who had battled a potentially life-threatening disease said:

> The last job I had was selling [appliances] ... and it was a very good job and I was treated very well and selling [appliances] is important ... But when you [are seriously ill] a couple of times your priorities shift, at least mine did. Your focus shifts and I've been given a chance now a couple of times to be here still and it just seemed I had to do something that was a little bit more important than selling. I had to do something that made an impact somewhere and maybe not for you but for me. So this is what I mean by meaningful ... and that's what I get to do here. (Interview A02)

Finally, for a much smaller group, meaningful work simply meant doing something they were passionate about. It had less to do with changing the world, making a difference, or helping others – and much more to do with their *own personal growth and creativity*. In some cases, the desire to do work they were passionate about was paramount, far more important than earning a good income or a running lucrative business. Discussing this, one solo owner of an arts and crafts business said:

> There's no question that I would love to have my visa paid off and my line of credit and my overdraft and you know those things. But it's not got anything to do with why I do what I do. It's the passion. It's purely what I get from it. (Interview B09)

Independence

Having *independence* was also an important motivator for the vast majority of women. Nearly 80 percent cited it as a very important reason for becoming self-employed and there was little difference between solo self-employed and employers in this regard. In discussing independence, women spoke about having the autonomy to 'control your destiny' and 'call the shots.' They also highlighted many different aspects of independence they enjoyed: *having the freedom to make short and long-term decisions, shape the goals and priorities of the business, and set standards and parameters for how work was done*. One noted that she liked 'the fact that I'm able to set, to decide for myself what I want I to do, with whom' (Interview A14). Another especially appreciated having the freedom to do 'what I think is right' (Interview C15).

When talking about independence, many women often spoke not so much in terms of what self-employment provided, but what they had been lacking in previous work situations. Said one woman who had worked in a large government department:

> I've always wanted to be able to do the job as I think it should be done ... And I don't want some bureaucrat sitting in Ottawa, telling me 'Oh that's not ..., you should done ..., we should follow this format. (Interview A14)

Another woman who had worked in a smaller organization had experienced a great deal of frustration around the lack of independence in her previous job:

I was dealing with the board and they hired me for my brains but they wouldn't ever let me use them. Every time I turned around I had to check with them and they were always questioning everything ... it was just stupid. (Interview B20)

Speaking more generally to the issue, another woman who had previously worked in the private sector remarked:

I think probably a lot of people go through this. At some point you decide that you don't want to be part of 'Corporate Canada,' you don't want to just be another employee and that you want to be able to call the shots yourself. And if you make a mistake, well then you make a mistake, but at least it's you that's making the mistake. (Interview B10)

These comments suggest that independence is not just a feature attracting women into self-employment, but a feature that also pushed or encouraged women to leave previous jobs.

In contrast to those who saw the desire for independence emerging from a previously constrained job situation, in a smaller number of cases women saw the desire for independence more as a feature of their personality. Speaking about this the solo owner of a retail shop said:

Since I can ever remember, I have to be in charge. I'm one of those people. I don't take orders very well. I'm extremely organized, I'm usually doing eighteen things at once ... I like to be responsible. So a business just seems the natural way to go. (Interview A02)

A few others, like Susan quoted at the start of this chapter, attributed the desire for independence to personality and the environment in which they grew up.

While independence was generally taken to mean 'independence in the workplace,' it is important to note that for two women, both solo self-employed, independence related much more to family situation and personal relationships. This echoes findings by Goffee and Scase (1999: 658) where some women pursued self-employment as a way to escape dependency on a spouse or partner. For example, one woman had pursued self-employment to gain independence from her children and partner and to create an identity beyond that of a mother and partner. Speaking about her decision to enter self-employment after being a full-time, stay-at-home mother, she said:

> I was almost anachronistic in my own time because I was a stay-at-home-mom, at a time when there were very few except for someone who was dedicated to being mom only. And I, I'm not sure how that is but I thought that you should be able to do both. Have something challenging and still be a parent. (Interview A08)

Another woman, who had a small clothing business, was drawn to self-employment as a way to gain financial independence from her husband. Explaining her decision she said:

> at that point and time I was home with no financial wherewithall whatsoever, with these two little kids and I really couldn't do anything more than grocery shop without really taking a look at the hard dollars and cents issues. And I didn't want to ... I wasn't happy with that at all, because that puts you in the position of no power and money is power. And sometimes when, regardless of the reasons why, there's one person who holds purse strings within a relationship or a marriage or a partnership, that can become an issue. So I thought to myself, 'I want some financial independence and it will help so I can do the things I want to do.' (Interview B15)

Though small in number, these comments highlight another way in which independence can be interpreted, and how it can motivate women to become self-employed. In this respect, one can argue that the traditional interpretation of independence in most studies is a gendered one, and should be broadened to better account for women's experiences.

Flexibility, Work-Family Balance, and Ability to Work from Home

Many studies emphasize the importance of flexibility and work-family balance for self-employed women. This was the case for many women in the study, though there were important differences between employers and solo practitioners. Whereas three-quarters of solo women cited flexibility as an important reason for becoming self-employed, this was so for just half of employers. There were more similarities with respect to work-family balance, which was important for 50% of solo women and 44.4% of employers. But ability to work from home – which is closely tied to issues of flexibility and work-family balance – was much more important for solo women (41.9%) than employers (28.0%). This is not surprising given, that very few employers operated in home-based locations whereas the bulk of solo women did.

Many comments on flexibility and work-family balance concerned women's desire to be *available to their children*, especially when they were young. Fairly typical was this solo woman who began her home-based business in order to give her young family priority: 'The flexible schedule was hugely important because when they're little they have many more things that they need. Kids need things now, not tomorrow but right now' (Interview A08).

Another woman who had been self-employed for over twelve years, in two different businesses, had started her business for similar reasons: 'I think the main reason that I started doing it was because I wanted the flexibility to be able to be home with my kids when they were small and I think I've kind of grown into it' (Interview B01).

But even women with older children emphasized the importance of flexibility. One employer who ran a non-traditional business said: 'I have two teenagers and if you think little kids need you, I think teenagers need you more than ever, so it's really important for me to be home for them or to be available for them' (Interview B19).

Another solo practitioner highlighted the benefits of a flexible schedule, not just for her teenage daughter but also for her aging mother:

> My mother is still alive but she has got to the point where she needs care and attention. And I'm right now facing a very real challenge of having her come and live with me because she's unable to cope on her own. This would not be a possibility if I were working outside the home. I would be trying to throw money at a solution instead of being accessible. And, as I said, I don't think it was a bad move for my daughter who hadn't seen me. I'd been getting up, getting dressed and disappearing for 15 hours a day all of her life. It certainly created a relationship that was needed at that particular time. (Interview C10)

Clearly children and family were the primary reasons for valuing flexibility, work-family balance, and the ability to work from home. But some women also used these features of self-employment for other purposes – to make time for *themselves, their hobbies, volunteer work, and friends* or to *schedule work and vacation* to suit their preferences. Illustrating this one woman in a solo-based consultancy explained her more flexible approach to work:

> If it's a nice day and I want to do something outside and I don't have clients to see, I'll take the afternoon off and then I'll catch up in the evening if I have work to do. So I could be working 'til midnight but I've taken the time that I need for myself. (Interview A14)

In a few cases, women took an occasional afternoon in the summer to play golf or soccer. Another woman was able to take short breaks in order to fit her volunteer work with sick children around her business day. Although the time away from work was usually short, and typically made up at a later time, these women valued their flexibility and ability to use time as they wanted.

Another feature some women valued was scheduling work and vacations around personal preferences and 'their best time of day.' Said one solo woman with a home-base business:

> Flexible schedule, ability to work from home and work-family balance, they kind of all go together. If I want to get up in three in the morning and work, I can. But if I had an office, I probably wouldn't be able to. And if I want to work through supper or whatever, if I want to take a break in the middle of the day and run out for four hours, I can do it. And that's one of the perks I think of being self-employed. (Interview B08)

Several women were early risers and liked to take advantage of this time to work. One woman in a solo design practice said: 'I like to get up at 5:00 a.m. and that's when I do my paperwork and all the ugly stuff that I don't like to do' (Interview C08). Another woman in a solo-based practice explained:

> If I'm going to be awake I go ten steps and I'm in my office and I work. And through the summer I've sort of got into the habit of working from 4:00 a.m. and when I'm tired I'm here and I go lie down. Which would be very hard to arrange in a more structured environment, you know. (Interview C10)

Flexibility mainly provided personal and family benefits to women but, in some cases, it also helped to attract clients. Speaking about this, a solo owner of an accountancy business said:

> If I wanted to do my work in the middle of the night, I could do it. I didn't have to answer to anyone. And that, the flexibility, is what brought me my clients. Because they could phone me at night, they could phone me

on the weekend, they could see me when it was convenient for them, not when it was convenient for me, not during office hours. And they all came to me via somebody else so they knew I worked at home and had little kids and they accepted that. (Interview B06)

As her business grew and became more successful, however, the situation became more difficult to sustain, and finally the benefits of flexibility and work-family balance eroded. Reflecting on this she said: 'Work-family balance, well it was good in the beginning, but now it's too much work.' Speaking about this same phenomenon, another woman remarked:

Everybody says well, if you go into your own business you'll be able to work part-time, have the kids at home and all that. And you honestly believe that when you first start it … and then you get into your own business and if you're not in demand, then it probably does work really well. But if you're in demand in terms of people actually liking your service and they get to know you as a provider, that makes it harder because you don't want to put restrictions on your time. Typically you are working always to the fact that tomorrow you may not have somebody requesting it. (Interview C13)

Several other women discussed this paradox – of having entered self-employment and small business in order to gain greater flexibility and work-family balance, only to find out that it was an illusion (Interview A04). While the potential for flexibility and balance exists, many women could not take advantage of it, or sustain it, as the business grew and became more successful. In these cases, a primary motivation to enter self-employment eventually becomes a source of job dissatisfaction.

From Pull to Push

Clearly the factors pulling women into self-employment are multifaceted and complex. For example, independence means a number of different things, from a lack of freedom in past jobs, to a desire for more control at work, to greater autonomy at home. But what about the push factors previously discussed? What types of motivations do they reveal?

On the face of it, the survey findings are in line with existing evidence in Canada suggesting that only minority of workers have been pushed into self-employment. But questions can be raised about the interpretation of these responses. Perhaps one of the most interesting and important finding is that in the interviews, over one-third of women who became self-employed in the 1990s mentioned some type of push factor in discussing their work history and pathway into self-employment. This is the case despite the fact that a much smaller number of women reported in the survey that job loss and a lack of work opportunities had been very important reasons. Using the interviews alongside the survey data, it is possible to gain greater insight into this discrepancy, expanding our understanding of the constraints facing women, the variety of ways in which they may have been pushed into self-employment, and the extent to which these factors have been adequately captured in existing research.

Job Loss and Limited Work Opportunities

Recall that the interviews were conducted in the late 1990s, several years after provincial and federal restructuring has dramatically reshaped the Albertan economy. Those who had *lost their jobs* and immediately moved into self-employment were quick to identify economic constraints as a very important factor. Said one woman who had been laid off from her job in the education sector: 'Job loss, that was the reason why I opened by business ... I had thought about having a business earlier. I just knew it was very hard particularly in my profession. That's why I didn't do that until the last moment I was really forced' (Interview B04). While several women had lost jobs due to public sector restructuring, some in the private-sector were also indirectly affected by government cutbacks. Recalled one woman who lost her job with a medical supplier:

> It was when the [Alberta] government was cutting back on health care, so all the medical companies were cutting back jobs, so there weren't any ... I looked at other jobs ... which were a substantial drop in what I was making and I thought, 'Well if I'm doing to make a drop like that, I'm not going to do it working for somebody else. I'm going to start my own company.' And there was an ad in the paper for people that had been displaced in health care that wanted to start their own business ... so I called that and started the next day. (Interview B13)

Another woman seeking to enter the health sector after completing her degree started her own business because of *a lack of job opportunities*:

> There were cutbacks in every field, you know, medical, health related professions ... And it became apparent to me that I was not going to get a job in Edmonton, or probably even Alberta in the foreseeable future. (Interview C12)

Others in private-sector jobs experienced downsizing or downturns in their particular sector, leading to job loss and subsequent self-employment. Said one: 'Being unemployed ... I felt really vulnerable and useless ... I just wanted to take my life back ... I just needed to do something to help' (Interview A09).

In this climate it should not be surprising that, in at least one case, a woman noted that it was not *actual job loss*, but the *fear of layoff*, that prompted her to become self-employed: 'There was a lot of talk about downsizing. That was in the early 1990s and I just thought maybe it was the time to make the choice rather than being laid off' (Interview C13).

It needs to be noted, however, that not all women who faced some type of economic constraint indicated that job loss or no other work opportunities were very important reasons for becoming self-employed. There are several possible reasons for this. In some cases there was a *time lag, or an indirect path*, between job loss and self-employment. Some women, for example, undertook short-term positions, or took a break, before becoming self-employed. One woman became self-employed well over a year after losing a permanent job. This time lag seemed to decouple the act of job loss and the act of becoming self-employed in her mind:

> I did a couple of jobs and those were short-term. Then I decided I needed to have something that would give me independence of thought and get me away from crazy employers, and so at that point I went into the current business that I am in. (Interview B23)

Another, who had lost her job in the health sector, described herself as becoming self-employed by default, after taking on a number of temporary work assignments: 'No job opportunities and job loss, those really were part of the initial thing. And then I sort of fell into all of this' (Interview A07).

In a couple of cases, women did not lack job opportunities but instead faced a decision of relocating to another city or department, or 'taking a package.' Recalled one former government employee:

In 1995, our department laid off most of its staff. They kept just a few staff members and we were all given the choice of moving ... taking a package or going to work in another department ... So I took the package that they gave, which came in very handy in starting my business. (Interview A14)

Two others, despite losing their jobs, seemed to view it positively, as an opportunity to do something else. For example, one former government worker explained that while government cutbacks forced her decision, 'I thought to myself I need the change' (Interview C09). Along the same lines, another displaced health care worker said:

I have no regrets. I know a lot of people who were very hurt and very disappointed and bitter when they lost their jobs during the cutbacks. But I was quite happy ... the timing was right for me to move ahead. (Interview A06)

Lack of Positive Work Environment and Independence

In exploring push factors in the interviews, a second observation that emerges is that job loss or a lack of other work opportunities is only part of the story. Two of the factors that were cited as very important for the vast majority of women – positive work environment and independence – have often been interpreted as pull factors in existing research (Statistics Canada 1997). But it is clear from the interviews that for some women these had operated to push them out of their former jobs into self-employment. Interestingly, Reed (2001) finds similar patterns for some of the New Jersey women in her study, noting their dissatisfaction with a lack of independence and workplace hierarchy and politics.

An important theme that emerges from the interviews concerns the *erosion of working conditions and working environment*. In this respect, a positive work environment was more about a rejection of their current jobs than an attraction to self-employment per se. For several women who had worked in the public sector, their workplace had become a difficult, stressful place. Commenting on her former government job, one woman noted that 'the stress was incredible' (interview C09). Another former health care worker said: 'The politics in the hospital, it's just unbelievable you know. People not happy, there's no job security now' (Interview A06). Another woman who left health and social services to go into an entirely unrelated field observed that government in the last twelve years has just been decimated and I just felt, you know, as a worker there is more on your shoulders and a lot of not very smart decisions being made. And so I think I felt like I wasn't in control and there was just more work coming at me. So that was a negative kind of push out. (Interview C01)

Those in private-sector companies also commented about their working environment. One woman described her former workplace as 'so negative it was just disgusting' (Interview B20). Another woman remarked 'there's a lot of things that don't advance the work and in the end contribute to a great deal of stress' (Interview C10). A third woman who had left a job in a private business services firm explained: 'Some parts of working there were great. But other parts were not, they weren't. And if you are going to be stressed, you know, after a while you realize that this is not good for your body and general health' (Interview A11).

While many of the comments related to work environment suggested that stress, insecurity, and workload operated as a negative push into self-employment, a few women also noted *difficulties with supervisors and superiors*. For example, one woman, who had worked formerly in the legal sector, left her job after a change in supervisors made her life unbearable:

Positive work environment, that was really the instigating factor ... my self-esteem was being battered and I couldn't stand it. I was twice as smart as my boss, ten times more experienced, but she delighted in making me feel small. (Interview A18)

Another talked about a very unhappy situation, working for a 'queen bee,' and leaving when she saw no way out (interview C18). Summing up this view, a third woman explained how her bad boss had been one of the motivators in becoming self-employed:

I don't want to have any more bosses. In my last job, I had one good boss and one bad boss ... and I just kept thinking ... what can I do to minimize this boss's part of my life? Well the fact is, in a job, there is no way out. You can't get away from the boss. You can do your best but they're still there. And I thought, I don't want this any more. (Interview B11)

In addition to the theme of working environment, many comments were also raised around issues of independence. While the interviews suggest that a desire for independence was a strong pull factor for most women, for some a lack of independence in their previous job had been a powerful push. One of the recurring themes in this regard was a lack of decision-making ability. One woman, who had previously worked in a large corporation in the private sector, said:

> they basically wanted me to be a robot and I looked at people there who had been there for years and that's what they were – robots. And I thought, I'm too passionate, I can't do that. I wanted to learn and grow and find out about a lot of different things. (Interview B20)

For another woman who had left the health care sector, a key issue was that workers had 'lost their independence.' Expanding on this same point, another former government worker recalled:

> I felt stifled in my previous work in that often decisions needed to be made and it was such a lengthy and at times unproductive process. So the idea of being able to just make decisions ... I wanted more of that in the workplace ... I felt frustrated with decisions that were being made that were just out of my control, and that I could see weren't very good decisions. (Interview C01)

Speaking to a related issue, another ex-government worker noted that she did not want to be 'compromised by the public system. I don't blame the individuals involved, it's not about that. It's about the government not providing enough and the public service burning out the people that are there' (Interview C03).

In addition to a lack of decision-making power, several other women noted the frustration of dealing with *overly bureaucratic workplaces*. For many of them, growing administrative and bureaucratic demands in their former jobs had been highly taxing, taking pleasure away from the work that they saw as meaningful and important. One former health care administrator spoke angrily about the 'nitpicking stuff that didn't really help patient care.' Describing her past work, she said:

> I just got so sick of the bureaucracy. You had to have ten sets of minutes ... and I got so sick of all that because a lot of times you were just holding [meetings] because you needed to. It was just a formality ... So just the bureaucracy of it all and 'total quality management.' I meant there's

another one that's enough to drive you to the mental hospital. (Interview A03)

Importantly, it was not just women who had been employed in public sector organizations who raised this issue. One women formerly working in a private firm in the area of human resources said: 'To make a difference I don't want to go through layers of bureaucracy' (Interview B02). Another former manager in a private business services firm said simply:

Other than having people around on occasion, there's not much I miss about the structure and the politics and the meetings and the time wasted. There used to be a great deal of frustration when you go in with five things to do and end up at 5:00 p.m. with the same five things to do ... which is typically what happens in large organizations. (Interview C10)

Taken together, these findings suggest that existing research may underestimate the extent to which women have been pushed into self-employment. This is not to say that the majority of women in this study were forced into self-employment – on the contrary, the bulk chose to become self-employed largely for positive reasons. But the interviews do show that economic constraints shaped the context in which at least one-third of women made their decision, even if not all indicated these as very important in their initial survey responses. Moreover, beyond job loss and a lack of work opportunities, there were other push factors for some women that were related to working environment and a lack of independence. These are important issues that deserve greater attention in future research.

Conclusions

Returning to the questions posed at the start of this chapter, what conclusions can we draw? Has women's presence within the entrepreneurial economy been fuelled by a growing attraction to self-employment? Or has it been forced by the circumstances of economic restructuring, downsizing, and constraint?

Certainly on the surface it would seem that push factors have not been the primary motivators for most women in the study to start their own business. On the contrary, a majority of women were motivated by a desire for challenge, a positive work environment, independence, and meaningful work. Encapsulated within each of these motivations is an even greater variety of factors, suggesting a multitude of reasons that may attract women to such work. Yet, notwithstanding women's apparent desire for self-employment, it is clear that economic constraints played a critical role in the decisions of some women, and that these constraints are not always readily articulated or observed. While 15 to 20% of women indicated that job loss and a lack of work opportunities were very important factors in prompting their self-employment in the survey for this study, a more detailed excavation of women's motivations in the in-depth interviews suggests that roughly one-third faced some type of economic constraint. This is not to say that these constraints were the primary, or only, impetus for this group, but rather to note that they shaped the context in which these women made their decisions.

Beyond clarifying the relative importance of what are fairly clear-cut push factors such as job loss, the interviews also show how some reasons that are typically regarded as pull factors – for example, independence and a positive work environment – operate as a powerful push into self-employment for some women. Negative work environments, a lack of independence and decision-making ability, and overly bureaucratic organizations are all highlighted by a number of women in the interviews. So, too, was a lack of independence at home. Presumably such motivations are captured as an attraction, or pull, towards self-employment in most research to date. But this clearly distorts women's experiences, or at least minimizes or disregards important constraints and limitations they face. These findings suggest a need to broaden and rethink current conceptualizations of push and pull factors, and to further explore how these factors are intertwined. To the extent that they highlight the importance of factors such as negative work environments, they also underline hidden costs of restructuring for employers and organizations in terms of a deteriorating workplace climate and the loss of knowledgeable, qualified staff.

These findings illuminate several limitations of the commonly used methodological approaches for capturing the ways in which individuals become self-employed. As we can see, existing surveys and aggregate analysis often define push factors in very narrow terms, asking, for example, about unemployment or lack of available work, while ignoring other factors, such as eroding working conditions, job stress, and insecurity that may partially push individuals to start their own businesses. Surveys also pose problems of interpretation. As the women's comments suggest, response categories such as independence can mean very different things to different people. Surveys may also oversimplify the complex array of factors shaping self-employment decisions, by asking typically for the 'main reason' why an individual became self-employed.

Having seen the paths women took into self-employment, and the reasons motivating their decision, a remaining question concerns how push and pull factors shape their eventual satisfaction with self-employment and their success. For example, do women like Nadia, forced into self-employment by job loss or a lack of other employment opportunities, have a more difficult time establishing a viable business than those, like Susan, who start a business on their own accord? Are they as satisfied with their income, job security, and ability to save for retirement? And do they experience the same satisfaction with the intrinsic features of their work, such as independence, creativity, authority, personal fulfilment? In the next two chapters these questions are explored in more detail.

4 'I Love What I Do!' Job Satisfaction and the Creation of Meaningful Work

It is a search, too, for daily meaning as well as daily bread, for recognition as well as cash, for astonishment rather than torpor.

Studs Terkel, *Working* (1972: xi)

As work becomes about both making money and finding meaning, free agents are expanding the American work ethic – and sometimes turning it inside out.

Daniel Pink, *Free Agent Nation* (2001: 84)

I think you do a lot of growing when you are self-employed. You get pushed and stretched in ways that you wouldn't be otherwise ... And you do things than you never thought you'd be doing ... That's satisfying – thinking you just never, never could do this. And then there you are, doing it.

(Jean, Interview B13)

If we judge simply by their growing presence and entrance into self-employment and small business, it would seem that women are making important inroads in the entrepreneurial economy. But we also need in-depth measures that will let us assess issues such as job quality and satisfaction. Listening to Jean, above, discuss her five-year-old business leaves no doubt she relishes her work and the challenges it brings. A bright, lively woman in her thirties, Jean juggles her work as business owner, mother, and wife, raising a toddler with her husband, while overseeing an educational services business that employs four other people. Asked to rank her job satisfaction she ticks 'highly satisfied' along a range of items – day-to-day work, independence, authority to make decisions, opportunities for creativity, personal fulfilment, work-family balance and working from home. It's not all been smooth sailing, she laughs. Some areas need work and there have been some nightmares along the way. But all things considered, she's happy. 'It's fulfilling,' she says with visible satisfaction, 'because you've seen something that's grown from nothing to the size that it is.'

Jean's story provides an important window into the experience of self-employed women in Canada. So, too, do the stories of other women in this study. Currently we have little detailed information on job satisfaction and job quality for the self-employed in Canada, for either women or men. The same is true in many other countries. Existing studies of job satisfaction, for instance, have not always distinguished between paid employees and the self-employed. And more focused studies of self-employed workers have not always probed deeply into the issue of job quality and satisfaction, either focusing on some job features to the exclusion of others, or asking fairly general questions, such as 'How satisfied are you with your job?' (See Spector 1997 for a useful overview of job satisfaction research and measures.)

Breaking new ground, this chapter offers a detailed picture of the daily working lives of self-employed women and their sources of job satisfaction and job quality. It begins by exploring the work self-employed women do on a daily basis and the hours they devote to their businesses. It then turns to examine their satisfaction with what sociologists of work call 'intrinsic job features' – such as independence, opportunities for creativity, authority, personal fulfilment, work-family balance, and time for self. In addition to drawing on in-depth interviews, this chapter also presents new, previously unpublished data from the CPRN-Ekos *Changing Employment Relationships Survey*, which provide a valuable window on the job quality of self-employed women in Canada.

'I Do Everything': Daily Work and Rhythms

Before looking at how self-employed women feel about their work, it is important to provide a snapshot of the kind of work they do. Perhaps one of the most striking features of their daily working lives is the breadth of activities they are involved in. This is especially the case for solo self-employed women who, in the words of several respondents, are a 'one-woman show.' Not only are solo practitioners responsible for carrying out their *core business activities* – whether it be providing accounting services, doing home inspections, producing food products and garments, or writing project reports – but they also liaise with clients throughout the day, in person or by phone, fax, or email. In addition, they are constantly juggling an array of tasks that come with running their own business, such as ordering supplies, paying bills, invoicing customers, marketing, networking, trouble-shooting technology problems, and dealing with tax and other legal requirements. In many cases, solo women handle all of these tasks alone, with only occasional support from family or friends. In some cases, women contract out some of their work, but this is not a common practice – with the exception of bookkeeping and the production of year-end financial statements, with which many women do get help.

Not surprisingly, given the range of their work, solo self-employed women often had difficulty describing a typical day. A woman who worked from a home-based office responded:

> There is no typical day and I think you'll find that ... for most women who are self-employed, especially in small business, because you do everything. I do my own accounting, I do my own marketing, I do my own research, I do my own writing, I teach the classes and meet with clients. You know, at this point I do everything, so there is no typical day. (Interview B01)

Another woman, in a four-year-old home-based accounting business that had grown rapidly, described a similar situation:

> I do everything, e-v-e-r-y-t-h-i-n-g. It's got the point where ... I may need secretarial assistance. But as for now, filing, typing, phone answering, photocopying, bonding, as well as preparing and doing all of that, all of that stuff ... Very much hands-on, the whole works. (Interview C10)

On first thought, one might expect the daily work of female employers to differ, given that they have employees, but this was often not the case. Instead the majority of employers – about 60% – followed a pattern similar to solo self-employed women, carrying out a wide range of tasks, including core business activities, client liaison, business operations, as well as managing and overseeing employees. For example, one woman who has run a design firm with her husband for the past thirteen years described her typical day as a 'hodge podge':

> My days are usually filled with a variety of things. It's very seldom that I would focus on the same thing all day, which sometimes drives me abso-

lutely bonkers because, you know, you don't get the satisfaction of actually starting and finishing something. (Interview C11)

Another women in a five-year-old design and manufacturing business with eight full-time and nine part-time employees itemized her day, noting that she still did 'everything, yes. We're still hands-on in terms of everything, except bookkeeping because ... we're just not wealthy enough' (Interview A01). In another case, the head of a thirty-year-old business had only recently changed her daily work activities so that she could focus on developing new products:

> Well, I am very fortunate that I have incredibly excellent staff and I have someone who basically runs the company. And she's been here for a couple of years now which frees me up to do what I enjoy doing [which is making our products] more exciting, to make them fun ... So I'm basically doing what I want to do and I'm really, really fortunate because I didn't do that most of the time. Most years there was just myself and a couple of part-time people and it was, roll up your sleeves and do everything yourself. (Interview B21)

'I Just Come In and Live Here!': Working Hours

Along with the wide variety of work, self-employed women also typically work extremely long hours, with the exception of part-time workers. Roughly one-third of solo women worked part-time, for an average of nineteen hours per week. But the majority of women worked full-time, and very long hours at that. Indeed, as Figure 4.1 confirms, the full-time women in the Alberta study worked much longer than Canadian women generally, whether full-time paid employees (who work just under forty hours a week) or full-time self-employed (just over forty-five hours a week). As we can see Alberta women who were full-time solo workers clocked fifty hours a week, while employers (none of whom were part-time) put in nearly sixty hours weekly. It is important to note, however, that amongst solo workers there was a wide range of working hours, and that less than half worked over forty hours each week. In contrast, there was far less variation amongst employers, with well over 85% working over forty hours weekly. In short, work hours were more polarized amongst solo women, whereas amongst employers there was a clear and strong pattern towards very long hours.

Figure 4.1
Mean Hours Worked by Self-Employed Women in Alberta, 1999, and by
Women who are Self-Employed and Paid Employees Canada, 2000

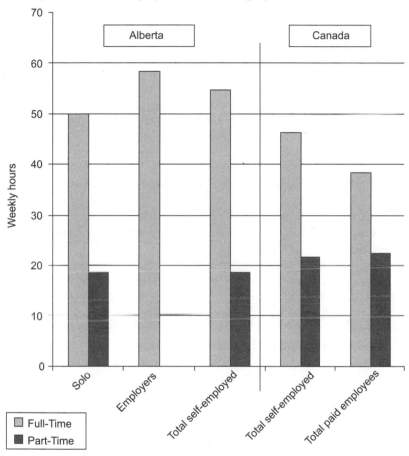

Source: Comparative data for Self-Employed and Paid Employees, Canada, obtained
from 2000 Survey of Self-Employment and 2000 Labour Force Survey (see HRCD,
2002:79).

These findings mirror other research, suggesting that the self-
employed typically work long hours, especially compared to paid
employees (OECD 2000a: 170; Perrons 2003). For example, the *Survey of
Self-Employment in Canada (SSE)* suggests that self-employed women
working full-time spend about 20% more time on the job each week

than those in paid employment. Though the longer hours of the self-employed are well established, some caution is warranted on precise figures as some women, especially those working in a home-based business, may carry out childcare and household work (for example, meals, laundry) alongside business activities. This layering of tasks, which women speak about at length in later sections of this chapter, may lead to some overestimation in working hours spent on the business – although it needs to be acknowledged that the working hours spent on household and caring work are equally important, and speak to the intensity of women's work lives in juggling paid and unpaid work simultaneously (see Adams 1995: 94–9, for a valuable discussion of the demands on women's time). As the OECD (2000a) notes, while there is little doubt that the self-employed work considerably longer than paid employees, there is evidence from time-use studies that the hours worked by the self-employed tend to be overestimated in surveys. Still, the OECD's own data suggest that female solo workers in Europe clocked 20% more time (forty hours) than women working as paid employees (thirty-three hours), and female employers a staggering fifty-two hours.

In speaking about the time they devoted to their work, two issues were central for the women in the study: first, the sheer *length of hours*, and second the *volatility or fluctuations* in working time. Those working long hours had little time for anything but business. In the most extreme case, a solo self-employed woman struggling to keep her business afloat was working nearly eighty hours a week:

> I work from morning until late night. I'm still behind ... Because everything, everything ... I have to do myself. From bookkeeping, to cleaning the office, to looking for materials, to looking for customers. So it's quite time-consuming. I also work on Saturdays, so practically in terms of vacation, I don't get any vacation. It's extremely hard. (Interview B04)

In addition to working long hours at her commercial office, she also routinely took work home in the evenings, doing new designs, paper work and developing promotional flyers and marketing ideas. Describing a typical evening she says:

> And when I come home, it does not mean the work is over. Because quite often I have to work on new designs, so I try not to waste time in the office because only there I can do technical work that I cannot really take home. (Interview B04)

Not all solo self-employed women faced a situation of excessively long hours, however. As noted previously, one-third of solo self-employed women worked part-time and another one-quarter worked close to forty hours. But long hours were a standard feature of the working lives of employers, most of whom worked over forty hours each week. When asked about her working hours, one employer laughed and said: 'Do you believe I don't even know? I just come in and live here!' (Interview C15). Another said simply: 'Too many ... too many, and my family will say that too, way too much.' Another went through a mental calculation, describing a typical working day:

> Right now, I feel like I am working part-time because I think we're proba- bly only working maybe fifty-five to sixty hours a week. Because we start work generally at 6:30 in the morning and we're leaving early now so 5:30, 6:00, we're out of here because it's summer and it's so short that we want to enjoy it. And we've worked six days a week, so I guess we used to work maybe seventy hours a week. It's a lot. (Interview A01)

Despite working very long hours, a few employers did take time out during the day to attend to personal or family errands, illustrating the layering of business and personal activities mentioned earlier. Said one woman who typically worked about nine to ten hours a day:

> I try and schedule myself so that I can get some work done at home, and then come here. And then I try to free myself up by the evening time. So, you know, you get a lot of independence by scheduling yourself. Although I wouldn't say I can do whatever I like, but at least I can work around it, compared to being in a nine-to-five job. (Interview B07)

In another case an employer had recently begun experimenting with taking one day off a week in order to reduce her weekly hours:

> I work probably forty-five to sixty-five hours a week. I am trying this year to work just four days a week, to take off every Monday and leave it, and just feel more refreshed. I'm getting older. I recognize that I want more balance in my life now in terms of time away. (Interview B02)

Most employers, however, seemed to take little time away from their business. In one telling example, an employer explained to me during our interview that this was her day off. In addition to doing a ninety-minute interview for this study, she had also spent several hours beforehand working with her business partner to check on another location and take care of all the things they could not get to on their regular days at work (Interview A10).

Beyond the length of working hours, a second theme that emerges in relation to the time women devoted to their businesses was the *volatility of working hours*. This was especially the case among solo self-employed women, though some employers mentioned this as well. In some cases, the fluctuation and volatility of hours was due to the nature of the business; for example, several women ran seasonal businesses, such as accounting and tax preparation services or real estate and design services, that were especially hectic at certain times of the year. In other cases, the fluctuations were due to the success or failure in attracting clients and projects, and generating new business.

Many solo self-employed women noted that their hours varied widely, and that it was important to 'make hay while the sun shines' (Interview B15). For example, one solo self-employed woman with an accounting business worked fairly steadily throughout the year, but saw her hours spike at tax time:

> There are days obviously that are shorter and days that are longer. In April, between April and June is a very intense period there. You know it's easily fifteen, sixteen hours a day and then you take it easier ... But there's no shortage of things to do, I can assure you. (Interview C10)

Another solo self-employed woman was very busy in the fall and winter, but much less so in the spring and summer: 'It varies depending on the time of year. In the fall it's really, really busy. So I may work sixty or seventy hours a week during the fall. As well in January and February ... that's a really, really busy time for me' (Interview B10).

In other cases, however, solo self-employed women experienced fluctuations in their working hours that were highly unpredictable. Explained one woman with a home-based health practice:

> It changes from week to week, without a doubt. There are some weeks that I easily put in eighty hours because in my business, I'm it. I'm the one that does the books, I'm the one that has to figure out the forecasts for the next year ... to make sure bills are paid, I'm the one that before people come in has to make sure the carpets are clean, the bathroom is clean. I don't have support staff, so I'm it ... But then there's some weeks, you know, I don't have anybody and it's just like you scratch your head and say 'Why is nobody coming?' (Interview B03)

Like solo self-employed women, employers also noted fluctuations in their working hours but more typically these served to increase, rather than decrease, their workloads. While in some cases fluctuations were tied to industry cycles, in other cases they stemmed from the demands of a specific project, and attempts to 'grow the business.' For example, one employer in the educational services sector had seen her hours rise sharply as a result of a larger project her business had taken on:

> This year because we're working very hard to get a specific project done, I'm working probably ten to twelve hours a day, weekends included ... And I don't intend on doing this very much longer you know, just until we finished the project. In about a year, I'm going to start slacking off to do work when I want to and holidaying when I want. (Interview B21)

In another case, hours varied due to the cyclical nature of the business, making for very intense periods of work followed by periods of rest.

Job Satisfaction: Canadian and International Trends

Given the nature of their daily work and hours, how satisfied are self-employed women with their working lives? Is the variety of work, challenge, and independence a source of satisfaction? Or do these factors, combined with long hours and insecurity, act as a source of dissatisfaction and stress? Existing data, both in Canada and other countries, provide only a general picture, suggesting higher job satisfaction on the part of the self-employed but offering few insights into why this is so.

A brief overview highlights some of these key trends, as well as current gaps in our knowledge. Research by the Canadian Federation of Independent Business (CFIB), for example, shows that the self-employed and small business owners are highly satisfied with their work, much more so than employees. A CFIB survey in the late 1990s, at the height of the self-employment boom, found over 90% of small business owners and self-employed workers fairly or very satisfied with their work. This compared to just 70% of employees in the public sector, 76% of employees in medium-sized companies, and 84% of those in large firms (CFIB 2002, 1999).

Data from the Canadian Policy Research Networks (CPRN) job quality website also reveal higher satisfaction amongst the self-employed (CPRN, nd). Overall, 85% of self-employed workers are satisfied or very satisfied with their work, compared to 69% of employees who are satisfied or very satisfied. Recent research by Finnie et al. (2002) con-

firms similar trends using longitudinal data from the National Graduates Survey (NGS) to track graduates from 1982, 1986, 1990, and 1995.
Self-employed workers had much higher satisfaction than employees,
regardless of gender or educational level. Of particular interest, those
exiting paid employment to become self-employed reported increased
job satisfaction, while those exiting self-employment for a paid job
reported a decline.

One of the most important recent studies, the *Survey of Self-Employment in Canada (SSE)*, unfortunately did not ask about job satisfaction
but instead what respondents liked best and least about self-employment. For women, what was liked most was independence (28.1%), flexible hours (17.0%), challenge and creativity (13.3%), balancing work and
family (12.4%), and working from home (11.5%). What was liked least
was the uncertainty and insecurity (20.9%), long hours and lack of time
off (16.6%), income fluctuations (11.7%), lack of benefits (9.9%), and
stress (6.9%). Compared to men, women placed less value on independence, and somewhat more value on flexibility, work-family balance,
and working from home – no doubt reflecting gender differences in
family responsibilities (see Vosko and Zukewich 2003). In terms of dis-
likes, women and men were more similar, with the exception of long
hours and lack of benefits, which were more disliked by women.

Outside of the Canadian context, existing evidence also points to
higher job satisfaction among the self-employed. OECD data for the
European Union, for example, indicate that 45% of employers and 38%
of own-account workers are very satisfied with their work, compared
to just 30% of employees (OECD 2000a: 171). For reasons that are
unclear, women appear to be more satisfied than men with self-
employment, with 52% of female employers (compared to 42% of male
employers) and 44% of solo women (compared to 35% of solo men)
being very satisfied with their work. Comparative research by Blanchflower and Oswald (1999, 2001) also confirms higher satisfaction
amongst the self-employed in the United States (1999) as well as sixteen European countries. But again the reasons for this higher satisfaction are not explored.

Job Satisfaction and Job Quality: Sharpening the Picture

Global measures such as those discussed above are helpful for establishing key differences between the self-employed and paid employees, but
they lack the kind of detail that we really need to assess job satisfaction
and job quality (Spector 1997; Rose 2003). In this respect, the standard

global question used to gauge job satisfaction – 'Overall, how satisfied are you with your job?' – typically produces positive results, even though other indicators may suggest important sources of dissatisfaction (Krahn and Lowe 2002: 428–30). A more effective approach, the 'facet approach', offers a more nuanced picture, probing satisfaction and dissatisfaction on specific dimensions or facets of the job (Spector 1997: 2–4). This approach, using data collected from the CPRN-Ekos *Changing Employment Relationships Survey*, offers new and valuable insights into the work experiences of self-employed women in Canada,[1] as we can see from Table 4.1.

Looking first at the global measure, 'How satisfied are you with your job?,' we see a striking difference, with much higher satisfaction among self-employed women (85.7%) than female employees (68.2%). Moving to examine specific facets of work, we see a more detailed picture that suggests some reasons why self-employed women may be more satisfied with their work. While many dimensions of work are probed in this table, three main clusters stand out. The most critical relates the *capacity for control and self-direction*, items captured at the top of the table. Here we see striking differences, with self-employed women being far more satisfied than female employees with the control they have over their schedules and the freedom to decide how to do their work. A second critical source of satisfaction relates to *positive work environment*, which resonates with discussions in chapter 3. In particular, self-employed women are far more likely than female employees to agree that they have a healthy work environment and good communication with co-workers. They are also far less likely to agree that morale in their workplace is low, as noted on the second-last item in the table. Finally, a third source of satisfaction revolves around *interesting work, recognition, accomplishment and skill*, items appearing in the middle of Table 4.1. In particular, self-employed women are more likely to report feelings of accomplishment, recognition for work well done, interesting work, high skill levels and opportunities to develop skills and abilities.

Perhaps surprisingly, the two groups are much closer in their assessment of *work-family balance* and *stressful and hectic work*. Among self-employed women, slightly more agreed their job allowed them to balance work and family life, compared to employed women. Similarly, both groups were almost equally likely to rate their work as stressful or hectic. The fact that work-family satisfaction is not higher amongst self-employed women is puzzling, given that it is an important motivator for some. This may be a reflection of the long hours worked by

TABLE 4.1
Job Satisfaction for Self-Employed and Paid Employees, Women, Canada, 2000

	Paid employee	Self-employed	Difference
% satisfied or very satisfied with their job	68.2	85.7	17.5
% who agree or strongly agree			
You can choose your own schedule within established limits	44.6	82.1	37.5
Your job allows you freedom to decide how you do your work	69.0	92.1	23.1
The work environment is healthy	73.5	90.7	17.2
Your job requires a lot of physical effort	38.6	55.0	16.4
Communication is good among the people you work with	80.2	96.4	16.2
Your job gives you a feeling of accomplishment	83.6	95.0	11.4
You receive recognition for work well done	75.9	87.2	11.3
The work is interesting	83.1	93.0	9.9
You are free from conflicting demands that other people make	54.9	63.3	8.4
The work environment is safe	86.4	94.1	7.7
Your job lets you develop you skills and abilities	81.2	88.7	7.5
Your job requires a high level of skill	73.4	80.7	7.3
You have access to the information you need to do your job well	88.0	95.0	7.0
I feel very committed to the kind of work I do in my job	90.0	96.4	6.4
The people you work with are friendly and helpful	92.3	98.5	6.2
Your job allows you to balance your work and family or personal life	79.1	83.0	3.9
You get the training needed to do your job effectively	77.7	77.0	-0.7
Your chances for career advancement are good	48.8	46.1	-2.7
Your job is very stressful	63.8	61.0	-2.8
Your job is very hectic	77.4	74.2	-3.2
Your job requires that you do the same tasks over and over	61.5	57.7	-3.8
The pay is good	66.8	60.7	-6.1
Your job security is good	72.2	63.8	-8.4
It would be difficult for me to cope financially if I lost my job	71.5	51.9	-19.6
The morale in your workplace is low	32.2	8.3	-23.9
The benefits are good	62.7	27.0	-35.7

*All statements were answered using 5-point scales where 1 = strongly disagree and 5 = strongly agree.
Source: CPRN-Ekos *Changing Employment Relationships Survey, 2000* (n = 2118)

many self-employed women, which would also explain assessments of stressful and hectic work.

Finally, one area where female employees clearly have an upper hand is around *pay, job security, and benefits*. As we can see at the bottom of the Table 4.1, self-employed women were far less likely than female employees to agree that their pay was good, their job security was good, or that they received good benefits. The gap on benefits is particularly striking, and reflects a significant issue in terms of job quality.

This information helps to deepen our understanding of job satisfaction among the self-employed. Building on this more detailed picture, we can move to an even more useful way of gauging job quality and satisfaction, looking at what can be called a job quality deficit.[1] This measures the difference between what people *have* in a job and what they *want* in a job – essentially the gap between their reality and their ideal. In calculating a job quality deficit, we use measures of what people have in a job (as shown in Table 4.1) and what they *want* in a job (additional measures from the CPRN-Ekos *Changing Employment Relationships Survey* not shown in Table 4.1). In addition to measuring the deficit, we also combine some of the individual, but related, facets shown in Table 4.1 into several key indicators. For example, the facets pertaining to pay, benefits, and security are combined into the dimension of extrinsic job rewards. The advantage of this approach is that we have a more robust, multi-dimensional, measure by which to gauge key differences in job quality.

Using this approach provides a rich snapshot. As we can see from Figure 4.2, women who are self-employed or own a small business have much smaller 'job quality deficits' than paid employees on several key dimensions of work. In particular, this is the case for work environment, intrinsic rewards, psychological attachment, and work-family balance. The first of these, *communication*, captures the extent to which one works with friendly and helpful people, has good communication with colleagues or clients, and supportive work relationships. Here just 3% of self-employed women report a large job quality deficit on this item compared to 15% of employees, suggesting a very tight fit between their actual and ideal work situation. The second indicator, *intrinsic rewards*, includes the opportunity for interesting work, training, skill development, and accomplishment. Here less than 6% of self-employed women report a large job quality deficit, compared to 14% of employees. *Psychological attachment* involves one's work commit-

Figure 4.2
Job Quality Deficits for Self-Employed and Employees, Women, Canada, 2000

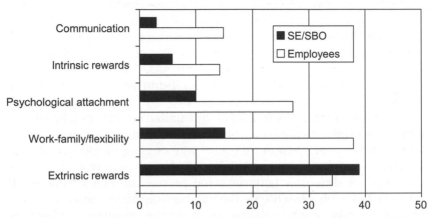

Source: CPRN-Ekos *Changing Employment Relationships Survey*, 2000 (n = 2,5000);
Hughes, Lowe, and Schellenberg, *Women's and Men's Quality of Work in the New
Economy*. Ottawa: Canadian Policy Research Networks, 2003.

ment and involvement, a sense of shared values and respect. On this
item, just 10% of the self-employed report a large gap, compared to a
very high proportion of nearly 30% of employees. Finally, *work-family
balance* includes the ability to choose one's schedule, balance work and
family, and have some influence on one's working life. Here 15% of
self-employed workers report a large job quality deficit, compared to
nearly 40% of employees.

There is just one area where self-employed workers and small business owners are more likely to report larger job quality deficits than
employees, and this is on the item of extrinsic rewards. This refers to
good pay and job security, an issue taken up in Chapter 5. As we can
see, almost 40% of the self-employed and small business owners report
a large job quality deficit on pay and security, compared to 34.1% of
employees.

To a large extent, these findings on job quality deficits are mirrored
in findings from the women in the Alberta study. Overall, their job satisfaction is exceptionally high with respect to the nature of the work
they do, their independence, their authority to make decisions, and the
personal fulfilment from their work. However, there are also important sources of difference, in particular, those between employers and
solo women.

TABLE 4.2
Satisfaction with Intrinsic Work Features, Alberta Study (% 'satisfied' or 'very satisfied')*

	Solo self-employed	Employers	All respondents
Independence	93.8	86.2	90.2
Opportunity for creativity	96.9	92.9	95.0
Authority to make decisions	96.9	89.7	93.4
Nature of day-to-day work	84.4	86.2	85.2
Work and family balance	68.8	51.7	60.7
Time for self	38.7	17.2	28.3
Personal fulfilment	90.6	96.6	93.4
Total (n)**	32	29	61

*Respondents indicated satisfaction on a five-point scale, where 1 = very satisfied and 5 = very unsatisfied.
**Response on each item varies from 58 to 61.

Excavating Job Satisfaction: The Study

In order to more fully excavate job satisfaction and job quality issues we now turn to the Alberta study. Here we collected data in two ways in order to learn more about this important issue. First, following standard survey approaches, we had women complete a brief survey at the start of the interview which asked about satisfaction with a limited number of work facets (for example, independence, day-to-day work, and so on). Midway through the interview, we reviewed and discussed these survey responses in detail with the women in order to learn more about source of satisfaction and dissatisfaction in their work.

Table 4.2 shows the responses to the initial survey items. As we can see, there are many parallels to the CPRN-Ekos survey. Overall the satisfaction with various aspects of self-employment is very high, for both employers and solo self-employed. Nearly all women were satisfied or very satisfied with their opportunities for creativity, their authority to make decisions, and a sense of personal fulfilment from running their business. Satisfaction was also very high in terms of their independence and the nature of their day-to-day work. Likewise, fewer women were happy with their ability to balance work and family, though the majority were satisfied or very satisfied. Where satisfaction fell most dramatically, however, was in terms of time for self, with just 28.4% of women agreeing they were satisfied or very satisfied.

An important insight from the Alberta study, not captured in the CPRN-Ekos data, concerns similarities and differences between employers and solo women. Overall, solo women were more likely to be satisfied with specific facets of their work. While satisfaction with the nature of their day-to-day work was roughly the same, slightly more solo women than employers were satisfied with their independence, and their authority to make decisions perhaps reflecting the advantage of working alone. Satisfaction with work-family balance and time for self was much lower for both groups, but here as well solo women were happier with their balance between work and family and the time they had for themselves. Indeed, the only item where employers were slightly more satisfied was personal fulfilment.

While the survey responses offer useful benchmarks on specific areas of satisfaction, they provide little detail as to how women experience these work dimensions, or why they find them particularly satisfying or dissatisfying. In order to deepen our understanding of these issues, the following sections draw on the in-depth interviews to explore these items in more detail.

'Master of My Own Fate': Independence

The desire for independence was a significant motivator for many women to become self-employed. But while satisfaction with independence was exceptionally high for both solo women and employers, there were differences in what they seem to find satisfying about it. Solo women were far more likely to gain satisfaction from having the independence and freedom to *shape their working environment* – for example, the hours they worked, the location they worked from, or the ability to more easily combine their business and family responsibilities. Even where they did not take advantage of this freedom, there was still satisfaction with the *potential* to be able to do what they wanted to. Said one woman who operated a five-year-old restaurant, 'I am satisfied with the level of independence I have because I can theoretically work the hours I want to – I can decide which hours I want to work and which ones I don't' (Interview C18). Others talked about being able to work at odd hours, juggle their work schedules, see friends, and operate in less conventional ways.

In addition to fashioning work environments that suited them, some solo self-employed women found satisfaction in *not having to deal with bosses and supervisors*. Said one woman: 'I'm a flexible person but I have pretty clear ideas and I have been frustrated many times at not being able to follow ... the way I saw things' (Interview B23). Yet, even though this independence was important for most, a few mentioned that it was 'a double edged sword.' Explained one solo woman, 'That's one of the setbacks is there's no one behind you pushing you to do it. You have no boss that says you do this or you're fired you or you have a week to handle this. You're on your own. There's good and bad in it' (Interview B08).

In contrast to solo self-employed women, employers were far more likely to talk about independence in terms of *shaping and building their business*. All but one or two comments dealt with this aspect. Said one woman who operated two retail stores with another female business partner, 'To me, it's the freedom and independence and being able to do what I want to do. If I get an idea I can bring it out here ... When you're working for someone else, you can't' (Interview A10). Another women working in the health care field said: 'I do like the independence, you know, in that I get to think about and decide what happens ... and how' (Interview A17). Another employer in a human resource company who had 'locked horns' many times with her previous employer, relished her independence:

> I can change. If I don't want to do this business, I can do another business tomorrow. I like setting goals and being responsible for achieving those goals ... I like being able to set the direction, change the direction. I like the developing of relationships. I like the challenges, I really do. (Interview B02)

Unlike solo women, just two employers spoke of having the independence to create their own working environment, such as by finishing early for the day, or more easily combining their work with raising their children. In short, for employers independence seems to be appreciated as a tool to grow and shape their business, while for many but not all solo women it offered a means to work differently and create a more balanced lifestyle.

'We're Very Creative': Opportunity for Creativity

Of all areas, creativity was the most satisfying for the women in the study – 95% were satisfied or very satisfied with the creativity in their work and there were fairly small differences between solo self-employed and employers in their survey responses and interviews. Women spoke of creativity in two different ways. For most, opportunities for being creative came through the *developing the products or services* they offered, and coming up with *new ideas*. This kind of creativity is critical for business success (Ward 2004). But a smaller group also noted that they found many opportunities for *creativity in their business operations* – for example, in activities such as marketing, promotion, and creating a visual image for their business. Notably, just one or two individuals indicated that they did not find their work that creative.

In terms of creativity in developing products and services, many women were involved in businesses that were creative at heart. Several ran restaurants or food-related business where creating delicious food and a warm, appealing atmosphere were keys to success. Other women worked in interior design, clothing design, or product design, where creativity and innovation were critical. In some cases, creativity involved making beautiful and appealing products. Said one employer in a design and manufacturing business, 'We're very creative, we have to be. It makes or breaks our business' (Interview A01).

Another employer working in the architectural industry said:

> There's a lot of creativity associated with it ... When you're on the creative side you're designing, you're trying to refine something, and in terms of colour schemes and materials, you have to think it through. The process is not something that you can say will just take five and a half minutes. It's something that could happen very quickly or could take a bit of time. (Interview C11)

In other cases, creativity was linked to *problem solving*:

> When I come up with a solution – that makes me really happy! So I think that is probably the strongest thing I do and, of course, I do it on my own terms. (Interview C06)

> In terms of opportunities for creativity, there's lots of opportunities for that. You know, just coming up with ideas and we're always looking at ways that we can improve what we're doing. (Interview B13)

Others discussed a link between creativity and independence:

> Creatively I have a lot of room and I love that. (Interview A15)

> Opportunity for creativity, well I think it's great because I can get to do

whatever it is I want to do. And whatever I can visualize and do, I can decide it and I can create it. (Interview B20)

Not all women spoke of creativity, however, in terms of the product or services they offered. For a small group, opportunities for creativity came largely through the *operation of their business* – for example, in marketing and promoting their businesses. One woman, in explaining at length a number of innovative promotions she had done, noted:

Opportunities for creativity come into play especially in marketing. I love different ways of marketing ... This is my creativity. I see something that I think would be appropriate for my clients and that's what I do. (Interview B14)

For other women creativity came in identifying and developing new clients: 'It's very creative because some times you run out of friends, you run out of cold calls, then what do you do? Then you have to be creative, right?' (Interview C09).

Although nearly all women, whether employers or solo self-employed, spoke highly about the opportunities for creativity in their work, there were one or two who felt the creative demands in their work were minimal. Said one woman working in the health care field: 'There is creativity involved in the work but I wouldn't rate it as particularly high' (Interview A17).

Such comments were rare, however, with most women feeling their work was very creative. This raises interesting links with recent arguments by Richard Florida in *The Rise of the Creative Class*. While arguing that the new economy is fuelled by a 'super creative core' of highly educated knowledge workers, Florida also suggests strong links between self-employment and creative work. This is not only the case for highly educated, professional 'free agents,' but also for some traditional service workers who are highly entrepreneurial, pursuing creative work in their own businesses in order 'to get away from the regimentation of large organizations' (Florida 2002: 77). In his view, these types of workers form part of the creative class, being creative not only in the work they do, but the way they do it.

'My Way': Authority to Make Decisions

Having the authority to make decisions was a source of satisfaction for the vast majority of women. But this was slightly truer for solo self-employed women than for employers. While nearly all of the solo self-employed women (96.9%) were satisfied with the authority to make decisions, this was also the case for 89.7% of employers.

In speaking about their satisfaction, both solo self-employed women and employers made many similar comments. A number of women identified themselves as 'someone who liked making decisions' and noted the satisfaction they got from making decisions about the type of work they would do, the running of their business, or the way they planned their day. Several employers also emphasized this as a feature of their personality. As one employer of a manufacturing firm said very honestly: 'I like being in charge. I like making decisions' (Interview A01). Other women explained: 'I'm a real independent kind of person, I'm kind of a lone flyer in many ways. I love to do things my way ... I like to make the final decisions. I like to have that control and the fulfilment of what I've done' (Interview B17).

For some women, the satisfaction of making decisions was largely a function of not having to deal with a boss or employer who would direct the way work was done, or the goals that were being set. In this way it was linked to independence. For one solo self-employed woman it was important to be able to use her own judgment in deciding how to approach a problem: 'I'm the only one who makes the decisions about the business. I don't get anyone who pretends to know something ... and try to force me to apply some procedures that are absolutely not acceptable' (Interview B04).

Some employers also discussed their satisfaction in these same terms:

I like setting goals and being responsible for achieving those goals. I don't like somebody telling me, well we did X million last year, we have to do X million this year ... I don't like that, I like to be able to set the direction. (Interview B02)

I find it very satisfying because I don't have to go to any higher ups ... because I know. And that helps instead of you waiting days and days to get approval. There's a time you have to make the decision fast enough to make a good deal and I know I've got that right to do it. So that helps a lot and I feel very satisfied with that. (Interview B07)

In one case, the satisfaction with making decisions came from the broader context of a women's life. This was a young single mother who had struggled with unemployment, illness, and finances before starting a home-based communications business:

> I don't have total authority because on a client's work, of course, the client's authority is final. But I like the authority to take charge of my own stuff, which I haven't always had. I mean when you're a single mom on and off of assistance as employment allows, you don't always have that kind of authority. But when I can say, 'No, I'm going to buy this for promotional reasons,' that's nice decision-making authority, that's good to have. When I have the authority to sign and apply for credit on my business's behalf, that's kind of nice when you get it. (Interview A15)

Where the most notable differences emerge between those women working alone and those employing others is in their discussion of the *downside of having authority*. While a few solo self-employed women noted this, it did not appear to be a significant issue for them. Typical of their comments were: 'If I make a mistake, I have to live with it' (Interview A16); or 'all the decisions that are made in my company are made by me, good, bad, or whatever, they're mine' (Interview B08).

In contrast, employers spoke at much greater length about the downsides of having authority, emphasizing both the *risks* and the *isolation* of being the final decision-maker. It would seem that their ambivalence stems in part from their responsibilities towards employees and the larger potential risks they face. Said one small employer in a business providing educational services: 'We've made mistakes that have been costly ... So that's why I've learned about the authority to make decisions, that you have to make sure that you're stepping back and looking at it' (Interview B13). Another employer spoke at length about the risks of her manufacturing business:

> I live and die by all of the decisions that I make, right? And, you know, if I bid a job wrong, I eat it. That's all there is to it. If I haven't been paying attention to the numbers, if I made a brain-dead error, well then, you know, it's me who has to come up with figuring out how to do that. And when I make errors, if I make an error, these are huge contracts that go out of here. I mean really big numbers that scare people to death ... Not many individual women can say that they're in a position where they make decisions about three hundred and four hundred thousand dollar contracts on a monthly basis. But that's the two-edged sword ... You live and die by your own decisions and if I'm good at that then I have nobody

to blame but myself and that's very good. But I have also nobody to talk
to, to keep me on the straight and narrow. (Interview B19)

Other employers also noted the isolation that came with making
decisions, and not having colleagues to help them work decisions
through. As this employer and owner of a one-year-old food-related
business explained:

Sometimes that's really hard because you have to make all of the decisions. Like, speaking of the challenges, like I sometimes find that really
hard. Like now I'm making a decision about staff and I've had my strug-
gles. It's like 'Am I going to make a good decision?' There's no one to
really sort of weigh that with. (Interview C01)

For another employer the downside also extended to her personal and
family life: 'It's nice to make a decision but sometimes I get home at
night and someone wants me to make a decision and I just think "No, I
don't want to make any more decisions!" I'm tired already, you know?'
(Interview C13).

'Slave to a Schedule': Work and Family Balance

Given that so many women worked long hours, and that the vast majority had children, we might expect very high dissatisfaction with work-
family balance. But overall, many women were satisfied, although this
differed notably between solo women and employers. While nearly 70%
of solo women were satisfied or very satisfied with their work-family
balance, this was the case for just over half (51.7%) of employers. Part of
the difference is no doubt due to the fact that many, though not all, solo
women had a different work set-up than employers. Roughly three-
quarters of solo practitioners worked at home, and one-third worked
part-time, averaging about nineteen hours each week. In contrast, there
were no part-time employers and those working full-time worked
nearly sixty hours a week, compared to fifty hours for full-time solo
women. In addition, only a few employers had home-based offices.

In discussing their satisfaction with work-family balance, many
women, especially solo women, highlighted the benefits of working at
home and being able to more easily blend their work and family responsibilities. During the day, laundry could be run while business calls

were made, or reports written. During breaks, children could be picked up from school, or taken to activities, and then work resumed later in the day when they were asleep. One woman with children aged seven and nine explained her satisfaction with being self-employed as a financial consultant in the context of her family life:

> Work-family balance, yes, it is very important to me. Had I been single, I don't think that is an important issue. I may still want to be self-employed because of the satisfaction again, but the flexibility and the ability to work from home would not be an issue. But because I am a mother and a wife, it is important. I can be doing my laundry, the supper cooked, and I am still working. (Interview B14)

Other women noted the flexibility their work allowed them to be involved with their children's activities at school and in the community. Said another woman with a seven-year-old child who had been in a home-based business for seven years: 'If I want to say "Oh, I think I'll go help out at his school today, it's nice to be able to do that or take off early and pick him up to go and do something." ... This way I can work whenever I want' (Interview B20).

A woman who shared the parenting of her eight-year-old with her former spouse emphasized how important it was to have a home-based business:

> Because I have a small child and I want to have some involvement in his school and things like that and because as a single parent there is the juggling of parenting responsibilities between me and his dad at different places, I need that flexibility ... It gives you more control of when you work. It's again, it's another factor of flexibility. If I want to do my database searches at 1:00 in the morning, I can do that. (Interview B23)

While the benefits of more easily blending work and family tasks were most discussed by solo women, at least one employer in a home-based business noted these benefits as well. With two children aged eleven and fifteen, she had been self-employed for six years, working in a home-based office and hiring contract employees throughout the year for the various projects she organized and managed. While she was currently evaluating whether to move into an outside office, she still felt strongly that there were many benefits to working at home, both in terms of blending activities, and saving time getting to and from work. Discussing the pros and cons, she said:

> We're just evaluating whether we'll move or not. But the pleasure and the time that you save like the hour drive, I mean, that's an hour I can take the dogs for a walk, I can clean the kitchen, I can throw in a couple loads of laundry. The flip side of that is in many ways that's harder on me. It would be nice just to go to work and forget about everything. But that's what the appeal was in the very beginning, that I didn't want to have to go into an office and put in all that time and effort. (Interview B17)

The downside that she alludes to – of running a business within a home – was one that many women spoke about, even if they were generally satisfied with the balance they had between family and work. Despite the benefits of working from home, difficulties arose when the demands of work and family came into conflict, or there was a difficulty containing the demands of clients and the business. One woman, who had been working in a home-based business for four years, while raising her teenage daughter alone, noted these tensions:

> Work and family balance is much more satisfying here. Still, I can tend to be absorbed in my work. There are certain times I just can't spend time, it is out of balance, the workload at times of the year. There's no helping that. (Interview C10)

Another woman with a home-based legal practice said, 'It's funny how when you're self-employed you think you can be very flexible, but sometimes you can't because your clients don't want you to be' (Interview A18).

Demands could be especially intense in the early stages of business start-up, or when businesses were growing rapidly or facing difficulties. One woman who had been running a home-based communications business for a year and a half, while raising a seven-year-old, discussed the difficulties of protecting family time from her business:

> I'm still finding it hard to keep the evenings and the weekends to my family but I'm working on it ... I am training myself not to check faxes, not to check emails, not to go down there on weekends. It doesn't always work. And sometimes I do have to meet clients in the evening in my family time but I try really hard not to. I'm trying really hard to separate that now.

Now that it's not a baby, it's not an infant any more, I'm trying to wean it into more of a regular schedule. (Interview A15).

Another woman with a three-year-old, who had recently moved her home-based business to an office location, also noted the difficulties of the initial start-up:

Work and family balance. I would say that's been a struggle but now it's not a struggle because when you first start your business, it's all consuming. And it is a strain on your family ... because it's hard to shut it off. Your office is in your house and you go by and you want it to be successful so you just focus, focus, focus ... So the balance between work and family was a struggle at first ... I've had to learn that you put so much time in and then you have to say that's it. (Interview B13)

Beyond the demands of a young business, pressures to earn sufficient income also had the potential to jettison work-family balance. Despite working part-time, one woman in independent sales still found that the promise of work-family balance and flexibility in self-employment was more illusory than real:

I like the flexibility although I will honestly say that sometimes that can be a trap because if you want to make it worthwhile from a financial standpoint, sometimes you have to become a slave to a schedule in order to make it work ... And I find that I have to be really, really disciplined to say 'No, I only work on Tuesdays and Thursdays. If Tuesday and Thursdays don't work for you, then I'll adjust my schedule' ... But that means I have to adjust the whole week. (Interview B15)

Whatever the drawbacks, they seemed to be outweighed by the advantages of a home-based business. In fact, those who were dissatisfied with the balance between their working and family lives were far more likely to be solo women who did not work in a home-based situation, or employers who typically did not. A common source of their dissatisfaction seemed to be a *lack of time* to devote to their family responsibilities. Speaking about this, one solo self-employed woman with three grown children who had been running her own business in a location away from her home for the past five years said:

I have no time for my family. I feel like my family concerns are on hold because the business consumes so much of my time. The job I am doing is a twenty-four-hour job and that does not leave much time for myself or my family ... even if I am not at work I still am thinking of it or doing work at home. (Interview C18)

Employers, even small-scale ones, were also more likely to experience 'time famines' (Perlow 1998) and face difficulties shutting off the demands of their businesses. In the words of one woman, who ran a small practice with one employee in the city centre: 'Work and family balance? What balance? I'm working!' (Interview A17). Another employer who had built up her business over the past seven years and had two children under the age of three spoke about her difficulties of being unable to take time for family, even if she had the independence and authority to do so. Reflecting on the birth of her children, she said:

I never expected whatever happened to me is that I'd have a baby and be back at work one week later. You know, I always thought that I was going to have the flexibility to take a lot of time off and not worry. It just doesn't happen. Once you've got your name in the workplace, there's demand and if you don't fill the demand, they're going to go somewhere else. (Interview C13)

Dissatisfaction was also more evident for women whose work involved a great deal of 'face time' with clients, or who were tied to an office or store location. Comments such as this were typical:

I do have flexibility but I don't. I mean if I have an appointment you can't very well just cancel it. (Interview B03)

I have to be here, I have to open the office, I have to do the work, so I cannot really close it and go do something else. (Interview B04)

There are times that the staff don't show up and you have to do their shifts. There is a downside to it too. (Interview B07)

My schedule is highly inflexible right now. Most of the time I have to open the shop ... If I sleep in, there's no sales, and that's not good for business ... But in the long haul I imagine this providing me with a schedule that gives me more control. (Interview C01)

Finally, it should also be noted that while many women were concerned with the issue of balancing work and family, some simply were not. A common stereotype of self-employed women is that they become self-employed in order to juggle work and family demands. But as the analysis in the previous chapter has shown, there are many different reasons why women become self-employed, and often they are a complex combination of factors. In discussing work and family balance, a few women made it clear that work-family balance was simply not an issue for them. One woman who had been in a home-based business for three years and had grown step-children made it clear that her career was the priority:

> Work-family balance, that's not important to me. I don't really think about work-family balance. My career has always come first ... My step-children don't live with us and I purposely did not have children of my own. I was one of those women that chose not to because I knew that my career was going to be very, very important to me and I didn't really want to start trying to 'balance' things. (Interview B10)

Another business owner and employer who did not have children and had devoted well over twenty years to her business, while her husband worked in another profession, said: 'Our work is our life, so it's pretty hard to get a balance when you're both very much involved in something as creative as this' (Interview B21).

'No, It Just Doesn't Happen': Time for Self

Without doubt, the greatest source of dissatisfaction for all the women in the study was with the amount of time that they had for themselves. Among solo self-employed women, just 38.7% were satisfied or very satisfied with the time they had for themselves, while for employers this figure fell further to just 17.2%. Despite these low rates of satisfaction, however, there were some women who felt that self-employment provided them with more than enough time for themselves. In some cases, it stemmed from the flexibility and independence of their work, as well as the growing independence of their children. For example, one solo self-employed woman explained:

> If my friend calls and says, 'Can we get together for coffee or something?' it's not an issue. I can do that. I like that, you know? It's kind of nice because I'm almost fifty and I've always worked at least two jobs, And so I've become more jealous of my time ... And I think my kids are older too

so they're not demanding on time and I have more freedom and I appreciate that. (Interview A09)

In a few cases, women seem to have made a conscious decision to cut back on their work hours to have more time for themselves. Noted one solo self-employed woman:

Time for myself is really important. I don't like working nine to five with three weeks only holidays. One of the things I like most about being self-employed is I can take a five-week holiday and I can take a week off here and I can take a week off there. The only thing that suffers is my own income. (Interview A13)

One employer, discussed earlier, had just begun a reduced work week of four days in the previous year. But cutting back on hours, in order to have more time for one's self, was relatively rare. In some cases, women's income was a key part of the family income, and cutting back hours was simply not an option. Discussing this, one solo self-employed woman said:

My works depends on me and for a number of years my husband was self-employed and I was the main breadwinner in the family, so you have to really keep that in mind that you're supporting other people. So just to decide today, 'Oh well, I'm going to take an hour off and go sit down by the river,' I would never do that. You just can't afford to do that ... So time for self is a tough one, yeah. (Interview B12)

Indeed, most of women in the study found themselves extremely pressed for time. This should not be surprising given the number of hours most women worked. Recall that while one-third of solo self-employed women worked part-time (an average of nineteen hours per week), the majority of women worked full-time, and very long hours at that – with solo self-employed women working roughly fifty hours, and employers working close to sixty hours each week. Between the two groups the depth of dissatisfaction was much greater amongst employers. Even so, a number of common themes emerge.

First, in many cases, women simply faced *too many demands on their time* from work, family, and other sources, and had simply given up on finding time for themselves. This echoes recent findings that self-employed Canadians are more likely to be stressed by too many hours or too many demands than are paid employees (C. Williams 2003). As one solo woman explained: 'I'm very dissatisfied with time for self ... Because of family, work, clients, customers, everything else, I find that they take precedence. I have to literally, physically force myself to say, 'Go and get your hair done' you know?' (Interview B14).

An employer echoed the same sentiments: 'My kids come first. My work here comes second. And what's leftover is for me and that doesn't wind up being, well actually what's left after that I have to sort of pay attention to my husband? ... So time for myself, no, it just doesn't happen' (Interview B19).

Drawing *firm boundaries between work and family life* was also difficult for many self-employed women, regardless of whether they had employees or not, or worked in a home-based business or in a location away from home. Reflecting on this, one solo self-employed woman who worked in a shared location with a number of other health care practitioners, and routinely took promotional and accounting work home with her, said:

> There's a thing about self-employment or your own business, that you're never free from it. If you have a nine to five job, you go to work, you go home, you don't take anything home with you. You don't have to worry about it, you finish it there. Whereas this one, you have to continuously get involved with whatever you're doing   It's always with you. (Interview A06)

For another solo self-employed woman, the difficulties in finding time for herself were linked to the inability to set limits on her availability to clients:

> They know that if it's absolutely necessary, they can see me on a Sunday afternoon or a Saturday morning and that's wonderful. But, on the other hand, I also do resent sometimes not being able to leave the message that 'The office is closed. The office is closed. I'm not here. Go away. I don't feel like it right now.' So staying motivated is difficult ... there are times when you just simply run out of energy. (Interview C10)

Seepage of work into family time was not just limited to solo self-employed women, as many employers also noted the need to bring work home that they were unable to accomplish during the day. Said one employer, with twenty-two employees:

I had a weekend off this weekend and I haven't had one in a few weeks. It's been working, doing some harried deadline. Most of them are proposals for new projects, because if you can't get it done during the workweek, you spend your nights working. And so it's something that I really wish I could turn back the number of hours worked and I still wish I could because I'm getting, I'm not saying I'm getting older because I feel very good, but it's just one of those things where I could use more time. I definitely could. (Interview C11)

In some cases women tried to carve out more time for themselves by hiring extra staff. For example, one previously solo self-employed woman had hired a part-time employee to take care of bookkeeping and administrative tasks in her office. But hiring employees did not always free up time. As an employer with half a dozen employees explained:

In the last year I've really expanded in terms of my employees ... and I had a perception that it would make me have more time to do other things. And I really thought I would be able to spend more time with my kids and I'd have less decisions to make and have more input from other people. But you end up dealing with a lot more of people's problems and you end up being a human resource person more than an entrepreneur. (Interview C13)

'I Love What I Do!': Personal Fulfilment

Regardless of the time stresses they faced, nearly all of the women gained enormous personal fulfilment from their work. Over 90% of solo self-employed women and 96.6% of employers were satisfied or very satisfied with the sense of fulfilment from their work. In speaking about this aspect of their work, women highlighted several different issues. Some women expressed fulfilment with their *work as a whole*, without distinguishing between specific aspects. Others noted that they gained fulfilment especially from *working with and helping their clients*. While employers and solo self-employed women did not differ in this regard, they did differ in the fulfilment they got from *running a business*. Whereas some solo self-employed women did not find the operational aspects of the business fulfiling, several employers spoke very specifically about the personal fulfillment and growth they got from the challenges of running and developing a small business.

In talking generally about personal fulfilment, most women were extremely enthusiastic. Said one woman who had been solo in a human resource practice for the past five years: 'I absolutely passionately love what I do everyday. It's just great fun. I have that personal fulfilment because I am doing what I love' (Interview B18).

Many employers echoed the same kind of enthusiasm. Said a more recent employer in the food sector: 'I have great personal fulfilment. I feel like I've finally found something that's good for me' (Interview B11). Another employer with a six-year-old business in the communications and events industry said: 'I love what I do and, yes, I would like to make more, but how many people can say when they get up in the morning ... Yeah, I want to go to work today, I love what I do' (Interview A11).

Helping clients was often given as a key source of personal fulfilment, both by solo self-employed women and by employers. One woman in a solo counselling practice talked about the fulfilment she got from working with her clients, as they dealt with personal, family or career concerns:

> There are certain people that just click, they shift their understanding of how life works or what their value is, what their purpose is, how to do things, how to communicate, it just opens up a new world to them and they take off! And it's just like magic and that's what I absolutely love, you know? (Interview A04)

Another woman who worked in a solo practice as a financial adviser explained:

> I enjoy it tremendously. I enjoy working more with people who are starting out, who want to go, because my satisfaction comes from seeing a result ... to me, the satisfaction, the reward of seeing somebody succeed is so much more important to me than my personal reward in terms of the monetary. (Interview B14)

Several employers also expressed the same types of sentiments.

If there was any area where solo self-employed women and employers differed somewhat, it was concerning the fulfilment they got from *running a business* as opposed to doing *a specific type of work*. When asked if she found her work personally fulfilling, one solo self-employed women replied: 'When it comes to what I do, yes. But when it comes to the business, no. If a project is extremely hard and I did well, there's lots of satisfaction ... *lots* of satisfaction. But all together with the business, not at all' (Interview B04).

Another solo self-employed women when asked about personal fulfilment said: 'I'm kind of halfway there ... I love certain parts of the business but I'm still not quite there, I don't have the ideal business yet. I'm not doing everything that I want to do' (Interview B10).

In contrast to solo practitioners, several employers highlighted the fulfilment they got from running the business itself and attending to operational issues. Said one woman with a five-year-old business that employed seventeen people: 'It feels good and I'm employing people and helping the economy. It makes me feel quite good even through we're still poor (laughing)' (Interview A01).

In some cases, the women linked their business growth with their own personal growth and fulfilment. Said one woman who has run and owned two retail stores for seven years: 'I notice I've gotten very confident. Before I used to hesitate in making decisions, but now I'm not scared to tell anything to anybody' (Interview B07).

Another small employer who ran a bakery said:

> I don't think I could have imagined ... I feel like I've pushed out in every direction of myself as a person and that's what been really stressful because I wish this would be happening slower and maybe one piece at a time. It's just a phenomenal learning experience ... The challenge is making the things and then the challenge of trying to breathe life into a business. (Interview C01)

Exploring Differences in Job Satisfaction

Looking at the overall picture of the women in this study, what comes across strongly is how satisfied they are with the intrinsic features of their work. For the vast majority, self-employment and small business ownership appears to provide a clear route to the independence, control, creativity, work environment, and personal fulfilment they desire in their working lives. This is evident not only in relation to the Alberta women, but also in terms of the national level data from the CPRN-Ekos survey. But there are also sources of dissatisfaction, most notably in the areas of work and family balance, and time for one's self. This is especially true for employers, who work longer hours and are far less satisfied with their ability to balance work and family demands, and to find time for themselves. Employers also appear to differ somewhat from solo self-employed women in their satisfaction with authority, relishing the challenge of building a business but articulating feelings of greater isolation and responsibility towards employees in their decision-making. Compared to the solo self-employed, they also seem to get greater satisfaction from the work involved in building a business and dealing with business operations.

It is possible that many other differences exist between women, or that some of the difference describe above are actually artefacts of other more important factors. In order to examine this further, in this final section we compare the Alberta women's responses on job satisfaction across several different factors. Some of these are business related – for example, work status (part-time or full-time), business tenure (numbers of years in business), business location (home-based or office-based), income, and reasons for becoming self-employed (forced or voluntary). Others are socio-demographic, such as age, education, visible minority status, and presence or absence of children. Because of the small size of the sample, it is not possible to control for several factors at once or probe these very deeply, but looking at these factors one by one to some extent clarifies what shapes self-employed women's job satisfaction.

In terms of socio-demographic factors, for instance, age does not appear to influence satisfaction in any clear or significant fashion, which is different from most findings of paid employees where satisfaction increases with age (Krahn and Lowe 1998: 408–10; Spector 1997). Perhaps this reflects the greater independence, freedom, and complex work the self-employed, have regardless of age, compared to employees where this type of work is more typical of senior (and hence older) employees. On the other hand, education does seem to have some impact. Women with a high school education are more satisfied with their day-to-day work, independence, work and family balance, and the opportunity to work from home. But they are less satisfied than better-educated women with the authority to make decisions. Visible minority women are slightly less satisfied with their independence, and more dissatisfied with their work-family balance – the latter perhaps linked to slightly longer working hours (about two hours on average each week) and a lower likelihood of working from home. Finally, having children is related to higher satisfaction in some areas, though again perhaps differently than we might expect. Those with children are more satisfied with their day-to-day work (87.0% compared to 71.4%), and their balance between family and work (63.0% compared to 42.9%), suggesting that self-employment may help to some extent in the 'struggle to juggle' (Hall-Hoffarth 2003). But, interestingly, the presence of children does not seem to have any impact on satisfaction with working from home (73.3% compared to 75.0%).

Turning to business-related factors, working in a home-based business does relate to much greater satisfaction with work and family balance (77.8% compared to 47.1%) and time for oneself (42.3% compared to 17.6%). No doubt this reflects the ability to more easily blend work and family tasks as discussed in previous sections. Though differences by business tenure are small, those with older businesses are less satisfied with finding time for themselves, and with managing employees. Perhaps not surprisingly, the part-time workers are much more satisfied with work and family balance (72.7% compared to 58.0%) and time for themselves (54.5% compared to 22.4%). Because all part-timers in this study are solo workers, we also compare part-time and full-time solo workers on these items. Those working full-time have lower rates of satisfaction, suggesting that it is not solo work per se, but the shorter hours of some women that create greater satisfaction. Here we may be seeing differences between what have been called 'lifestyle entrepreneurs' (those who intentionally enter business to better balance work and family, and make time for themselves) and those solo workers and employers with a more traditional business approach based on the 'clockwork of male careers' (Hochschild 2003: 238).

Of all factors shaping differences in satisfaction, however, the most important relates to the reasons why women entered into self-employment in the first place. Dividing the group into 'forced' and 'voluntary' self-employed in Table 4.3, following the typology developed in Chapter 3, we see that 'forced' or 'necessity entrepreneurs' are notably less satisfied on most items. In particular, they are less satisfied with the nature of their day-to-day work, their independence, creativity, authority, work and family balance, personal fulfilment, and working from home. The only exception is time for themselves, which may not necessarily be a positive outcome but instead reflect their difficulty attracting business. Despite these differences, it is important to note that their levels of satisfaction still remain relatively high, with the exception of work- family balance and time for themselves. In this respect, forced entrepreneurs share with those who enter self-employment voluntarily a positive experience of self-employment, at least in terms of intrinsic job quality.

TABLE 4.3

Satisfaction among Forced and Voluntary Self-Employed, Alberta Study
(% 'satisfied' or 'very satisfied')*

	Voluntary	Forced	All respondents
Nature of day-to-day work	86.7	75.0	84.2
Independence	91.1	83.3	89.5
Opportunity for creativity	97.7	83.3	94.6
Authority to make decisions	97.8	83.3	94.7
Work and family balance	66.7	50.0	63.2
Time for self	27.3	33.3	28.6
Personal fulfilment	95.6	83.3	93.0
Working from home	84.0	66.7	80.6
Total (n)**	45	12	57

*Respondents indicated satisfaction on a five point scale, where 1 = very
satisfied and 5 = very unsatisfied.
**Response on each item varies from 55 to 57, with the exception of
working from home (31 responses).

Conclusions

This chapter sheds new insight into the job quality and satisfaction of
self-employed women. Offering new data on these questions, it provides strong evidence that self-employed women are typically more
satisfied with their work than female employees – at least as far as the
intrinsic dimensions of work are concerned. For instance, nationally
representative data from the CPRN-Ekos *Changing Employment Relationships Survey* reveal an almost twenty-point gap in the overall job
satisfaction of self-employed women (85.7%) compared to female
employees (68.2%). On specific facets of work, it also finds self-
employed women far more satisfied with the control and influence
they have over work schedules, and how they do their work. They are
also more likely to agree that they are part of a healthy workplace,
where morale is high and one feels committed, respected, recognized,
and to feel that there are opportunities for skill use, development, and
recognition in their work.

Combining these specific indicators to measure job quality deficits –
the difference between what women 'have' and 'would like' in a job –
shows that self-employed women have much smaller job quality deficits in key areas, such as intrinsic rewards (interesting work, training,

skill development), communication (working with friendly and help-ful people), psychological attachment (shared values, commitment) and work-family flexibility (control over schedule). Where there is a huge job quality deficit is in extrinsic work features (pay, job security).

Why self-employed women derive such satisfaction from their work is made clear through the in-depth interviews. While probing a more focused set of issues, the interviews illustrate the critical importance played by factors such as independence, authority, interesting work, and opportunities for creativity and personal fulfilment. Listening to women talk helps to unravel how specific factors – such as independence and control over their work lives and environment – contribute to satisfying, meaningful work. The interviews also illustrate how different facets of work may be valued in distinct ways, and helps identify where there are consistent patterns of difference and similarity between employers and solo women. On this latter point, employers seem to gain more satisfaction from building a business; their discussions of independence, authority, and personal fulfilment all revolve around this point. In contrast, solo women seem to value these features more for enabling them to do the work they want to do, in the way they want to do it. Not surprisingly, solo workers are less apt to highlight the downsides of independence and authority, such as isolation and being responsible for others.

Perhaps the greatest surprise in terms of satisfaction is with work-family balance and time for one self. Media and popular accounts routinely portray self-employment as a way for women to 'have it all.' And while the CPRN-Ekos data indicate that far fewer self-employed women experienced a job quality deficit in work-family balance (15% compared to nearly 40% of women in paid employment), the Alberta study highlight some concerns. This is especially true for female employers in the study, just half of whom were satisfied with work-family balance, and only 17.2% with the time they had for themselves. Here solo women fared better – over two-thirds were satisfied with their balance between work and home – but they were clearly gaining balance at a personal cost, with almost two-thirds dissatisfied with the time they had for themselves.

Given the hours and intensity with which many of these women worked, especially employers, the findings are understandable, but also underline some of the pitfalls of independent work. They also echo broader concerns over the growth of long working hours in Canada and other countries (Statistics Canada 2003a; Lowe 2000; Duxbury and Higgins 2001), and the 'time bind' (Hochschild 1997) and 'time famines' (Perlow 1998) experienced by individual workers and their families. Interestingly, they also run counter to optimistic accounts of self-employment, such as Daniel Pink's *Free Agent Nation*. Drawing on Nippert-Eng's work, which identifies 'integrating' or 'segmenting' strategies towards work and family, Pink suggests self-employment offers an effective means to 'blend,' rather than simply to 'balance,' work and family life. But the findings here suggest that for some work-family balance is not always achieved or comes at the cost of time for one self – an issue less commonly acknowledged or explored.

Without doubt the most important area of difference the study highlights is between those forced into self-employment and those who entered willingly. Of all factors shaping differences in satisfaction, this difference was most crucial. While still fairly satisfied with their work, necessity entrepreneurs were less happy with the nature of their day-to-day work, their independence, creativity, authority, personal fulfilment, work-family balance, and working from home. Ironically, the only area where they were more satisfied was with time for themselves, but even here only one-third expressed satisfaction. To what extent they were satisfied with their income and job security, of course, remains a critical question – one to which we now turn.

5 Players or Paupers?[1] Income, Job Security, and the Negotiation of Risk

There's no unemployment insurance, there's no health care, there's no anything else. There's no sick pay, there's no anything to fall back on if things
aren't going well.

(Carmen, Interview B23)

For me, my job is more secure if I have my own business. And a lot of people
think it's so scary. But for me it's scarier to be working for somebody who's an
asshole. When there's downsizing, rightsizing, whatever you want to call it ...
I'm more secure working how I am than if I had a 'real' job.'

(Kate, Interview B20)

Clearly the majority of women involved in self-employment and small
business ownership are highly satisfied with their work. They enjoy
the variety of activities and challenges they face each day, the freedom
and flexibility they have, and the opportunity to do meaningful work.
But how are they faring economically? Do they earn good incomes? Do
they make a reasonable return on the long hours they work? Are they
able to save for retirement? Do they feel secure in the work they are
doing?

Exploring this issue reveals a range of experience, with some women
struggling while others prosper. At one end of the spectrum are
women like Carmen, quoted above, who is deeply dissatisfied with her
financial situation. A single mom in her early forties, Carmen has a
low, unpredictable income and is without health care and other benefits that many, though not all, employees in Canada enjoy. Just two
years into her business, she knows the early stages are hard, but finds

her lack of security unsettling. Business is seasonal, and payments are often delayed or late. 'You never know when you're going to get paid next,' she says, 'and that's very stressful, because you know your own bills can't get paid on that basis.'

Far away, at the other end of the spectrum, are women like Kate, who is 'very happy money wise,' enjoying the success of her seven-year-old production company, and earning more than the average Canadian woman, whether self-employed or working for an employer. A single mother too, with a school-aged daughter to support, Kate knows there are risks in self-employment, but still feels she is more secure than if she was working for someone else. 'Making money this year was very easy,' she says, 'all I had to do was answer the phone.' Though not one of the self-made millionaires touted in the press, Kate is nevertheless comfortable and happy. 'I'm a single mom and I'm paying my mortgage. I'm not limited financially at all with what I want to do. For me that's success.'

While Kate and Carmen reflect two very different faces of the entrepreneurial economy, their experiences are in line with academic and policy research that point to growing polarization among such workers, and in the labour market overall. At the heart of this debate are questions not only about the job quality and economic returns offered by non-standard or precarious forms of work such as self-employment, but about the changing patterns of inequality emerging in industrialized societies. Within this debate, self-employment is often assumed to be contributing to the bottom end of a polarized job structure. But there are reasons to question the simplistic conflation of self-employed with bad jobs. Recent research suggests there is considerable diversity amongst the self-employed (Kalleberg et al. 2000), making it difficult to generalize. Moreover, beyond basic statistical indictors, we do not have a great deal of detailed information about the economic situation of self-employed women, or the extent of their satisfaction and dissatisfaction with their short- and long-term financial security.

Working towards this goal, this chapter explores questions about income, job security, and risk, drawing on existing studies, survey data, and the in-depth interviews from women in the Alberta study. As a starting point, it considers what existing research has to say about these issues, and assesses recent national trends with new data from the *Survey of Self-Employment in Canada* (*SSE*). It then focuses on the Alberta women's experiences with what sociologists of work call 'extrinsic job features,' such as income, job security, and the ability to save for retirement. Extending the discussion beyond income offers a broader perspective on economic polarization, illuminating the short- and long-term consequences of self-employment and small business ownership for women, and the extent to which it can be considered risky business.

Economic Polarization, Self-Employment, and Small Business Ownership

Debates over a more polarized and unequal distribution of earnings first emerged in the United States in the early 1980s through the work of 'deindustrialists' such as Bluestone and Harrison (1982) and Kuttner (1983). Since then numerous studies have confirmed that trend in the United States (Grubb and Wilson 1989; Schwartz 1992; Ryscavage 1995; Levy and Murnane 1992; Danziger and Gottschalk 1993), Britain (Westergaard 1995; Sherman and Judkins 1995), and other industrial-ized nations (Gottschalk and Smeeding 1997). In Canada, existing studies confirm the general trends. Analysis by the Economic Council of Canada and Statistics Canada, for example, found growing earnings inequality and polarization from the mid-1960s to mid-1980s (ECC 1991). More recent analysis suggests growing inequality in family income in the 1990s (Picot and Heisz 2000; Statistics Canada 2003d).

How do self-employed workers and small business owners fit into this picture? Generally speaking, studies of self-employed workers find that they earn less than their paid counterparts,[2] suggesting they are contributing to the bottom layers of a more polarized earning structure. One of the most in-depth analyses to date found a 35% earnings differ-ential between employees and the self-employed in the United States throughout the 1980s and 1990s,[3] though unfortunately these findings are for men only (Hamilton 2000). Not only do the self-employed have lower initial earnings, they also have lower rates of earnings growth as well. This trend is assumed to be a voluntary trade-off between mone-tary and non-pecuniary rewards, especially to the advantage of being one's own boss (Hamilton 2000), even though data are not offered to support such interpretations.

Turning to specific studies of women in self-employment and small business ownership, we see relatively low earnings and a more pro-nounced gender gap of the self-employed compared to wage-and-sal-ary employees (Carr 2000; Devine 1994a, 1994b; Bird and Sapp 2004). Reviewing trends in the 1980s and early 1990s in the United States, Carr

(2000: 215) found a gender gap in business receipts and/or income of 27% in 1980, 35% in 1982, to 46.7% in 1990, leading her to conclude that 'despite the health of the small business sector, ownership does not currently provide women with levels of economic success comparable to men's.' In her view, earning differences are largely attributable to the smaller size of women's business, their location in traditional sectors, such as retail trade and services, and 'compensating differentials' between monetary and non-monetary rewards, in particular flexibility and work-family balance.

In Canada, research on the self-employed also points to lower average earnings, as well as to income distributions that are far more polarized, with the self-employed more concentrated at the low and high ends of the income distribution. (Belcourt 1991; CFIB 2002; HRDC 2002; Hughes 1999; Statistics Canada 1997; Thrasher and Smid 1998). Reviewing studies from the 1970s and 1980s, Belcourt found that 30% of small business owners were unable to make enough money, and that this reason was the most frequently cited for exiting their business (52). Even when women did earn more as entrepreneurs than as employees, they still earned less than their male counterparts. Although Belcourt argues there is potential for greater wealth through women-owned business, it is difficult to understand why she draws this conclusion. One-third of the two hundred women she studied in the 1980s received no compensation from their business, and only 6% earned an annual income of $80,000 or more.

When we turn to the self-employment boom of the 1990s, low earnings remain a concern. In the mid-1990s, for example, median earnings of the self-employed were roughly two-thirds that of paid employees (Statistics Canada 1997; Hughes 1999). More significantly, nearly half of the self-employed earned under $20,000 a year, whereas this was the case for just one-quarter of employees (Statistics Canada 1997). Reflecting a more polarized earnings distribution, the self-employed were also over-represented at the upper income levels, with 6.4% earning over $80,000 a year, compared to just 2.7% of employees (Statistics Canada 1997; Hughes 1999).

At first glance these trends suggest that self-employed workers and small business owners are far more likely to contribute to the bottom layer of the earning gulf – even though a much smaller group are also doing very well. But within these aggregate trends are important differences both between and among solo workers and employers. For example, in terms of average income, solo workers make 68% the income of employees, while employers actually earn 22% more than their employed peers (Statistics Canada 1997; Hughes finds 55.6% for solo and 102% for employers). Employers are also far more likely to earn high incomes – just 2.3% of solo workers made more than $80,000, while this was the case for nearly one in ten of employers (Statistics Canada 1997; Hughes 1999).[4]

The gender gap in earnings is also larger amongst the self-employed. In the mid-1990s, self-employed women working full-time earned 64% of men's earnings, compared to a gap of 73% for employees (Statistics Canada 1997: 25–6; Industry Canada 1998). Average incomes for self-employed women are particularly low in certain sectors, such as personal services and retail, and for those who are younger, working in a home-based business, or raising a child alone (Industry Canada 1998). Not surprisingly, women earning above average incomes are more highly educated, and located in the knowledge sectors of the economy, such as computing services, business services, architecture and engineering, accounting, and advertising (Industry Canada 1998).

It is interesting to note that these findings concur with some popular writing on women's entrepreneurship in Canada. In their 1998 book *Smart Women*, Thrasher and Smid explore what they call women's 'dirty little secret' – the fact that despite entering self-employment in droves, women are still making very little money (see also Church 1998; Fowlie, 1998). Speaking about the potential for self-employment to reduce the earnings gap between women and men, Thrasher says: 'The one real hope that we had of women climbing out of that hole in a hurry was entrepreneurship and it seems as if it's just digging them deeper.' Drawing on interviews with one hundred women heading businesses ranging from start-ups to million dollar companies, Thrasher and Smid argue that low income is the result of a several factors. These include women's socialization, non-financial motivations for seeking self-employment, a tendency to under-price, and a lack of management skills needed to grow a business.

The Current Picture: National Trends

Whatever the reasons behind these trends, we see some emerging consensus on income patterns for self-employed women. But most research has focused on trends in the 1980s and early 1990s, leaving open the question of whether recent years have seen significant change. Information from the *Survey of Self-Employment in Canada (SSE)*

Figure 5.1
Income for Self-Employed Women, Full-time, Canada, 2000

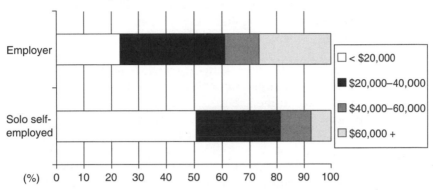

Source: HRDC and Statistics Canada (2000), *Survey of Self-Employment in Canada*

provides the most up-to-date information available, tracking patterns at the end of the century in 1999 (HRDC 2002).[5] Like past research, however, it suggests marked polarization and low incomes, with over one-quarter of the self-employed (men and women) earning less than $20,000 a year. Again, there are key differences between employers and solo workers, with more than one-third of solo workers making under $20,000, compared to just 14% of employers.

If we focus further on women's earnings, looking only at those who work full-time, we see even greater disparities. As Figure 5.1 shows, solo women are heavily concentrated at the bottom end of the income distribution. Roughly half make under $20,000, and another 30% make between $20,000 and $40,000. Just fewer than 20% earn incomes higher than $40,000. In contrast, employers do much better. Just one-quarter fall in the lowest income bracket and another quarter earn $60,000+.

Certain factors help to explain some of the variation we see. Multivariate analysis of the *SSE* by Devlin (2001) find that years in self-employment and higher-skilled occupations have a positive effect on earnings, while being an immigrant has a negative effect (see also Li 2000 and Frenette 2002 on immigrant earnings). Pathways into self-employment also matter; quitting or losing a job has no impact on earnings, but being retired, unable to find work, or preferring paid work brings lower income levels. Comparing women and men, Devlin (2001) finds that marriage results in lower earnings for women but not for men. However, women who enter self-employment because of a lack of paid employment earn the same as other women, whereas men earn less. Learning appears to have more benefits for women than men; higher education, formal training, and informal training all boost women's incomes, whereas for men this is the case only for formal training.

A valuable aspect of the *SSE* is that it provides additional information about the financial situation of the self-employed, extending the traditional focus beyond income to critical questions about retirement savings, financial difficulties, coverage for dental, health, and disability insurance, and interest in income insurance programs. This is an important feature, as past research suggests reduced access to standard economic benefits amongst the self-employed. For example, analysis by Lowe and Schellenberg (2001) shows that less than half of the self-employed have medical/dental coverage (20% through own, 25% through spouse) compared to 90% of those in paid employment (72% through own, 18% through spouse). Solo practitioners are far less likely than employers to have their own coverage. The self-employed are also typically excluded from government funded benefits such as paid maternity benefits and unemployment insurance, an issue we take up in Chapter 6.[6]

On these issues, the *SSE* highlights a number of concerns. For example, in terms of dental and supplementary health insurance, just one-third of the self-employed are covered by dental insurance, and just 40% have supplementary health insurance. While the level of coverage is similar for women and men, it is much higher for employers than for the solo self-employed, and also rises with income, occupation, and membership in an association. Of critical importance, women are far more likely to rely on a spouse for benefits: over 70% of women were covered by their spouse's plan, compared to 45% of men (HRDC 2002: 52). Yet women and men share similar reasons for not having their own coverage. Roughly 40% felt it was too costly and 20% not worth the cost (41).

Disability insurance is another area of concern. Here just 40% of the self-employed are covered, but men (43.1%) are far more likely than women (28.6%) to have insurance. Notably, this difference is not due to variation in the types of occupations held by women and men: even in the same occupation, men are more likely to be covered (HRDC 2002: 55–4).

Another issue of importance about which we know little concerns retirement preparation. Data from the *SSE* show that 90% of the self-employed have saved in some way for retirement. Unfortunately, information was not collected about the value of these assets, making it impossible to assess whether savings are adequate. Men (92.0%) are somewhat more likely to save than women (88.5%) but the main difference lies between employers and solo workers (HRDC 2002: 57, 105). Among the assets held by the self-employed, in order of decreasing importance, are equity in a home or business, RRSPs, other savings, assets such as land or rental property, and a pension from a previous job.[7] Though relatively small in number, about 9% of the self-employed have not been able to save for retirement at all. In nearly three-quarters of these cases, this is simply because they cannot afford to do so (HRDC 2002: 107).

One final issue on which the *SSE* sheds light is the financial risk of self-employment and small business ownership. About 40% of self-employed Canadians have experienced some financial difficulties in the past, with this being less likely for women (34.7%) than men (41.9%), but more likely for solo workers (41.7%) than employers (37.2%). Of note, those forced (56.5%) into self-employment or discouraged by it (48.9%) are at greater risk than those who have chosen self-employment (32.8%) or adjusted to it (41.4%). Typically, the self-employed deal with financial difficulties in several ways: by reducing personal and family expenditures (51.3%), borrowing money (37.2%), using savings (26.5%), relying on other sources of income (15.3%), selling assets (11.5%), and cashing in RRSP (11.6%).[8] In borrowing money to cope, women were less likely to rely on financial institution than men (55.9% against 70.3%) and more likely to rely on family and friends (51.0% against 35.3%) (HRDC 2002: 97–8).

Income and Economic Security: The Study

While the *SSE* provides useful baseline information to assess the economic security of Canadian women who are self-employed, it tells us little about how they experience the financial side of self-employment. For instance, how do women feel about the incomes they are earning? How do they feel about the security of their job and business? What concerns, if any, do they have about their lack of benefits? How satisfied are they with their ability to save for retirement? Moving from the national picture to the women in the Alberta study allows us to begin sketching some answers to these questions.

Before turning to these questions, however, how does the Alberta group compare to national trends? In many ways the women in the study closely resemble the national average, as Table 5.1 shows. For example, personal before-tax income is somewhat polarized, reflecting both highs and lows. Nearly 30% of the women made less than $20,000 per year, and just under 30% made over $60,000, with the remaining 40% earning between $20,000 to $60,000 a year. In keeping with national trends, there are important differences between solo workers and employers as well. Far more solo workers made low incomes (less than $20,000 a year) than did employers. At the upper income levels, well over one-quarter of employers made $80,000 a year, compared to just 7.4% of solo self-employed women. Despite these broad similarities, there are somewhat more high-earning solo women in the Alberta study. It should also be noted as well that, while the vast majority of women earned all of their income through their business, a few had second jobs or received pensions from previous employment. Taking these women into account, employers on average made 86.1% of their income from their business, while solo workers made 71.1%.

Income levels provide one indicator of economic security. But we also wanted to know how women feel about their income, job security, and financial futures. As Table 5.1 shows, in response to questions about their satisfaction with income, less than half reported being satisfied or very satisfied. This varied notably by self-employment status, with just over one-third of solo women reporting satisfaction, compared to 57.1% of employers. Further reflecting their dissatisfaction with income, just one-third of women were happy with their ability to save for retirement. Again differences between solo women (26.7%) and employers (41.4%) are striking. Equally striking, but equally surprising, given debates over the risks involved in self-employment, the majority of women (60.3%) were satisfied with their job security. This was much more the case for employers (70.4%) than for solo women (51.6%), perhaps reflecting differences in their business tenure and stability. Despite the low levels of satisfaction on income and retirement savings, a majority of women (65.6%) were also satisfied with having financial responsibility. Interestingly, on this item the satisfaction levels of solo women and employers converge.

A final issue, which ties into issues of financial adequacy, concerns the ways in which women financed their business (multiple responses were allowed). Here we can note that while more than one-quarter of women had financed their business through a bank loan, and 15%

TABLE 5.1
Financial Background and Extrinsic Satisfaction, Alberta Study*

	Solo self-employed (%)	Employers (%)	All respondents (%)
Own income before tax			
1–9,999	22.2	14.3	18.2
10,000–19,999	14.8	3.6	9.1
20,000–29,999	11.1	10.7	10.9
30,000–39,999	18.5	10.7	14.5
40,000–49,999	7.4	10.7	9.1
50,000–59,999	11.1	7.1	9.1
60,000–69,999	7.4	7.1	7.3
70,000–79,999	0	7.1	3.6
80,000 plus	7.4	28.6	18.2
% of income from business	71.1	86.1	78.5
% 'satisfied' or 'very satisfied' with**			
Level of personal income	37.5	57.1	46.7
Job security	51.6	70.4	60.3
Ability to save for retirement	26.7	41.4	33.9
Financial responsibility	65.6	65.5	65.6
% financing business by (n = 60):			
Commercial bank loan	10.0	46.7	28.3
Community loan fund	6.7	3.3	5.0
Government loan fund	3.3	16.7	10.0
Personal credit (Visa, etc)	40.0	43.3	41.7
Line of credit	13.3	3.3	8.3
Student loan	0	3.3	1.7
Total (n)	32	29	61

*Response rates varies from 55–61.
**Respondents indicated satisfaction on a five-point scale, where 1 = very satisfied and 5 = very unsatisfied.

through a government or community loan fund, the most common way of financing was through personal credit. Again, there are important differences between solo self-employed women and employers. In particular, far more employers (46.7%) than solo self-employed women (10.0%) had used a commercial bank loan for financing their business. But roughly equal numbers of solo workers and employers had used personal credit cards at some point to finance their business.

While these survey responses provide valuable information on specific levels and areas of satisfaction and dissatisfaction, they provide little insight into how women feel about the extrinsic aspects of the self-employment and small business ownership. In order to deepen our understanding the next sections draw on the in-depth interviews to more fully excavate such issues as income and financial security, job security and risk, retirement saving, and financial responsibility.

'I Am Really Barely Making It': Income and Financial Security

Even though more women were dissatisfied than satisfied with their incomes, we should not lose sight of the fact that many women were content with their financial situation. Again, this reflects the polarization within women's self-employment, where some women manage to earn a good living, while others seem to face a constant struggle. As a rule, those women who were financially satisfied were far more likely to be employers and to have businesses of longer tenure. One employer, who had been in business for more than twenty years, was currently very satisfied with her financial situation, noting: 'When it's good, it's good. When you're doing well and when the economy's good, you can make a really good income' (Interview B16). Another employer with a booming retail business felt the same: 'I feel *very* satisfied with that ... I never realized how well off you can be if you can run a business properly, you know? It's given me a lot of satisfaction' (Interview B07).

Earning a good income also provided a sense of security for some, as one employer noted in linking the two: 'I always did want to be financially above the average person and I think I've achieved that. I've created my own job security' (Interview B22). Another employer, though satisfied with her income, highlighted the hard work and hours she put into her business: 'It's good' she said 'but I've had to earn it' (Interview A12).

Though solo women were less satisfied with income than employers, there were some who were happy with their financial situation. Without exception these women all had higher than average incomes, in the range of $30,000–$39,999 to $80,000+. Not all of these women were long-established business owners. In one case, a quite recently established solo woman seemed almost surprised by her success: 'I had no idea I could make that kind of money and I had no idea that it would come that easily. I found it a little shocking when I saw my six month halfway statement because I had already made $45,000' (Interview C08). Another woman, already earning a very good income and expressing high levels of satisfaction, still felt she could do even better: 'Right now I'm comfortable. I'm very comfortable. But I would like to make more. I mean, it would be nice if I could put more away and invest a little bit more in terms of different things that the bank will offer, you know?' (Interview C14).

For some solo women, high satisfaction was not just the result of earning a good income, but a greater feeling of control, that they could earn what they deserved. Discussing the link between earning and effort, one woman in independent sales explained:

> It only depends on yourself, right? If you are employed by other people, you're controlled by other people. Even through there's a pension, when they ask you to leave, you leave. Here, if you work hard, it's going to come. It all depends on yourself, right? You have nobody else to blame. (Interview C09)

None of this is to deny the broad current of dissatisfaction felt by many women, most notably the solo self-employed.[9] Discussing her frustration with long hours, low income, and slow business growth, one woman highlighted the gap between skills and earnings as a key source of dissatisfaction: 'Level of personal income. I am *very* dissatisfied. For my education and so many years and money I spent on education and the time I spent here, the amount I invested, I am very dissatisfied' (Interview B03). Another woman linked her dissatisfaction to the time needed to build a successful business. While she greatly enjoyed the intrinsic dimensions of her work, especially her independence and authority, she was less satisfied with her financial situation:

> The only thing I'm not satisfied with is the money ... When you're in your own business, I keep telling everybody that just because you've learned these skills and you open your door, because you have a great product to sell, does not mean when you open the door, people are going to rush in. Don't expect that. I think a lot of people have that kind of idea ... That's not the way business works. You have to build it up. (Interview A06)

Other women also expressed frustration with slow business growth coupled with high, and perhaps unrealistic, expectations. Said one woman in an independent health practice that had been operating for less than two years: 'You have expectations of making money much more quickly than it actually happens' (Interview B03) It bears noting that these frustrations were not limited to the solo self-employed. An employer in a five-year-old travel agency voiced similar concerns:

> It's not as great as a lot of people perceive it to be ... I didn't come into this business saying 'Well, I'm going to make a million bucks for myself.' That wasn't the idea. It was that I just wanted to use my energies, do something ... It's just that it hasn't moved forward as much as I anticipated that it would have been by this time ... it just doesn't get any easier. (Interview C17)

Delving further into issues of income, several themes emerge that may explain the level of dissatisfaction many women express. One concerns the issue of *expenses,* and the difference in working as an employee, where a fixed payment is received, and a business owner, where income is determined not just by revenues but by expenses and the need for reinvestment in the business. This was especially true for young businesses struggling to start up, where unexpected expenses were a constant challenge. For example, one solo woman in a three-year-old health care practice had seen great success in attracting business, but found that anticipating and dealing with expenses was the difficult part of the self-employment bargain. Discussing her situation she said:

> In terms of income from what I make personally, I'm very happy. There is always room for improvement ... But I'm quite satisfied with that. It's just that I have a lot of expenses when you go into business ... I mean especially when you own the place. You have to pay rent, you pay utilities, you pay a lot of thing ... and it takes up a lot of money. (Interview A06)

Another solo woman, with a young two-year-old business, was deeply dissatisfied with her income, despite high sales. Recalling how she had struggled over the past year to meet expenses, she said: 'Well, money was coming in but I was spending way more. When I did my income tax, I was putting so much into the business, any money I got I was putting right back in' (Interview A09). For her, this was a significant problem as she was the main breadwinner for the family. For other women, however, such as the one below, a high family income allowed her to be much more relaxed and philosophical about this issue. Explaining why she drew no income from her young business, she said:

I didn't start a business to be a multi-millionaire. That wasn't my goal although I like money, it's important and it's not coming as fast as I'd like. But definitely the first year people start a business seriously and expect to make money, I think that's unrealistic because any money you make goes back into the business either to alter it because the original plan was not quite right, or to make it prosper in areas that need growth. And with growth, it takes money to make money, so in businesses that make an income and you put it back in the business, I don't see that as a loss, I see that as growth. (Interview B03)

Though coping with expenses was more difficult for younger businesses and for those who lacked family support, some veterans also voiced concerns. One woman, despite feeling generally satisfied with her income, still lamented: 'But at the same time, after ten years, I should have more to show financially than what I do right now, I think ... I've made a lot of money doing this, I really have, but I've spent a lot of money too' (Interview B15). Another woman far less satisfied, said simply: 'I'm dissatisfied about the finances. You take all the money and you put it back into the business. If this was not my business, I think I'd be rich' (Interview B24).

In addition to grappling with a new income equation, and keeping a handle on both revenue and expenses, another issue that emerges with respect to earnings is *non-monetary benefits*. Unlike paid employees, who are more likely to have supplementary benefits such as health care, dental care, vision care, and so on, self-employed workers and small business owners are often without these, unless they have coverage through a spouse's plan or through affordable plans offered by any associations to which they belong.[10] They also lack access to government sponsored benefits, such as employment insurance, in the case of business failure and job loss, unlike paid employees who find themselves unemployed. The insecurity felt by workers over this situation is well captured by Carmen, quoted at the start of this chapter, who lamented the lack of a social safety net to 'fall back on if things aren't going well' (Interview B23).

Though both employers and solo workers grappled with this issue, for solo workers the problem was especially acute. For example, one solo woman with a long-established private therapy practice talked in depth about the challenges facing self-employed workers and small business owners with respect to health care benefits, disability insurance, and sick pay. Not only are they vulnerable due to lack of coverage, but they have ongoing, often fixed, expenses even when they face sickness or disability. As she explained:

> It's difficult to make a living when you work independently ... you don't have benefits. I think that's probably the biggest problem, that I have no benefits whatsoever. So I don't have ... I pay for my own health care but I pay the minimal amount. I just had a friend who is in private practice as well and she did the smart thing because she took out disability insurance which was good because she just contracted an illness. But if I were to become ill, then what becomes of my office? I mean I can't pay rent, you know, I don't have sick leave. You don't get paid sick leave, so you know it's very tough that way. People that work for businesses don't realize the kind of benefits they get ... And I think that that's probably one of the biggest hardships with being in private practice. You have to make enough to cover while you're on holidays, to cover all of your expenses, this sort of thing, so financial responsibility, level of personal income, I could probably do better if I would work full-time for somebody else. (Interview B12)

For some women who were doing well, insurance of various forms could be purchased. Several other women, as we will see below, had coverage for health, dental, and other insurance through their husband's plans. However, those on more limited incomes simply could not afford coverage or did not feel the cost was worth the potential benefit. Explained one woman with a four-year-old business in legal services: 'My husband doesn't have benefits with his work and I don't have benefits of course. And so Blue Cross, I did the math and I'd have to be going to the dentist and doctor a lot more than I am to make it pay for itself' (Interview A18).

Beyond expenses and the lack of benefits, a third issue that many women faced was dealing with *fluctuations in income,* whether on a seasonal basis or tied to the business cycle. Again, this highlighted the difference in the circumstances when one was working as an employee where income was more regular and secure. As one solo woman explained, 'It would be so much easier if there was a regular pay check, regardless of what it was, coming through the door all the time as opposed to all this sporadic stuff where you get thousands one month, and then hundreds the next' (Interview B10).

An employer in a six-year-old communications business was also experiencing significant fluctuations in her business. Discussing income issues she said,

If you had asked me last year, I would probably have said that I was all right. But I'm not any more, so I'm finding ways to improve that. I'm not just saying 'Oh, I'm not happy with my income level right now' and not doing anything about it. I realize that I need to do something about it. (Interview A11)

For another employer, who has weathered significant ups and downs in her twenty-three years of business, past downturns had forced her to sell her home:

Before, money was growing on trees, you know? And we were spending it as fast as we were getting it because we thought it was going to last forever. We bought a big house and ...[then the economy slumped] ... and we sold our house and used the money to keep the business going. We never did that again. (Interview B16)

Another employer also pinpointed the problem of volatility, noting that 'in terms of income, we can be up there and then down there very quickly' (Interview C11). Given this her satisfaction with income had varied through the years, 'We had a few very lean years and at the time I'd finished paying babysitters I barely had anything left to take home. But the last few years the economy has been good. The work has been good and so it's been very satisfactory' (Interview C11).

Given this dissatisfaction, it seems reasonable to ask why women carry on with their businesses? Why continue to work independently when it would seem far easier to work for someone else? One thing that may keep some women going is the *dream of their potential business* – the business they believe they will have someday. Like struggling artists, actresses, and musicians, who hold on to a belief that someday they will make it big, many self-employed women and small business owners held on to a similar dreams for their business.[11]

Illustrating this was one solo woman with a very young communications business who believed strongly in its potential. Despite an annual income under $10,000, she was not dissatisfied, saying simply: 'Personal income, it's going to grow.' To expand her business she was trying to attract larger clients and she felt sure it would come. 'It's the guy in the corner office I really want to win over' she explained 'and I've won over a couple of them already' (Interview A15). In another case, a solo woman repeatedly emphasized the potential of her business, despite her current low income:

> The opportunity to earn a lot of money with this I think will also be motivating, but it isn't right now because it's too new. It's not generating enough yet ... But working hard at this I think I can make more money that working at a job that says this is what your salary is. (Interview A08)

Another solo woman, though better off, also seemed to assess her financial situation in terms of her potential, rather than current, earnings: 'I know it's only going to get better. I've been planting a lot of seeds at this time, lots of samples going out, so this year's going to be better than last so I'm really happy about that' (Interview C06).

While dreams of the potential business were more common amongst solo self-employed women, a few employers also spoke about this and the need to be patient in the early stages. One owner of a two-year-old retail store was facing significant financial hurdles, but said simply: 'The money, that's coming. You know, you have to be patient' (Interview A02). Another employer in a young health care practice, who was doing nicely but still working hard to establish her business, also emphasized its future potential: 'I'm certainly not rolling in it by any stretch of the imagination and I'm still struggling to pay back my student loans, but I can see a lot of potential and doors opening for me in ways that they've never opened in my life' (Interview A17).

Beyond the dream of their potential business, another reason that some woman remained self-employed was that they were making a *clear trade off between monetary and non-monetary benefits* – in particular, trading off higher income for flexibility and the ability to better balance family and work. Speaking about the financial trade-offs that came with this, one solo self-employed woman explained why she felt so satisfied: 'I can work whenever I want and I just know that I won't earn as much money if family is more important, but money isn't that important' (Interview B20). Another solo self-employed woman was very explicit about the trade-off she was making between a higher income and a satisfying family life: 'I know that if some of my priorities are other than the business, then the income will as a consequence not be as high. And that's, you know, the bargain that I've made' (Interview A04).

Tied to work-family balance, a third reason women continue to be self-employed is that, in some cases, they were not the primary breadwinners and could *rely on their partners to provide financial support* and an adequate standard of living. Their goal was not to support their household, but to contribute in some way, earning a 'component wage' rather than 'full wage' (Siltanen 1994). Reflecting this, one employer noted:

'My husband makes really good money, so on a day-to-day basis I don't have to worry about it that much' (Interview A10). Another observed that her husband's wealth left her in a 'much softer spot' than most women (Interview A04). A few women also noted other sources of financial support, either through pensions (Interview A07) or inheritance (Interview A10).

Financial support was especially important in the early stages, when business income was low. For example, one solo woman, who had held a very well-paid management job prior to starting her own consulting practice, emphasized the importance of her partner's support:

My husband was employed through all of this. So we certainly weren't destitute. But I certainly felt guilty because we didn't have the disposable income that we had had when I was in a full-time management position ... So we did have a couple of rough, well not rough – I mean nobody was starving to death or not getting braces put on – but certainly our standard of living changed for our family. But again my husband was supportive and he said to me, 'You know, it takes three to five years to grow a business. Like you have to kind of stick it out.' (Interview A03)

Her business was now doing nicely but his support had been critical in the first few years. Another woman, though disappointed that her business was not more lucrative, also noted how her partner's job provided the economic security her own business lacked:

Because my husband is employed with a large, multinational corporation and has all the bases covered as far as employee benefits, health plans, eye plans, dental plans, RRSPs and stock purchase plans, and this and that and the other, I know that from that perspective, we will be far better than just OK in the long run. (Interview B15)

But relying on a partner for financial support could also be problematic, as the case of one employer showed. Having quit a well-paying job to open her retail business, her relationship then ended, leaving her in a very difficult financial situation. As she explained:

You know you go from making $50,000 a year, to making nothing. There's a big, big gap there and when I was living with my partner, his income was OK, so you noticed it but you didn't notice it drastically. But as of now I have no income. So now what do I do? (Interview A02)

Finally, another reason why some women continued to be self-employed is that they had not become self-employed for *monetary reasons*, and were not strongly motivated by financial rewards. Typical of this view were the following comments: 'I didn't start this business to be a multi-millionaire' (Interview B03), 'I want to work for more than money' (Interview B05), and 'The income side was not that important to me.' Explaining her satisfaction with an income under $10,000, a solo self-employed woman said: 'I didn't want to put very dissatisfied for personal income because I'm not. I guess I'm being pragmatic about it and then the reality is that it has so little to do with why I'm doing it that it's not really dissatisfaction. It's just more like 'How am I going to pay my bills?' (Interview B09).

Another woman noted how money was not a motivator and how this cut across common stereotypes of entrepreneurs: 'Money has never been a big driving, you know, important thing with me, which is weird. People dealing with entrepreneurs, those in business, find that really kind of derailing' (Interview C12).

Were the women in the study less motivated by money than other factors? Certainly their responses to questions about the reason for entering self-employment might suggest so. Recall from Chapter 3 that the desire for better income was important for just 31.7% of respondents., with slight differences between solo workers (28.1%) and employers (35.7%). In contrast, other factors such as the desire for challenging work, independence, and a positive work environment were important for most of the women. In researching this issue, Thrasher and Smid (1998) found the vast majority of women in their study were not motivated by financial concerns. Other researchers, such as Carr (2000: 217) have also suggested that women may be less interested than men in material gain. Citing evidence from Beutel and Marini (1995), Carr suggests that women may embrace values that are less materialistic, and more focused on finding meaning and purpose in life – what have been termed 'post-corporate' or 'post-capitalist' values (see also Fenwick 2002).

But others, including Carr, cite evidence that women are often motivated by the same concerns as men (see also Rowe and Snizek 2003). In keeping with this, some women in the study were clearly motivated by money and the potential for greater financial success. Said one solo self-employed woman of her $40,000 to $50,000 income: 'Level of personal income? Somewhat satisfied. But I want to be wealthy, very, very wealthy, so I'm never going to be very satisfied in that area' (Interview B10).

Data from the *SSE* also suggest that women are as equally motivated as men by financial concerns, though this was the main reason for entering self-employment for just 9.7% of women and 9.5% of men. While we cannot make gender comparisons for the Alberta study, we can see that there are clear, and identifiable, differences *between* women in terms of motivation. This may explain why some – though certainly not all – women remain self-employed despite low financial returns.

'The Whole World Has Shifted': Job Security and Risk

If satisfaction is relative to other available job options, this is no more apparent than in relation to job security. Despite the many risks involved in owning a business and being self-employed, almost two-thirds of the women in the study indicated they were satisfied or very satisfied with their job security – a finding that is truly surprising. Perhaps a key reason for this seems to be that job security is judged not in isolation, but through the lens of the changing corporate environment and economy, which in the 1990s saw significant turbulence and downsizing in both the public and private sectors. In this respect, Beck's 'risk society' is the background against which women evaluate their situation. This is clear from discussions on job security which were replete with references to growing upheaval and risk in the labour market. Said one woman: 'Job security? There's no job security, I don't think it's not only for me, it's for anybody' (Interview A11). Another refugee from the public sector said simply: 'There is no job security these days anyways. The whole world has shifted' (Interview A07).

Is it possible that more widespread precariousness makes self-employment and small business ownership seem more safe and attractive? Do perceived risks recede when you control your own employment, and have first-hand knowledge of how the business you work for – your business – is doing? To some extent this appears to be the case. But feelings of security also vary, making some key differences clear. In particular, employees are much more likely to feel secure in their work. Nearly three-quarters were satisfied or very satisfied with job security – a figure no doubt reflecting the longer tenure of their businesses, and their greater financial stability. In contrast, just half of solo women were satisfied with job security, but even this in some ways is surprising.

For those who did feel secure in their work, the following comments were typical: 'My job is as secure as I make it' (Interview A10), and 'My job is as secure as I work hard' (Interview A08). Over and over women expressed the view that they had made their own security through hard work, initiative, and enterprise. Explaining this, one employer said: 'It's as secure as how busy you want to be, what effort you want to put into it. So you really tap your resources. You tap your stamina, you tap your knowledge, your alertness. Everything. You just tap in on who you want to be in business' (Interview B22).

Control was central to this feeling of security. Indeed, many women felt that by working for themselves they actually had more, rather than the same, job security as they had working for someone else. Illustrating this viewpoint is Kate, quoted at the start of this chapter.

While solo women most commonly expressed this view, employers were also wary about working for someone else. As one owner/employer of a five-year-old manufacturing business said in explaining her sense of security, 'I know I will always have a job. I may not make a lot of money, but I know that there's a lot of work to be done here' (Interview A01). Continuing on, she emphasizes her sense of control, and the perceived danger of working for others:

> I like to have a sense that I'm in control of my own destiny and that I'm not going to be laid off, you know? Big companies like to shuffle and I don't blame them. I mean who wouldn't want fresh young blood all the time? ... You can't blame the institution because young blood is good. I mean I have a lot of young blood here. But at least I'm in charge of my own blood, I mean I control it. (Interview A01)

Speaking again to the issue of control, another employer explained that she felt secure because she knew what was 'going on' in her own business:

> It's more secure than if you were working with another company where you never know what's going to happen. The company could be sold ... In your own business you know what's happening. But if you work for another company, you never know what's going to happen. (Interview B16)

Having a business also spread the risk around because women had many clients rather than just one boss. As the employer of a very successful accounting practice explained, she felt secure because she had many bosses, not just one: 'The whole hundred of them are not going to fire me at once ... And no one leaves, I don't lose clients because they don't go elsewhere. I typically lose clients because they go out of business. And I always have more coming in' (Interview B06).

Other women, while satisfied with their security, were still not quite as secure as they wanted to be. Compared to those discussed so far, they were more ambivalent. One solo woman with a fairly busy practice felt secure 'in terms of the fact that I can't fire myself,' but still needed more work to feel her business was established and secure: 'I would like to have a lot more work than we've got. I would like to be busy every single day of the week, or handing work off to other people. As it is, I've got enough to keep me busy but I still want more of it, you know? I still want more' (Interview A18).

Another solo practitioner, though generally satisfied with her job security, worried about fluctuations in her workload and finding new work as other projects ended:

> When a couple of days have passed in between one project ending, I go through two days of 'Oh, this is wonderful to have the time,' and then I start panicking, thinking, 'Oh my gosh, I don't have another project right now!!' But then lo and behold it turns up. So I've been very fortunate that way. I don't know how I'll be if I go for a longer period of time. Time will tell if that happens. (Interview C08)

Another woman saw her unease over job security diminishing over time as her business became more established. 'I'm more secure about the job now than I was two years ago but less secure than I would hope I would be in two years from now' (Interview A17).

In some cases, women seemed to feel secure not only because their business was doing well, but because they felt they could always go on to *do something else*. In this sense, self-employment and business ownership seems to have imparted confidence and skills in their ability to earn a living. As one employer in a very successful business explained, 'I don't even worry about it ... If it didn't work out tomorrow, I'd find something else. I know myself really well now' (Interview C13). Another solo women said:

> I suppose I'm as secure as I am motivated. If it is a concern, I think, 'What will happen to me as I age, or as my clients age and die, then what?' But I

think there's a general level of skills and I think also there's exposure to different kinds of work, different kinds of businesses. You're continually developing skills. I'd be surprised if I couldn't get a job ... so I'm not really concerned of being unable to support my family having gone to this extreme. (Interview C10)

In addition to these women, a few others had *other sources of support* that eased concerns about job security. For example, one married women working solo in a very non-traditional field said: 'Job security really isn't an issue. I suppose it will be more so perhaps when my husband retires, but at the moment we could live on his salary. So that's not applicable' (Interview A16).

Against these more positive assessments, however, there was also *discontent* about job security, particularly amongst the solo self-employed. Speaking about her struggling business, Carmen, quoted at the start of this chapter said: 'I'm *very* dissatisfied with job security. There is none' (Interview B23). Another woman who worked incredibly long hours in a commercial location said: 'Telling the truth, from month to month, I don't know whether I will have the business' (Interview B04). The same was the case for one employer who also had a retail location: 'There is no job security here because if the store doesn't make it, then I'm out on the street looking for work. So there is the risk. I try not to focus too much on the risks ... but people going into business have to be very aware of that' (Interview A02).

A key concern for many solo self-employed woman was *finding new clients and new sources of business.* For one solo self-employed woman in the health care field who was just starting out:

I guess the least satisfying part of it is that it's difficult to really get a foundation and make a valid connection to paying work, continual access to paying work ... So I think that the most frustrating is the access to continual sources of contracts that you know will pay money. (Interview B05)

This precariousness was also underlined by another solo practitioner:

Because I'm out marketing myself, I'm always concerned. When is the next contract going to be? And how big is it going to be? How long is it going to take? Etc., etc. So job security isn't something that I'm ... I don't know if I'll ever be really, really secure. (Interview B10)

In addition to accessing new clients and business, some women also felt vulnerable because the *business was totally reliant on them and their health*. Said one solo self-employed woman who had struggled with various health issues:

> I'm not very secure because job security is like 'OK, how much can you do at a particular time?' I'm very vulnerable because it's just me, and my business depends on my health being OK and me being able to produce. So I don't think I really have job security in that respect. (Interview A09)

In another case, an employer was suddenly feeling less secure as a result of an injury, underlining some of the dangers faced by the self-employed:

> The biggest negative that I've just discovered was a month ago I hurt myself and I missed three days of work. And that's when I started thinking about job security. Because, before that, it just didn't mean anything, because I'm making so much money that I think 'Oh, it doesn't matter. All my needs will always be met.' But I have no savings at all. (Interview C19)

'The Money's Just Not There': Preparing for Retirement

Beyond their income and job security, how satisfied are self-employed women with their ability to prepare for retirement? According to the *SSE*, 90% of Canadians who are self-employed have some savings invested for their retirement. Just 9% have not saved at all. While the actual amount of savings in unknown, the impression we get from this statistic is that the self-employed are making adequate preparations for their retirement. But in stark contrast, the Alberta study suggests that many women are ill prepared. Just one-third were satisfied with their ability to save for retirement – 40% of employers, and just one-quarter of the solo self-employed. This compares to recent findings for the Canadian workforce as a whole that two-thirds of workers approaching retirement age feel they have made adequate financial preparations to maintain their standard of living (Statistics Canada 2003b).

Delving further into this issue through the in-depth interviews, only a few women expressed confidence about their retirement planning. One of these women had started her business after retiring from a job in the health care sector and was already drawing a pension from her former job. A second was no longer saving for retirement because she had 'invested wisely' in earlier years (Interview C16). A third woman indicated she was well prepared for retirement before starting her business but understood the difficulties faced by many of the self-employed:

> I have my retirement taken care of so maybe it was easier for me to go in to become an entrepreneur. I just don't know a lot of entrepreneurs that are my size anyway, that have an additional ability to save for retirement because they're self-employed. That just doesn't seem to be the case ... But I'm not saving for retirement. I've already done that (Interview B10)

For most women, however, retirement saving was a significant challenge and a source of concern. Because of low income, many woman faced difficulties simply finding the money to invest in an RRSP. When asked about retirement saving, one solo woman said simply: 'Save for retirement? What retirement?' (Interview A13). Another explained that she wanted to save but simply could not: 'The ability to save for retirement – I'm not in a position to do that yet, so you know, I'm quite dissatisfied with that' (Interview B08). Lacking the resources for saving was highly frustrating for one woman who had contributed to an RRSP as an employee in the past: 'I don't make what I was making when I was working, or anywhere close. You know, so stuff like RRSPs, my husband still puts into those but I don't put nearly what I was putting in ... The money's just not there' (Interview B13).

Even when some saving had been done, many women worried that it was not enough to prepare adequately for retirement. While the study did not collect data on the amount of retirement savings, several comments highlighted women's concerns in this area. For example, one solo woman who had been self-employed for nearly two decades did not feel that she had accumulated enough savings to retire: 'I would have done a lot better probably if I would have worked for somebody else. I did start saving a little bit of money each month, but it's not enough and so I think that probably as I get older, that's one of the biggest drawbacks' (Interview B12). Asked if it was a concern, she replied, 'yes retirement ... I think I'll be working forever.' In some cases, the extra income they would have liked to contribute towards an RRSP was often needed elsewhere, either to invest in the business or to smooth out fluctuating income. One woman with a four-year-old solo consulting practice reported:

> When I'm juggling with so many things and trying to meet all my financial commitments – equipment that I buy, notes that I have to pay – I don't have extra cash to save for retirement. If I have extra cash I always

put it for June, the money for June and July, because I know my work will slow down. So in terms of retirement, self-employment is not the best way to save. (Interview A14)

Though many women expressed concerns over their situation, their ability to deal with it was *limited by the financial demands of their business*. As one woman with a young communications company explained, 'I can't see the point of worrying about it right now when the day-to-day needs have to be met. I think I need to look at it as part of a five year plan' (Interview A15).

More worrisome than simply deferring saving, several women had found it necessary to *use existing retirement savings* to either start up their business or keep it afloat during difficult times. When asked about retirement saving, one solo woman, a forced entrepreneur, in a three-year-old business, said: 'Ability to save for retirement? I don't think I will. I'm just dreading it. I'm forty-two now. I spent to open the business, I spent my RRSP money because I could not get any loans from the bank' (Interview B04).

In another case, a woman in a one-year-old home-based business had also made use of retirement savings from previous employment to help with the initial stages of start up. Asked if she was currently saving, she said, 'No, no in fact my savings, the savings that I had, have gone into building my home office and in doing advertising and covering the costs of continuing to keep going every month' (Interview B23).

While this was more typical of newly self-employed woman, there was at least one long-time employer in a similar situation. Explaining how she had kept her business of over twenty years afloat, in the face of growing competition from larger chains, she said: 'I've used up all my RRSPs and all that sort of stuff to put into the store, because you know when things are down, it's down. And you just have to survive it somehow' (Interview C15).

Though many women appear to be ill-prepared for retirement, a number seemed unconcerned, as they had financial support from their spouses. In this respect, retirement, even more than income, was a *joint venture*. When asked about retirement, one employer/owner of a relatively new restaurant said laughing: 'My husband's saving for retirement and I'm going with him' (Interview C02). Another solo woman in a home-based business explained her retirement approach:

I am married, so it's a collective retirement, OK? So this business, the ability to save, yes, I think that I can generate enough money that I'm also

going to protect my future income. But my retirement to me is connected
to the fact that I hope to retire with my husband. (Interview A08)

Several other women made comments along these lines, emphasizing
the critical role their partner's finances played in their future. Said one
solo woman in acknowledging the importance of her husband's support: 'Well my situation is different in that I'm not the primary income
earner. So, you know, a little softer spot than a lot of women might
find themselves in' (Interview A04). Another woman underlined a key
difference a partner made: 'Well I'm lucky because I've got a husband
who supported me ... But if you're a single person, solely dependent
on income of self-employment, especially in this kind of business, I
wouldn't advise it unless you've got a back-up' (Interview A06).

Beyond family support, a few women noted they were counting on
the *equity they had in their business* to provide for the retirement. This is
not surprising in light of findings from the *SSE*, which suggest the
most commonly cited assets of the self-employed are equity in a home,
cottage, or business (HRDC 2002: 58). Across the board, these women
were all employers – two in non-traditional fields – with much larger
than average businesses, and above average incomes. Explaining her
retirement preparation, one employer said:

> Basically this is my retirement, my business is my retirement savings plan
> ... My idea is that I work for another ten, twelve years full-time, build up
> the business, bring in my kids as they want to, if they want to, and con-
> tinue the business, not sell it, and just continue the business and draw an
> income from the business as the owner. Even if I let it slide, and let some-
> body else take it over, I still can draw income from the business. That's
> my retirement saving plan in a nutshell. (Interview B06)

For another employer in the manufacturing sector, the retirement plan
was linked to plans for business growth and entry into new markets:

> If the United States does open up to us, the business will grow at such a
> rate that it'll be beyond my capability, as simple as that. And somebody's
> going to have to buy me out and that would suit me just fine ... so that's
> the retirement plan, right? That's why you build the business, so that is
> the retirement plan. So that somebody can come along and buy your busi-
> ness for what it's worth and you retire on whatever that is. That's the way
> I'm looking at things. (Interview B19)

Whether 'whatever that is' would be enough to retire on remains an open question. Speaking to this issue, another employer in the computing industry said:

> At the end of the day, I'm sure I've got the equity and all that. So savings for retirement to me is not tangible; it's intangible. But I also know that I do have that. It's not really dissatisfaction, it's really more neutral, it doesn't mean much to me. (Interview A12)

Finally, another group of women indicated that they had *no plans to retire*. In some cases this was motivated by the love of their work and business. Explained one woman with a young health care practice:

> I probably won't retire until I'm ninety-two. I'll probably be working at least part-time, you know? Because that's what I do, I love it. I don't know how to not work which is hard to come to realize ... I mean if you like your work, why not continue it? What I would rather do is retire a little bit through the year. (Interview A17)

Another employer/owner of a retail store expressed the same view: 'My mom ... worked up until she was in her late seventies. And I can't imagine not working at something. I know that as I go along, what I worked at is going to have to change, but I can't imagine not working' (Interview A10).

In other cases, it was motivated both by a *love of work and the inability to adequately prepare*. As one employer in a manufacturing business said bluntly, 'I'm not saving for retirement cause I'm not going to retire ... and I haven't had the money to save for retirement. I'm just getting by at this point' (Interview A01).

It is interesting to note that despite the general discontent about retirement planning generally, only one woman brought up issues of government support. Pointing out that small business owners, as employers, contributed to the retirement planning of their employees, she raises a number of questions about whether there is an appropriate governmental role on this issue:

> Why hasn't the government put in some kind of mandatory pension plan for small business owners? ... What about the people who are the support system to the whole economy, the small business person, and there's no pension plan! If I didn't create my own pension plan, you know, what

have you've got left? You've got your EI. You've got your Canadian pension which is not a lot, it doesn't meet today's standards. And you've got your old age pension. That's it, my dear. So you're down to living on nothing (Interview B22)

Her comments raise a number of important policy issues that will be taken up in Chapter 6. At the heart are questions about how self-employed workers can ensure long-term economic security when they find themselves excluded or differentially included in some of the traditional safety nets that have supported other Canadian workers for years.

'You Are Always Worried': Financial Responsibility

Beyond concerns over income, security, and retirement planning, the self-employed also carry additional financial responsibilities and worries that escape most paid employees. Central here are responsibilities for keeping their business afloat, and paying employees, suppliers, and others. Given the financial difficulties many women faced, it seems paradoxical that nearly two-thirds expressed satisfaction with the financial responsibility of running a business. Even more surprising, there were no differences between solo and employers, which we might expect given the greater scale of business and responsibility employers had. How do we explain this?

To some extent it may be linked to women's ability to exercise independence and control – in this sense extending the control they had over their work to include their financial affairs. For example, as one solo woman explained when talking about financial responsibility, 'It's my choice, my decisions, and that gives me a certain satisfaction, I guess' (Interview A18). For a few women, being financially responsible was also satisfying because it was highly motivating. As one employer/owner of a human resource firm said: 'I like the responsibility, I like the complete ownership. I find it exhilarating. The fear of failure is a wonderful motivator you know and I make sure that it motivates me as much as it should' (Interview B02).

Most women who were satisfied with financial responsibility, however, said relatively little about why this was so. Instead, it was those who were dissatisfied that spoke at length. This was especially true of employers who were responsible not just to clients and suppliers, but also to their employees. Talking about this, one employer in a three-year-old health practice said: 'Financial responsibility is scary, it really is. And that's part of why I don't want to bring somebody on full-time right now' Another employer in a travel agency emphasized the stress involved: 'You're always worried about "Will I be able to pay the rent?", "Will I be able to pay my staff?", "Do I have to lay off?" that kind of thing' (Interview C17). Echoing these comments, a restaurant owner and employer recalled her first year in business: 'I'd lay awake at night wondering how I was going to pay everybody. It's unbelievable, the first year' (Interview C02). Another employer in the manufacturing sector, though now more established, recounted similar experiences:

> Financial responsibility, I hate it. I would like somebody else to be in charge of that. And of course, who can be? Because when you own the company, you are financially responsible to your employees, to your mortgage company, to your bank to pay back a loan ... Especially when you're starting because it's tough and you're scrambling for money and you're thinking 'Oh my God, I hope these people pay their bill because I've got these expenses coming up and it's pay day and you know it's levelling out.' So I don't have that stress every pay day that I used to have of 'Oh my God!!' But, boy oh boy, that's a part of the business that I really wish somebody else could have done because I didn't like it. (Interview A01)

For solo women, financial responsibility also brought stress, but it was more self-contained, relating to covering costs and ensuring adequate income for themselves from month to month. In some cases, as these two solo women show, dissatisfaction was directly linked to *low income levels* or *fluctuating income*:

> The financial responsibility is also something that I am not satisfied with because since I make such little money it becomes difficult at times to cover the bills and this becomes a really challenge when the money coming in does not match the money that needs to go out to cover expenses. (Interview C18)

> There's always a few months in the year that you're not making as much as you know, a certain amount. So it's hard, it's very stressful and I don't like that. (Interview C14)

In other cases, a *lack of financial skills* was the issue, as for this solo woman with a clothing design business: 'I don't like the responsibility, the financial responsibility ... In order for the business to flourish, I would probably have to have somebody help me with that end of things' (Interview A09).

In another case, it was the result of *changing family circumstance*:

> I think when I started it was exciting and now it's stressful and probably I find that because I have two babies, and I find it somewhat more stressful that I'm responsible for a whole family. When I was single, it didn't matter. Now I think, 'My God, they've got to eat' and stuff like that. So I do find it, I think now, a little bit more pressure-filled ... So having the kids I think has definitely changed my focus. (Interview C07)

With respect to financial responsibility, a further issue raised by several women was the use of *personal lines of credit or credit cards*. As noted previously, just over 40% of women used some form of personal credit at some point to help finance their business. For some women this was not a concern. Said one woman in a solo business: 'So putting myself and my credit cards on the line, I mean it's there but everybody does it and it's not a huge deal in the scheme of things' (Interview B09).

But for others, such as this solo consultant in human resources, the use of personal credit was a source of stress, making her feel out of control:

> The biggest challenge that I have right now is my finances because I have used my personal line of credit. I use my credit cards a lot and I want to be able to get out of that situation. So I'm giving myself two years to try and work that through. So finance is a big challenge. I think because what I've found as a self, especially as a sole proprietorship, I think it's very difficult to get loans from the banks. You know you talk to them and you can see in their eyes, they're thinking of corporations. They're not thinking of the single individual sitting in front of them and especially a woman and a woman of colour. I think it's so much more difficult to even start talking about loans because bank managers don't take you seriously. (Interview A14)

Exploring Differences in Income and Economic Security

What conclusions can we draw about the short and long-term economic security offered by self-employment and small business ownership? How are women faring in the entrepreneurial economy? Are they earning good incomes? Can they prepare for retirement? Do they feel secure in the work they do? Exploring these questions reveals no black and white answers, no clear-cut signs of either emancipation on one hand, or marginalization on the other, for women over all. Instead, what we see are some key dividing lines between women and tell-tale signs of polarization, in terms of income levels and satisfaction with income, job security, and retirement savings.

Overall, employers are doing much better than solo women in terms of earning power. They are much less likely to earn low incomes, and far more likely to be satisfied with most extrinsic aspects of their work, except the ability to save for retirement. In contrast, the majority of solo women are not satisfied with income, job security, or the ability to save for retirement. And while there is an elite group of solo workers – about 15% – who earn $60,000 per year, nearly twice as many – about 36% – are earning under $20,000 annually. If any surprises emerge, it is the much higher than expected satisfaction with job security among both employers and solo women. Much of this seems a response to growing precariousness in paid employment generally during the so called nasty nineties, where organizations downsized and laid off workers. In this context, owning and running a small business may not feel like a risky endeavour, but may instead seem to impart a sense of control in a turbulent world.

Though differences in financial situations are strongly shaped by one's status as either solo worker or employer, other factors may help to explain the variation and polarization we observe. In order to explore this further, we can examine women's extrinsic satisfaction by taking several factors into account. Some factors are *socio-demographic*, such as age, education, visible minority status, and presence or absence of children. Others are *business related* – for example, work status (part-time or full-time), business tenure (number of years in business), business location (home-based or office-based), income and reasons for becoming self-employed (forced or voluntary). Because of the small sample , it is not possible to control for several factors at once, but looking at these factors one by one does help to clarify what shapes women's feelings about their economic security.

In terms of socio-demographic factors, age, education, and the presence of children all have an influence. For example, age influences satisfaction with income and job security (though interestingly not with one's ability to save for retirement). Younger women are generally more satisfied with their income and job security, perhaps reflecting lower expectations at the start of one's working life. Education operates in a similar manner, less educated women being more satisfied than college and university educated women with their income and job security, as well as their ability to save for retirement. Surprisingly, in light of studies on gender and race in the labour market (Das Gupta 1996; Vosko 2002), visible minority women have incomes similar to the sample as a whole, and were more likely to be satisfied with their income. This reflects the higher education and a greater presence of employers amongst visible minority women in this sample. Immigrant women (a somewhat different group to visible minority women) had somewhat lower incomes, with satisfaction levels similar to the sample as a whole, clearly reflecting the greater number of solo workers in this group. Finally, having children is linked to lower satisfaction with income, and somewhat lower satisfaction with retirement savings, but makes no difference to satisfaction with job security. Nearly three-quarters of those without children were satisfied with income, while just 43.4% of those with children felt the same. No doubt this reflects the trade-offs many women with children are making – the bargain between lower earnings and greater work-family balance. But it also suggests that women experience some discontent with this trade-off, or at the very least a feeling that earnings potential is hindered by operating a business in this way.

In terms of business-related factors, working in a home-based business or on a part-time basis does not appear to influence satisfaction with income, job security, and retirement savings, with one exception. Part-time workers were much less satisfied with job security (40.0%) than those working on a full-time basis (64.6%). Perhaps this reflects involuntary part-time status for some women, or perhaps some concern over the ability to sustain or grow a business on a part-time schedule. Far more important in shaping satisfaction with economic security, however, were factors such as business tenure and reasons for becoming self-employed. Women in younger businesses (up to five years) were much less satisfied with income and retirement savings than those with longer tenure (six years and more). Just one-third of women in newer businesses were happy with their income, compared to nearly 60% of older business. For retirement, just one-quarter were satisfied with savings, compared to roughly 40% of more senior businesses.

As in Chapter 4, however, the most influential factor for satisfaction was one's reasons for becoming self-employed in the first place. Using the typology of forced and voluntary self-employed, we see striking differences. Only 16.7% of those forced into self-employed were satisfied with their income and ability to save for retirement, while for those who entered voluntarily, the figures were 54.5% and 41.9% respectively. Moreover, while just one-third of those forced into self-employment were satisfied with their job security, this was the case for over two-thirds of those who pursued self-employment and small business ownership on their own accord.

Conclusions

Compared to the Chapter 4, which showed how much women enjoyed the work they do and the independence and challenge they have in the workplace, the results from this chapter provide a far more measured account of the entrepreneurial economy. In particular, what they suggest is that while there are many successful women in small businesses and solo practices earning good incomes, there are also a significant number who are struggling to make ends meet, and who face significant challenges not only in terms of meeting their immediate needs and securing a good standard of living, but in making adequate preparations for their long-term financial security. This latter group is largely ignored in media accounts of women's entrepreneurship which, for obvious reasons, prefers to focus on the success stories. Women like Oprah Winfrey are routinely splashed across media pages as example of women who have made it in conventional terms, earning huge incomes from businesses they have started from scratch. Media lists such as *Chatelaine's* 'Top 100 Women Entrepreneurs' keep such women firmly in public view.

But if the findings here suggest anything, it is the need to recognize the great diversity within women's self-employment and small business ownership. At one end are the conventional success stories, what have been called high flyers, bosses, gazelles – women entrepreneurs establishing highly successful businesses, who are interested in expanding their businesses by exporting to new markets, investing in new technologies, and securing new sources of capital. Their experiences are quite different from those who may be lifestyle entrepreneurs or business moms, working in a home-based business in an effort to gain better balance between family and work. Both of these groups are different still from necessity or forced entrepreneurs who have become self-employed due to downsizing and job loss, and who appear to face significant risks in terms of their short- and long-term economic security. And all of these groups differ still from an emerging elite of highly skilled, educated female 'free agents' or 'one woman shows' who in the new economy are managing to parlay their sought-after talent and creativity into lucrative solo careers.

Much like the media, which have failed to capture or convey these disparate images, public policy has also failed to come to grips with the complexity of the emerging entrepreneurial economy. While on one level encouraging self-employment and small business ownership, government has been slow to recognize the ever-rising proportion of workers in self-employment and small business ownership who fall outside a traditional employer-employee relationship, and therefore lack many of the benefits, protections, and social services that have traditionally been granted to Canadian workers through their status as an 'employee.' In a world filled with high flyers, this would not present a problem. But as the findings in this chapter show, the current situation in Canada is considerably more complex. How public policy can deal not only with growing numbers of self-employed women and small business owners, but with their wide diversity of needs and concerns, presents a considerable policy challenge. It is to this issue we now turn.

6 Building an Entrepreneurial Economy

The growth of small business is essential to job creation in Canada.
Growing Small Business, Industry Canada (1994b)

As a company I just see us growing and growing, you know?
(Lisa, Interview B17)

Why do I want to grow? I'm happy doing what I'm doing. I like being a 'one woman show.'
(Joan, Interview A03)

Discussing her plans for the future, Lisa is the classic example of a growth-oriented entrepreneur. In just six years she has built a highly successful business, earns a generous salary, and sees nothing but unlimited opportunities ahead to 'increase sales, increase revenues and grow stronger.' In marked contrast, Joan, who runs a thriving consultancy, has virtually no interest in seeing her business grow. Having worked for several larger organizations earlier in her career, she loves being a free agent, talking at length about the freedom and independence she enjoys. Business is booming, opportunities abound, but she's just not interested in expanding. 'Why do I have to think about growing?' she asks when discussing her plans for the future. 'I just like working by myself.'

Lisa and Joan's differing approaches to growth shed important light on recent efforts to build a more entrepreneurial economy in Canada. Taking direction from the enterprise culture spawned by Thatcherism in mid-1980s Britain (Burrows 1991a, 199b), Canada, like many other industrialized countries, has placed great emphasis on the small business sector, moving away from attempts at direct job creation in favour of a less interventionist, more market-oriented, approach where small and medium sized businesses acts as the engine of economic growth (OECD 2000a). Not only has self-employment been promoted to the Canadian population generally, it has also been encouraged as a way back into the labour market for unemployed and laid-off workers – most notably through the federal government's self-employment assistance benefit that helps unemployed Canadians start a business (Graves and Gauthier 1996; Orser and Hoggarth-Scott 1998). In these initiatives and others, Canadian policy has drawn from the micro-enterprise movement in other developed and developing countries as a way to reduce unemployment and poverty, and fuel economic growth (Calmeadow 1997, 1998; Grameen Bank 2001; McMichael 2000; Raheim and Bolden 1995; for critical reviews of such programs, see Ehlers and Main 1998; T. Williams 2003).

In Canada, the policy emphasis on self-employment and small business can be seen on a number of fronts. In the mid-1990s, when self-employment was growing rapidly, federal government policy documents such as Industry Canada's *Growing Small Business* (1994b) and *Building a More Innovative Economy* (1994a) set out goals for creating an economic environment more supportive of small business. Key recommendations included reducing taxes, providing financing, reducing regulatory and paper work burden, and making business-related government programs more efficient and effective (Industry Canada 1994b: 9). Such thinking built upon growing evidence from most OECD countries showing that small and medium-sized enterprises (SMEs) made up the majority of enterprises in most countries and were key contributors to job growth (OECD 2000c, 2000d; Baldwin and Picot 1994). It also built upon influential books such as David Birch's 1987 *Job Generation in America: How Our Smallest Companies Put the Most People to Work*, which sang the praises of small business (cited in Parker 2001). In addition to policy and academic writing, the merits of the entrepreneurial economy have been well profiled in the media and popular writing. News article such as 'Small Business a Big Deal to the Economy' (Howell 1999) and 'Small Firms Big Job Creators' (Little 1994) are just a few examples in the Canadian context. Together these public discourses suggest a need for policy regimes to better support small business and new enterprise – in particular, a paring back of the interventionist, managed welfare-state government in favour of a laissez-faire, entrepreneurial model where small business plays a key role (Parker 2001; Audretsch and Thurik 2001).

Women have often been an important focus of these policy initiatives. Nowhere is this more apparent than in the creation of the Prime Minister's Task Force on Women Entrepreneurs which was commissioned in November 2002 by then Prime Minister Jean Chrétien and chaired by MP Sarmite Bulte. In announcing the task force, Chrétien argued that women business owners were playing a key role in the development of a more innovative, entrepreneurial economy. As he noted:

> In the Speech from the Throne, we identified innovation and learning as priorities for the government and set ambitious national targets aimed at making Canada one of the most innovative countries in the world by 2010. But we cannot achieve these targets alone. As an important source of talent and creativity, women entrepreneurs have much to contribute to this important goal. (Canada, Privy Council Office, 19 November 2002)

The task force report, released in October 2003, provides powerful testimony to women's contributions, documenting a remarkable range of business activity by women across the country. Since coming to office, the Martin government has affirmed its commitment to action on this issue. In October 2004, a follow-up conference to the task force, Sustaining the Momentum: An Economic Forum on Women Entrepreneurs, brought together researchers, policy-makers, and practitioners to consider policies to help Canadian women's business thrive. International activities such as the April 2004 Tri lateral Virtual Summit and the June 2004 OECD Conference on Women Entrepreneurs have also kept this issue on national and international policy agendas (see Project Tsunami 2004).

Amidst these encouraging assessments and actions on the issue of small business and female enterprise, however, some commentators have questioned the role small business and self-employment is playing in the new economy (Finlayson 2003; Parker 2001; Ehlers and Main 1998). In 'The Myth of the Entrepreneurial Economy', for example, Parker argues that small firms typically fail to live up to their billing, as the vast majority are not particularly innovative, do not contribute disproportionately to employment growth, and do not engage in progressive employment practices. Canvassing the performance of small firms in France, Germany, Australia, the United Kingdom, and The United States, Parker argues that it is not 'small business in general,' but a tiny group of dynamic small firms that are responsible for the bulk of innovation and employment growth in these economies. In her view, it is this select group that government policy should target, rather than promoting self-employment and small business across the board. Lending credence to these concerns in the Canadian context, recent analysis by Baldwin and Chowhan has linked falling productivity to growth among the self-employed, observing that 'almost all of the difference in labour productivity between Canada and the United States in the 1990s can be attributed to the greater growth of self-employment in Canada and the poorer income performance of this group' (2003: ii).

Other commentators, while noting the vital role small organizations play in industrialized economies, acknowledge there is significant instability and turnover in this sector. As Aldrich (1999: 12) notes, small businesses are started and disbanded at a high rate; in the United States in the 1990s only half of businesses succeeded and fewer than one in ten grew in size. Along similar lines, the OECD found significant flows both in and out of self-employment, with only one in thirty solo workers becoming employers each year (2000a: 167). Other writers have also noted 'the very uneven employment-providing potential of small firms and [the fact] that many owner-managers neither seek nor desire employment growth (Baines and Wheelock 1998: 590–1; see also Storey 1994; Industry Canada 2004). Yet while few small and micro-businesses grow to be large, those that do receive disproportionate attention (Baines, Wheelock and Abrams 1997)

The importance of small businesses and self-employment to the economy thus remains a critical question. At present, politicians and policy-makers clearly assume SMEs are critical job creators, placing a great deal of policy emphasis there. But is this a valid assumption? Most SMEs are small and, while some seek and eventually achieve growth, this may not be the case for the majority. Equally important, while business start-up, growth, and expansion continue to attract the bulk of policy attention, critical policy gaps have emerged on other fronts – creating what Lowe (2002) has called a situation of 'policy limbo' for self-employed and other workers. These gaps can be found in broader areas of labour market policy that shape working conditions and social protection – for example, access to employment and income insurance, maternity leave, sick leave, disability, and retirement benefits. Though less directly tied to self-employment and small business in the minds of most Canadians, these programs play a key role in determining the quality of work. But this not because of what current policies do but because of what they fail to do for such workers. Built on the postwar premise that most workers are employees – typically in full-time, permanent jobs – existing labour policy routinely excludes the self-employed. As we will see, this creates significant problems in an economy where independent work is not only on the rise but also changing in critical ways.

In order to shed light on these issues, this chapter assesses existing policy and programs in light of women's experiences, aspirations, and needs. Given the current policy emphasis on business start-up, growth, and training, the first part of the chapter begins there, examining how well existing policy and programs mesh with Canadian women's own plans and goals. In particular, it provides an overview of existing programs designed to serve the SE/SBO sector, and then turns to examine the growth aspirations and the training needs of the Alberta women. Moving from 'what exists' to 'what is needed,' the later part of the chapter shifts to consider some key policy gaps that have emerged in Canada – in particular, the lack of access to adequate social protection for self-employed workers. Here I focus on three key issues: employment and income insurance; work-family leave; and retirement savings.

By examining these areas I hope to make clear the critical role policy plays in shaping the emerging entrepreneurial economy. Many studies of women's self-employment and small business ownership pay little attention to the larger political economy and policy context. But governments are key players in shaping the quality of work, setting regulatory frameworks, and incentive and disincentive structures. I argue here that one of the key challenges facing policy makers is to begin thinking differently about women entrepreneurs, not only recognizing their growing importance to the economy, but also the changing nature of self-employment and small business in the new economy, and the diverse aspirations and needs of such workers.

Business Start-up, Expansion, and Growth

Arriving at the Edmonton international airport, one of the first things that comes into view is a huge billboard proclaiming 'Entrepreneurship: The Spirit of the West.' Sponsored by the Government of Canada / Western Economic Diversification, it provides a toll free number to connect with '100 points of service working for you.' Currently across the country there exists a vast network of programs designed to encourage and support self-employment, small business ownership, and entrepreneurship. Programs exist at all levels of government and often work in partnership with other industry or non-governmental organizations (NGOs). Overall, the services provided are highly varied, ranging from financing for start-up and expansion, to business planning, coaching, mentoring, training, and advice on a broad range of business topics.

Itemizing these programs is a mammoth undertaking. A recent inventory of policies and programs done by Bell (2003a) for this project identified and documented literally dozens and dozens of programs operating at the federal, provincial/territorial, and local level. A similar inventory done by the Prime Minister's task force women identifies thirty-two pages of programs in federal departments alone (see Appendix 1 in Canada 2003; see also Stevenson 2004). While space considerations prevent replication of the detailed scan by Bell here, Table 6.1 provides a summary glance of some of the most important programs at the federal level. Table 6.2 outlines provincial programs using Alberta (which forms the backdrop of this study) as an example. In both cases the lists are selective only.

Looking at these programs, a number of features stand out. First, most programs take a fairly positive and active stance towards self-employment and small business ownership, encouraging business start-up through assistance with business training, development of business plans, and financing. Second, while many of these services and programs are available to all Canadians, a significant number are targeted at groups seen to be disadvantaged or marginalized in the labour market. This includes women, young Canadians, Aboriginals, the unemployed, disabled, and poor, as well as those living in rural areas or specific regions. Of particular interest amongst targeted programs is the Self-Employment Assistance (SEA) program which assists unemployed Canadians who are interested in becoming self-employed. Delivered differently in each of the provinces, as a result of the Labour Market Agreements (Lazar 2002; HRDC interview, 24 October 2001), individuals eligible for employment insurance may choose to enter into this program, gaining business training and support to develop a viable business plan and secure financing. As part of this program, participants receive ongoing business coaching and assistance, as well as financial support for up to fifty-two weeks. Other programs of interest included in Table 6.1 are those offered by the Business Development

TABLE 6.1
Selected Federal Programs for Start-up, Expansion, and Growth

---

1 HRSDC Canada – Self Employment Benefits/Assistance (SEA)
SEA offers income support, coaching and technical assistance to individuals who wish to become self-employed. It is open to anyone who receives employment insurance (EI) benefits and has not taken part in the SEA program in the last five years. To be eligible, participants must attend an orientation session, develop a viable business plan acceptable to HRSDC, start a new business or take over an existing one, and agree to work full-time in the business while receiving financial assistance (for up to fifty-two weeks).

2 Business Development Bank of Canada (BDC)
BDC is a commercial crown corporation that seeks to help small and medium-sized businesses to grow. It targets those in the start-up or early growth phase (first twelve months of sales) and offers financing of up to $100,000 to provide for working capital, acquiring fixed assets, marketing or start-up fees, or purchase of a franchise.
   In addition to their regular loan program, BDC also has the following programs:
   i. Co-vision: Start-up Financing Program: finances businesses in their start-up or early growth phase. Target manufacturing, distribution, service and tourism.
   ii. Young Entrepreneur Financing Program: provides start-up assistance of up to $25,000 to young entrepreneurs (eighteen to thirty-four) with a commercially viable business idea and a proposal that has realistic market or sales potential. Also offers management support and access to professional business management counselling.
   iii. Aboriginal Banking Unit: offers financing and consulting services tailored to Aboriginal businesses, on or off reserve land. Financing may cover fixed assets, start-up costs (up to $25,000), or intangibles such as R&D, or market development costs.
   iv. Micro Business Program: supports the growth and development of small and innovative micro businesses (fewer than five employees, annual sales under $500,000).

3 Industry Canada
Offers assistance through a variety of programs including:
   i. Canadian Small Business Financing Act (CSBFA): Assists businesses in obtaining term loans and capital leases of up to $250,000 for establishing, modernizing, and improving small businesses in Canada.
   ii. Aboriginal Business Canada: helps individuals establish or acquire a tourism business, a manufacturing business, a professional services business, a scientific/technical services business, a business that exports a product or service, or in limited situations a business that is linked to a specified major development. For existing businesses, may provide support for business planning, capital cost, marketing and business support financing related to assist with growth and expansion (e.g. new markets, improved processes, product development).

TABLE 6.1 (*Continued*)

---

4 **Community Futures Development Corporations (CFDC)**

CFDC promotes community economic development by organizing events, fostering cooperation and creating sustainable jobs and businesses. Its mandate is twofold: (ii) services for businesses (access to funding, technical assistance, support for local and young entrepreneurs); and (ii) services for the community (cooperation, planning, events, awareness, and local growth generating initiatives). CFDC loans assist entrepreneurs who may have difficulty accessing loans from traditional lenders. CFDC also has a youth strategy initiative with the mission to slow the exodus of young people to cities.

5 **Export Development Corporation (EDC)**
http://www.edc.ca/prodserv/womex/index_e.htm
Provides information and resources to assist women interested in exporting.

6 **Department of Foreign Affairs and International Trade (DFAIT)**
http://www.dfait-maeci.gc.ca/businesswomen/
Offers information through its website on exporting, available programs and services, key contacts, advance notice of trade events, and market leads and opportunities. Also provides access to research, reports, statistics, and newsletters such as *CanadExport Supplement – Going Global: World Markets for Women Entrepreneurs.*

7 **Western Economic Diversification Canada (WED)**
WED seeks to help small and medium enterprises in Western Canada grow, diversify, and create jobs. Western Canadian Business Service Network (WCBSN) consists of a network of business professionals to help with business planning and development, accessing capital, export or trade development, selling to governments, and providing information and links to government programs and services.
WED also provides specific programs focusing on targeted groups:
  i. Women: a pan-western Women's Enterprise Initiative which provides service such as financing, free business counselling, training, free business networks as well as other resource and referral information. Programs operate in British Columbia (Women's Enterprise Society of BC), Alberta (Alberta Women's Enterprise Initiative Association), Saskatchewan, Manitoba (Women's Enterprise Centre of Manitoba).
  ii. Entrepreneurs with Disabilities: offered through the Community Futures Development Corporations in specific regions, this program is designed to help Western Canadians with disabilities pursue their business goals and contribute to the economic growth within their communities.
  iii. Micro Business Loan program: Western Economic Diversification and the First Nations Bank of Canada administer, offers loans to help start-up or expand a business. The program is specifically designed to benefit people who operate or want to operate a business in Western Canada, and are enrolled in or a graduate of the Self-Employment Assistance program or similar entrepreneurial program, or referred to the First Nations Bank by WED

TABLE 6.1 (*Concluded*)

---

8 Atlantic Canada Opportunities Agency (ACOA)
Atlantic Canada has forty-one Canadian business development centres, which deliver programs and services aimed at helping entrepreneurs and would be entrepreneurs in Atlantic Canada. Technical assistance usually takes the form of information, counselling, and advice on small business matters. Financial assistance is typically in the form of a loan, but may also include equity or loan guarantees. The financial services are targeted to entrepreneurs who have difficulty securing capital through traditional sources of funding. All the loans are repayable and the maximum amount is $125,000.

   ACOA Business Development Program: provides assistance to small and medium-sized enterprises in Atlantic Canada to start up, expand, modernize and become more competitive. Non-profit organizations providing support to the business community may also qualify. Most businesses are eligible except retail/wholesale, real estate, government services, and services of a personal or social nature. The eligible activities may include business studies, capital investment, training, marketing, quality assurance, and not-for-profit activities that support business in the region.

Bank of Canada, Industry Canada and Community Futures Development Corporation, as well as those focusing on specific regions such as Western Economic Diversification and Atlantic Canada Opportunities Agency.

In addition to the emphasis on business start-up and targeted groups, a third feature to note about the programs identified in Table 6.1 is that there are a considerable range of services designed to promote business expansion and growth. In addition to many of the programs already discussed, which include such elements, there are agencies such as the Export Development Corporation (EDC) and Department of Foreign Affairs and International Trade (DFAIT) which provide information and support for those seeking business growth through export markets. While their services are open to all entrepreneurs, again there are also specialized information and services for women. For example, the Export Development Corporation sponsors educational activities and awards that encourage women to export (for example, the Canadian Woman Entrepreneur of the Year Award). It also runs the Womex initiative to ensure women's interests are well represented in EDC's activities (Canada 2003, Appendix 1: 35).

It is important to note that the programs outlined in Table 6.1 are dispersed across different government departments and agencies, with little apparent (at least to users) coordination between them. This was

commented on by the Prime Minister's Task Force on Women Entrepreneurs, which expressed concern about the lack of coordination and
uniform delivery:

> While some highly successful federal government support programs and
> policies exist to assist women entrepreneurs from start-up through to
> expansion, they are fragmented. Many are limited in their geographic
> scope or are delivered only on a regional basis. In general, programs are
> not available or accessible everywhere in Canada. A more coordinated
> and national approach to programs and support services for women
> entrepreneurs is required. (Canada 2003: 133)

Similar concerns were noted in the 2001 Canadian National Executive
Report of the Global Enterpreneurship Monitor (GEM) which men-
tions too many competing, targeted programs (Peterson 2001: 22).
Another issue of concern to the task force was the elimination of some
successful business training programs, such as those offered by the
Business Development Bank of Canada, as a result of government cutbacks in recent years (Canada 2003: 93).

Turning to the provincial level, using Alberta as an example (see
Table 6.2), there is a relatively strong complement of programs and
services available for women (see Bell 2003a), especially through the
Alberta Women's Enterprise Initiative Association which is funded at
the federal level through Western Economic Diversification. Other federal, provincial, municipal and industry partnerships, such as the Business Link and Alberta.First.Com, offer useful general resources. There
are also a number of micro loan programs, run by the private sector,
community groups, and NGOs, that provide important sources of
funding. Again, however, there appears to be a lack of coordination
between many programs. This is apparent in many interviews with
women in Alberta who describe navigating a rather complex course
between many different programs and providers, before finding
appropriate information and advice.

Finally, it bears noting that Tables 6.1 and 6.2 do not include a bud-
ding non-government sector of profit and non-profit groups catering
specifically to women business owners and entrepreneurs. Examples
include Women Entrepreneurs of Canada (WEC) and Canadian Association of Women Executives and Entrepreneurs (CAWEE). Many of the
major banks also have specifically targeted programs and websites for
women entrepreneurs, and have become interested in partnering with

TABLE 6.2
Selected Provincial Programs for Start-up, Expansion, and Growth, Alberta

1 Alberta Business Service Centre

The Business Link: offers information and advice on start-up, incorporation, financing, regulatory requirements, market access and exporting, as well as public and private sector programs and services. It is a joint venture between Western Economic Diversification, Alberta Economic Development, and the City of Edmonton.

AlbertaFirst.Com Ltd:. is a federal, provincial, municipal, and industry partnership, created to promote business and community development across the province of Alberta. It operates as a non-profit organization consisting of a consortium of 155 Alberta municipalities which Alberta Economic Development and Western Economic Diversification support. Through its website it provides information, statistics, profiles on key sectors, regions and communities throughout the province.

2 Alberta Women's Enterprise Initiative Association (AWEIA)

AWEIA provides women entrepreneurs with business resources, financing, coaching, information and networking opportunities. To be eligible for financing, businesses must be 50% women-owned, and operations must be 51% women-controlled. Applicants must be eighteen years and older, and operations must be in Alberta. AWEIA is not a last resort lender; the maximum loan amount is $100,000, with no minimum. Loans cannot be used to finance revolving lines of credit, multi-level marketing ventures, franchise fees, independent agents or direct sellers, tuition or educational training, purchase of goodwill, owners' salaries, or to re-finance existing debt. AWEIA also provides business resources, business planning, information about other sources of financing, networking opportunities, and one-to-one business coaching.

3 Edmonton Community Loan Fund

The Edmonton Community Loan Fund is an organization that provides capital and other support to socially responsible projects intended to improve the economic self-reliance and quality of life for low-income people, families, and neighbourhoods in Edmonton. Small business loans of up to $10,000 are available. Technical assistance and/ or mentoring programs accompany the loans.

4 Edmonton Mennonite Centre for Newcomers

The centre located in Edmonton, offers an entrepreneurship coaching program, which provides the business evaluation, step-by-step help writing a business plan, individual business advice, and referral on how to access small loans from community loan funds.

5 Business Micro Loan Program (MCC Employment Development MCC-ED)

MCC-ED is a Calgary non-profit organization that assists low-income individuals. They offer trades training, English for the Workplace, small business loans, and literacy for low-income individuals. The Business Micro Loan Program has existed since 1995 and its overall goal is to support disadvantaged entrepreneurs in the start-up or expansion of their businesses. The program utilizes character lending. The initial loan is up to $2,000, but once this loan has been repaid applicants may apply for a second loan of up to $5,000. MCC-ED also offers several small business workshops and offers technical assistance such as micro-business development and lending, security deposit lending to the homeless, financial literacy, asset development, and trades training.

women's organizations that support women entrepreneurs. For example, the Royal Bank of Canada has promoted various international trade initiatives with Canadian business women, and has been involved with the project *Beyond Borders: Canadian Businesswomen in International Trade* (DFAIT and the Trade Research Coalition, 1999). It also sponsors a website for women entrepreneurs which provides information on current research, resources and events. In addition to these national organizations, a wide range of groups also operate at local levels.

Assessing Women's Interest in Growth: Existing Research

Given the current policy emphasis on business start-up, growth, and expansion, one would expect a correspondingly high level of interest in these issues among women themselves. But while recent labour market trends suggest women are increasingly attracted to self-employment and small business ownership, existing literature suggests they are not necessarily growth oriented. Overall, women's enterprises grow more slowly than men's and are smaller, whether measured by number of employees, revenues, or profit level (Cliff 1998; Fischer 1992; Fischer et al. 1993; Kalleberg and Leicht 1991; Orser 1999). While some have argued that gender is not really of importance to size, if one controls for other factors such as industry, legal status, and so on (Jungbauer-Gams 1994), such arguments fail to understand gender as a *structural feature* in the self-employed and small business sector. For the most part, men and women do not run similar types of businesses, and businesses in those industries where women cluster tend to be smaller. Even if growth is planned, it is often very small-scale. In Canada, for example, Belcourt et al. found that many women business owners were interested in growth, but most had increased employee numbers only slightly. With three employees on average, each business had taken on the equivalent of less than one part-time employee in three years. Moreover, while 60% expected to hire more over the next three years, only 20% had intentions of moderate to high growth (1991: 24–5).

While much of the literature highlights the smaller size and growth of women's firms, and tends to regard it as a a problem (Cliff 1998), some research suggests that the situation is changing and that women's tendency to head smaller-sized enterprises may be a thing of the past. A study by the Bank of Montreal, for example, found that employment in women-led firms increased by 13.0% compared to 3.1% for all firms in the early to mid-1990s – four times the national average (1996: 6). Nevertheless, the bulk of existing studies in Canada do suggest that women are less interested in growth. Early studies such as those by Lee-Gosselin and Grise (1990) found that women were not strongly growth-oriented, and valued businesses that were small and stable. Fischer (1992) and Fischer et al. (1993) also observed different growth orientations between women and men, and note the difficulty in explaining why such differences exist. An early Ontario study, cited in Belcourt et al. (1991: 24), also found that women had modest growth expectations, hoping to 'make a living rather than make it big.' More recently, Orser (1999; 2004) has suggested that attitudinal differences may explain this difference. Putting a positive spin on this, Fenwick (2002: 718)) has questioned whether women are creating a different type of enterprise culture – a 'post-corporate capitalism' that is less focused on traditional values and benchmarks such as profit, growth, and size.

Some studies raise similar questions in other countries. For example, in Germany, Jungbauer-Gans (1994) found that women are interested in heading smaller enterprises, even taking into account difference in industry, education, experience, objectives, and support. In the United Kingdom, Carter and Cannon found that women tend to measure their current and future success less by growth than by other markers, such as the achievement of independence, personal satisfaction, and employment for the owner. However while growth is less important in the initial stages, it becomes more important in future goals (1992: 108–9). Another British study by Baines and Wheelock (1998; 2000) found that the majority of small and micro business owners (both women and men) do not aspire to business growth, and in fact many were uncomfortable with the idea of being an employer.

Notwithstanding these findings, some studies challenge the common portrayal of women as 'growth resistors'. In British Columbia, Cliff's study of male and female business owners found that both were equally interested in growth but approached it in different ways. Unlike men, women sought smaller businesses that would allow them to maintain control of the firm, contain working hours, and balance work and family life. Women were also more cautious about the risks of fast-paced growth, preferring a 'slow and steady rate of expansion' (1998: 523–4). Equally important, studies from other countries suggest diversity in women's interest in growth. For example, in New Zealand, McGregor and Tweed's study of eighteen hundred women and men found that women who had a mentor were far more likely to be 'expansionist' than other women or men. They argue that the decision to control growth may be a 'carefully considered and strategic choice' and ask whether 'growth orientation is and should be a universal aspiration for all small business owners' (2002: 423–4). In Britain, Baines and Wheelock (2000: 49) also found differences amongst female owners, with 25% being 'growth rejecters,' 50% 'growth ambivalent,' and 25% enthusiastic about growth.

Women's Attitudes towards Business Growth: The Study

Currently in Canada we have little information about the growth aspirations of women business owners, nor on the trends in employment growth, firm turnover, and tenure in women-led small businesses. While Statistics Canada and organizations such as the Canadian Federation for Independent Business (CFIB) provide some data, there is relatively little or no gender-based analysis. From the broad picture they provide, we know the majority of small or micro businesses in Canada are tiny, with fewer than five employees (CFIB 2002; Statistics Canada 1997: 37). According to the CFIB, three-quarters of Canada's businesses employ fewer than five people and 97% of all businesses have fewer than fifty employees. In Alberta, between 75% and 80% of businesses in the 1990s had less than five employees (Chambers and Rylska 2001:9; CFIB 2000: 1). But they played a growing role in job creation in the 1990s, generating some 43.5% of all jobs (Chambers and Rylska 2001: 16).

Despite this record, it is important to recall that the number of the self-employed who had employees fell throughout the 1990s, with most job growth taking place amongst the solo self-employed. While in the late 1980s, 45% of the self-employed had employees, this fell to 37.6% by the mid-1990s (Statistics Canada 1997: 37). The growth of solo work was particularly strong in sectors such as business services, health and social services, and finance, insurance, and real estate (Statistics Canada 1997: 37). According to the SSE, 40.5% of solo women reported that employees were not 'applicable to their occupation,' and another 9.5% did not want the responsibility of being an employer. A further 34.1% did not have enough business to hire employees, and 9.5% of women could not afford to (unpublished data). Beyond the growth of solo work, it is important to keep in mind that there is significant turnover in the SE/SBO sector. Analyis by Lin et al. (1999a) for the 1980s and early 1990s found gross flows in and out of self-employment accounting for 42% of the self-employed population.

Moving beyond this general picture, what insights do the Alberta women offer on issues of growth? Are they interested in expanding their businesses, or do they hold diverse attitudes towards business growth? Recall that the women in the study operate a range of businesses; half of them are solo endeavours, and the other half are employers, most with relatively small numbers of employees. Based on existing literature, we might expect fairly modest goals within this group, with the exception of some of the larger employers and perhaps one or two solo workers. Yet, in fact, nearly one-third of the women were interested in significantly expanding their business, either by developing new products, targeting new clients, or entering new markets nationally or internationally. Of the remaining women, over one-third planned to continue at present business volumes, but wanted to make key changes in their operations, such as partnering with others, hiring office assistance, or specializing in market and clientele. Just 15.6% of women wanted to continue their business as it was. The remaining 17.2% of women planned to move onto new things – retiring, moving into paid employment, and in one or two cases opening up a brand-new business.

Of the one-third of women interested in business growth, as we might expect, it was larger employers who were most interested in expanding into new markets. One was looking to 'the European market' (Interview A01), but most were focused on moving into markets outside of Alberta, either within Canada and/or the United States. This is in keeping with existing research that identifies the United States as the dominant market for Canadian women entrepreneurs (Canada 1999). One employer was already well under way with her plans for expansion in western Canada, but felt that she might need to adjust her original expectations with respect to entering the US market:

> My long-term objective was to have twenty offices within eight years and that may have been a little ambitious. I may have to adjust it. My next, after I do Vancouver, is into the US market. I'll begin my research there and of course I've got a much bigger country to work with there so I might be able to achieve the twenty. I would like to see us three years from now sitting with at least fifteen offices. (Interview B02)

Several other women were also highly growth-oriented but currently at much earlier stages of planning. For example, one employer in the manufacturing sector had identified the United States as a key market for her product, but had not yet done any detailed planning: 'The plan at this point is to explore moving into the United States. And that's a fairly ambitious plan all by itself. I haven't mapped out a strategy for that as yet ... But in the next couple of years, we're going to make a serious stab at moving some of our product into the United States' (Interview B19). In a few other cases, women were planning to expand within the province – for example, opening a location in Calgary – or to use the internet to develop a national clientele.

Pursuing national or international markets was more typically a focus of large employers. In contrast, most growth-oriented solo women were simply interested in taking on more clients, and larger projects, in the local market itself. Typical of this approach was a younger solo woman who was trying to expand her home-based communications business: 'I'd like to have some bigger projects and yet I realize until I upgrade my equipment, that I'm not really capable of too many of those. But that is a goal of mine, to start getting bigger clients, some midsize companies' (Interview A15).

This type of expansion presents challenges for solo women, who often lack capital and financial support. In addition to acquiring new equipment and hiring staff, expanding one's business also means potentially moving from a home-based to a commercial location. Thus, growth can be a mixed blessing, as this woman with a home-based business that employed one other person explained: 'When I did my business plan it became very clear to me that if I continued the growth that I am experiencing, which is 25–30% a year in the last three years, that I will need a commercial location' (Interview B06). For small home-based businesses, this type of decision is a significant one, both in financial, family, and personal terms.

Several other strategies were also mentioned for developing businesses. In some cases, women were trying to develop more lucrative products or services that would expand the business. For example, two women in service firms hoped to package their knowledge into a 'proprietary product,' enabling them to increase profits in a way that was impossible by simply 'doing more themselves' (Interview B04). One noted the inherent limitations of a labour-intensive, service business: 'That's something we'd like to do because the service business is really tough to make a lot of money' (Interview B04). Several other women planned to pursue new relationships and associations with partners and colleagues in an effort to build and generate more business. In some cases, this was the result of dissatisfaction with existing relationships; for example, one solo woman who already had an 'association' with two other solo workers was seeking a new arrangement because of dissatisfaction with one person's 'lack of participation' (Interview A18). In other cases where new associations were being pursued, solo women and employers were planning for succession, and were interested in building the business and bringing new people in, with an eye to retiring in five to ten years' time.

Given debates over women's growth orientation, it is interesting to note that several women, while actively planning to grow their business, also expressed reservations about expansion. One employer, for example, planning a new location in Calgary, felt she had to be 'really, really careful,' adding, 'I don't want to grow too fast' (Interview B11). Echoing these comments, a solo woman was grappling with the question of whether and how quickly to expand, concerned that she might jeopardize her already very successful business:

> The challenge that I have is, is it too much? Is it too big of a bite? And then you end up screwing up and all of your good work that you've done before developing competency and reliability goes down the tubes. So that would be the future challenge. (Interview A08)

Another employer of four people had set parameters on her growth, much in the way Cliff (1998) describes:

> Those types of headaches, once [the business] gets to a certain size, they would be so great that they wouldn't, for me, be worth it. And just the stress of it, it wouldn't be worth it to go beyond that. So probably about double what we are now is probably about as comfortable as I would feel going. (Interview B13)

Notwithstanding this ambivalence, these women were actively pursuing growth opportunities. In contrast, a second group (35.9%) were more interested in continuing their business at the same scale, while making important changes in its operation. Here the most important type of change was a shift in the mix of tasks and day-to-day work. For instance, a number of women wanted to move away from 'hands-on' work to pursue teaching, writing, publishing, and travel opportunities in their business field. Others sought a change in partnerships and associations, or products and services, not so much to grow the business so as to consolidate it or take it in a slightly different direction.

Other changes involved containing hours, changing locations, being more selective about clients, as well as getting additional help for secretarial or administrative work.

Reflecting the more modest aims of this group, several women discussed what they saw as the dangers of growing too large. For example, one solo woman in a very successful home-based business hoped to get some administrative help, and shift her client mix away from individuals, and towards larger corporate clients. But her goal in this was not to significantly expand the business – 'I don't want a big business, no' (Interview A04) – but rather simply to maximize what she could do herself. Another small employer of a thriving business hoped to experiment in some new directions, but did not plan to significantly expand.

> I do not know how I feel about expansion. This has been something I've been quite ambivalent about ... Because being more prosperous means making more ... means more people. Do I want that? I don't see this as ever being a huge business because it goes against the whole kind of philosophy and identity. (Interview C01)

Speaking even more directly to this theme was a third group of what can be called 'growth rejecters' (15.6%) who wanted to continue with their business exactly as it was. Two-thirds of these were solo women who were basically happy working on their own. One of these, Joan, mentioned at that start of this chapter, explained: 'I just like working by myself. I'm making enough of an income for myself and my family and you know I'm just not interested in that' (Interview A03). Speaking of an opportunity for expansion that she had passed up she said:

> I thought, you know, you really should look at that if you want to grow, and then I thought, 'Why do I want to grow?' I'm happy doing what I'm doing, being a 'one woman show.' So why do I have to think about growing? (Interview A03)

Echoing these comments, another solo woman noted her reluctance to hire employees even though her business had the scope to expand:

> If push came to shove, I would get somebody to help me on the secretarial side, but it's hard. As soon as you take on somebody else [to help with the substantive work], your liability goes up so much and you can't stand over them and make sure that they don't miss something. (Interview A16)

In another case poor health had dampened a solo woman's original plans to expand: 'It'll never be big business because I'm not physically or emotionally able to deal with big' (Interview A09). A few others in this group were older employers who were making plans to retire, and therefore were more interested in business succession than business expansion. Said one employer: 'I guess basically we want to give it five years and hopefully find someone else, you know, a younger partner or something, to pass the flame on to' (Interview C12).

A final group were seriously considering closing their business in order to take on new opportunities. In a few cases, women were planning to wind down, or sell their business, to retire. More commonly, though, women had taken, or applied for, a job working for someone else, after deciding they no longer wanted to work for themselves. In most cases, these women were motivated by better economic opportunities and securities provided by a paid job, along with a dislike for certain aspects of self-employment. For example, one solo woman had taken a job because it presented a 'great opportunity' but also because she disliked marketing her own business. As she explained:

> I obviously have the missing marketing thing. This is something one has to do and one has to be willing to do it you're going to be self-employed, to market, whether it's cold-calling people or whatever. But I watched my colleague do this stuff and it's like, she can do it. She's got this system, she's been doing it for twenty years, she's got all the different contacts which of course lead to more work. But do I want to build all that up? No. And that's part of the reason I took the job. (Interview A13)

Another solo woman had been recruited into an excellent limited-term job, though she continued her independent practice on a part-time basis. Now enjoying the stability of employment – 'the benefit plan, pension plan, and Blue Cross' (Interview C07) – she wondered whether she would ever return to her own practice full-time. Explaining the trade-offs she said:

> The reason I took it was because it's nice, steady employment with benefits and I don't work as hard as I do when I'm running my big practice. I wanted to take time out to be with my kids and stuff. But you get a bit spoiled and I guess one of my challenges is going to be, 'What am I going to do?' And venturing back into self-employment again, after having, I don't want to say it's an easier job, but it is, you know what I mean? And the security of it, there's commitment and all that stuff (Interview C07)

In addition to the security, she also felt a certain freedom from not being self-employed. Talking about returning full-time to her practice she said:

> I think, do I really want that responsibility? It goes back to that. I'm not quite sure I want to because I'm kind of enjoying my time without having it. When there are big disasters, I don't have to deal with them any more and I can still make good money. (Interview C07)

Her comments are particularly interesting in light of a fairly prevalent belief that self-employment – in particular, homed-based businesses – allows mothers to seamlessly combine work and family demands. While this may be a successful strategy for some, for others it is not always workable or ideal.

Training for an Entrepreneurial Economy

A critical question raised by attitudes towards business growth concerns whether women can access the type of training and skill development they need to achieve their goals. Of the one-third actively pursuing growth, for example, how easily can they obtain marketing and export training to expand into new markets, or management and human resource skills to deal with significant employee growth? Even for those women who are not growth-oriented, training and skill development remains important. The skill set needed to run a successful business is varied, making training a challenge. As one woman who advises business owners on tax and financial matters observed:

> Many people are trained to be nurses, doctors, or lawyers, but they are not trained in how to be entrepreneurs. So I'm sort of a business interpreter. They don't understand generally about accounting, a very low level of understanding of tax and the more complicated government makes it, the less they are likely to understand. So a lot of my work is really client education. Some of it is what I'll call confidential consulting. There's very few people that entrepreneurs can turn to discuss their business and know that it's not going any further ... And an entrepreneur has to have some knowledge in a lot of areas to succeed. Many, many requirements are not well understood. Workers' compensation, employee legislation, the legal organization of the business and agreements, tax planning, lots of things. You name it. That's the scope for general business services because people generally aren't well trained. (Interview C10)

Given this complexity, training is critical for individual success and for the overall productivity of the SE/SBO sector (HRDC 2002: 35; Hughes 2001; Orser and Riding 2003; Weeks 2000). But the training needs of self-employed women vary depending on their aspirations, as well as the knowledge and experience they bring into their business. For those with significant formal education, or extensive experience working for someone else in a similar field (Moore and Buttner 1997), training needs may be less pressing. Reflecting this, one woman owner of a retail operation said:

> I know people say training is very important but for me I worked [previously] as an office manager and accountant. I don't need any more training, I know how businesses run. ... But having a mentor would have been so helpful, you know, having somebody else who had started up a retail business and go through maybe a bit of what I've gone through would have been awesome and I wish that would have been there. (Interview A02)

Other women also drew heavily on previous work experience in running their business. In one case a solo woman had gained skills working for an entrepreneur before setting out on her own: 'He was a very difficult fellow to work for but it was very interesting in that he was forever starting up companies. So I got very used to starting things off, dealing with the bank, running horrible overdrafts and generally flying by the seat of the pants' (Interview A16).

Another woman followed a 'business incubator model,' using her former employment to acquire the skills and contacts she needed before setting out on her own:

> I really did it all myself. I had it in my head, my business plan, how I was going to market myself, where I was going to get my client base from. I really developed that prior to leaving on my own and I think I also got that because I did manage the department for [my previous employer]. So I was kind of self-employed, even though I was working for someone else. I was managing, I had to do the financial statements every year, I had to do the budgeting. I did everything in that department. (Interview C08)

For these women, training issues were not that significant, although it must be noted that none of them were aggressively pursuing growth.

But for other women, training was critical, either as they struggled to establish or stabilize their business, or sought ways to expand and grow. Indeed, among women overall, there was a very high level of interest in training, both formal (courses, seminars) and informal (reading, discussion). Many women mentioned workshops and courses they had taken either through local colleges or through women's support organizations. Others engaged in informal learning by networking, surfing the net, discussing issues with colleagues and customers, seeking mentoring, and even setting up advisory boards. Reflecting this activity are comments from women in a range of sectors, from professional free agents to those in the retail and personal service sectors:

> I spend at least two weeks out of every year doing training ... Usually it's way over one hundred hours per year because I have to report that to my association. (Interview C03)

> I go to school three or four times a year ... I am hungry for knowledge ... Picking up new things, seeing what's happening. (Interview C16)

> We've taken lots of courses ... and done different things like that all the way through ... You've just got to keep learning. (Interview A10)

> Well, it's just more or less learning as I go. (Interview A18)

This strong interest in training is also borne out in national statistics. According to the *SSE*, for example, nearly 80% of self-employed workers are involved in some kind of training activity (Hughes 2001: 15). Women's involvement with training is at a similar level to men's. Clear preferences exist for informal, over formal, types of training; for instance, just 27.3% of the self-employed had taken formal courses in the past year, compared to 52.5% who had relied on informal training. Certain kinds of informal training are also more popular than others, notably discussion with others (reported by 71.5%), followed by studying manuals (62.2%) and observing colleagues (42.1%) (Hughes 2001: 25). While training levels are high, however, access is very unequal, with those in professional, high-income areas far more likely to participate than those from low-income sectors. And, despite high levels of training, there is a sizable group (20%) of the self-employed who are not engaged in any training.

Two clear barriers to formal training for self-employed women are the time and costs associated with taking courses. This comes through clearly in the *SSE* as well as in the interviews with some of the Alberta women. According to the *SSE*, 42% of women (compared to 27.5% of men) indicated costs had discouraged formal training, while 57.7% of women (compared to 67.7% of men) noted time constraints (see also Statistics Canada and HRDC 2000; Rooney et al. 2003: 94). Neither of these is surprising, given what we know about the working hours and income levels of many self-employed women. Reflecting these types of issues, one woman, who entered self-employment through the Self-Employment Assistance Benefit program, spoke about her difficulties accessing the training she needed once she had started her business designing and sewing clothes. Being self-taught, she quickly realized she did not don't know enough and took a professional course to further develop her skills. While the course was extremely helpful, she faced significant problems in terms of the costs of the program and time lost to the business: 'I couldn't afford it but I didn't think I could afford not to do it.' Describing the difficulties for her business and family, for whom she was the main breadwinner, she says: 'It was invaluable, it really, really was. But I found that there was a lot of homework plus I was still working two days a week plus doing that one day a week and so I didn't take on a lot of other projects while I was doing it ... I wasn't actively working' (Interview A09). Given these constraints, she had not pursued further training despite knowing how helpful it would be:

> Certainly from the business end of things, I would definitely benefit from a business background. Marketing skills, that sort of thing, because you don't have a clue how to market yourself and if you're not marketing yourself properly ... your business never goes as far as it could ... So I would definitely need a better business background to really make it fly. (Interview A09)

While her comments capture the experience of low-income women, it is important to note that even women in professional, high-income businesses faced difficulties due to the high costs of training. For example, one financial planner attended many courses each year to keep up with financial trends and markets: 'I just attended a course and that cost me over $5,000 in one week ... So what we do and how we prepare ourselves for it costs a lot of money' (Interview B14). In addition to the actual cost of training, there is also the opportunity cost of lost income and time while training, as well as the difficulties finding temporary help to cover the business while away on workshops and courses.

Finally, an additional problem that emerges in the study of Alberta women is the mismatch in some cases between existing training initiatives and the aspirations and needs of women. Discussing this, for example, one woman had attended several meetings in a government-sponsored program but was disappointed at their lack of relevance. As she explained, 'I went to a couple of meetings but I didn't find them all that helpful ... I guess a lot of the issues that come up are related to the kind of business that you have' (Interview C01). More helpful for her was locating a mentor and colleague in the same field who she could talk with about common concerns: 'We can talk about production-related issues, supplies issues, staffing issues. So that's been a support' (Interview C01).

Mentoring was indeed mentioned and valued by several, though not all women were able to access it. But mentoring programs were not always successful, again underlining the need to understand the diversity among women entrepreneurs and to match them with appropriate resources. Describing her mentoring experience with a non-profit organization, one solo woman said:

> The mentorship program they had I think failed very badly. Not only with me. I talked to others who were on this program. It failed with everybody. It was a very good idea. But why did it fail? ... They didn't let us choose from the group of mentors who would be the best mentor for us ... And I got a mentor who didn't have the slightest idea about my field ... Someone from a huge corporation who could not relate to small business really. (Interview B04)

Recognizing some of the challenges women face in relation to training, mentoring, and networking, the Prime Minister's Task Force has made a number of recommendations. These include development of an effective and flexible training infrastructure that provides equal access to women; training programs that responds to women entrepreneurs' unique needs and learning styles, and include components on personal development and confidence building; development of on-line training that builds on existing programs developed by the Women Enterprise Initiatives; reinstatement of training from the Business Development Bank of Canada with special emphasis on women; and extension of the Self-Employment Assistance (SEA) benefit to women who are not eligible for employment insurance (for example, those returning to the workforce after raising children, those who have left work voluntarily) (Canada 2003: 97–8). In addition to training, the task force also emphasizes the value of mentoring – both face-to-face mentoring and e-mentoring – recommending the development of a national small business mentorship program in partnership with private and not for-profit sectors. They suggest it be modelled on the Business Development Bank of Canada's 'Step In and Step Out' program or the Canadian Executive Services Overseas (CESO) where retired executives share their expertise (Canada 2003: 88). In all of these recommendations the task force stresses the importance of ensuring training and mentoring opportunities are accessible to women across the country, especially those in rural areas.

These types of initiatives could play an important role in improving the productivity in the SE/SBO sector, offering a needed mix of formal and informal training, and the electronic delivery of programs that can overcome time-related barriers to training. In addition to these recommendations, however, several other initiatives seem key. Without doubt, the most important is training that can enable women to enter less traditional, more profitable business sectors, and that assists them with skill transfer, where they can enhance existing skills and parlay them into entirely new areas. Currently there are far too many women entering labour-intensive, low-profit areas in the SE/SBO sector. Training for non-traditional sectors would go a long way to improving the incomes and economic security of some women (Hughes 1990; 1995). In the 1970s and 1980s government training programs encouraged non-traditional choices for women, taking direction from the Royal Commission on the Status of Women. Existing programs, such as the Self-Employment Assistance program, should make this an explicit focus, providing training that steers women away from female ghettos. In addition, current programs that encourage non-traditional choices for women, for example in the trades and professions, should include components on self-employment and small business.

Second, the costs of training remain a significant barrier for self-employed women, especially for those at the low end of the earnings distribution. Recall that half of solo women made under $20,000 a year. For this group, absorbing the cost of training and forgone revenues is very difficult and in some cases impossible. While training costs are tax deductible, the development of other types of credit tools to fund training may hold promise. Suggestions that may be relevant for the self-employed include, Individual Development Accounts (IDA) that enable low-income groups to build up assets to finance learning, with these being matched by public contributions. Other tools such as Learning Accounts and Registered Training Plans may be beneficial as well (Betcherman et al. 1998). As with paid employees, it is those self-employed workers who need training the most who are least able to gain access to it (Hughes 2001; Lowe 2002: 99) Special attention should therefore be paid to helping low-income women, and focusing in particular on the one-fifth who engage in no training at all.

Of course, one way to make basic business training more affordable and easily accessible would be to open up existing programs, such as the Self-Employment Assistance (SEA) program, to a wider group of users. While this is recommended by the Prime Minister's Task Force, and would address concerns about gender inequities in accessing employment insurance benefits, there are reasons for caution here. In the Alberta study, several of the women who entered self-employment through the SEA were concentrated in very female-intensive, low-income areas, and generally struggled to keep their businesses afloat. Regardless of whether the program remains as is or is expanded to a broader set of users, it needs to develop a gender-based analysis of the SE/SBO sector, and to incorporate this information into its training and business planning for clients. In addition, the effectiveness of the program needs to be more thoroughly evaluated and publicly documented. Throughout the years there have been very few public evaluations of this program, and these have lacked a gender-based analysis (see, for example, Graves and Gauthier 1996; see also HRDC 1998 for reflections on own account self-employment generally). One notable exception is an evaluation made by Orser and Hoggarth-Scott in 1998. While highlighting the strengths of the program, in particular the longevity of SEA participants compared to other self-employed individuals, it also emphasizes several concerns, including the under-representation of women, visible minorities, and immigrants; inadequate and limited training; and the need for more comprehensive, multidisciplinary program assessment. Indeed, regular in-depth evaluation that includes gender-based analysis would provide useful insights on sectors where success is most likely and the types of training content and delivery that seem to be most effective.

Finally, existing training needs to be better matched to the needs and aspirations of women. As the Alberta study shows, there is a significant group of women who wish to expand their businesses and who can make good use of existing programs and information, such as those on exporting and entering new markets. But some of these programs need to be rescaled to provide a better fit for women entrepreneurs. As the task force points out, program criteria for company size or loan floors often render women ineligible because of their smaller size. For example, the Department of Foreign Affairs and Trade's Program for Export Market Development (PEMD) targets companies with annual sales of $250,000 to $10 million (Canada 2003: 117–25). These types of unintentional but systemic barriers should be addressed.

Concurrent with rethinking what growth-oriented businesses look like, there needs to be more recognition that some self-employed women are simply not interested in growth, preferring to consolidate or continue their business as it is, or to make small scale changes, such as shifting the daily mix of work they do, or entering into networking relationships that would allow bidding on larger projects without having to grow. All of these types of activity require training, but of a much different kind. Rather than dismissing these as low-potential 'hobby businesses,' government policy and programs need to better understand and respond to the expanding ranks of low growth and no-growth workers which form a key part of the entrepreneurial economy that has emerged in Canada.

'Policy Limbo' and the 'Do It Yourself Safety Net'

Writing about public policy, prominent analyst Judith Maxwell has observed: 'There are two kinds of time in policy analysis: long periods of stability like the post-war period, and spells of disruption, leading to a break in organizing principles for public policy' (Maxwell 2003: 12). Growing self-employment and small business ownership provides a perfect example of such disruption, laying bare the growing chasm between existing policy and emerging forms of work organization in the new economy. As labour and public policy analysts have increasingly noted, current policy reflects an 'old world of work' – male, blue-collar, goods-producing – where the standard employment contract was the norm (Fudge 2003; Gunderson 2002; Lowe 2002; Trudeau 2002). While this historical depiction is itself male-centred, reflecting a male norm that ignores the more flexible work historically done by women (see MacDonald 1991; Jenson 1989), it remains the case that the standard employment contract has served as the normative model that has informed both policy and legislative frameworks. With increasing

TABLE 6.3
Eligibility of Self-Employed for Selected Benefits

Employment insurance benefits	Typically no. Self-employed workers can be eligible only if they have insurable income from work under a 'contract of service,' *and* they must prove that their self-employment activities are 'minor in extent.'
Paid maternity leave	Typically no. Self-employed workers are eligible only if they meet the same criteria described above.
Paid parental leave	Typically no. Self-employed workers are eligible only if they meet the same criteria described above.
Compassionate care benefits	Typically no. Self-employed workers are eligible only if they meet the same criteria described above.
Paid sick leave	Typically no. Self-employed workers are eligible only if they meet the same criteria described above.
Canadian Pension Plan/ Quebec Pension Plan	Yes. Self-employed workers make a contribution based on their annual net earnings between the minimum and maximum amounts set for the year.
Workers' compensation benefits	Self-employed workers are not automatically eligible to receive workers compensation benefits, but they purchase additional personal coverage to attain benefits. The benefits only include wage loss, medical benefits, and rehabilitation (if the injury is long-term). There are no special benefits for self-employed workers.

numbers of workers falling outside the 'postwar Fordist model' of full-time, permanent jobs with a single employer, many find themselves with inadequate or little social protection. Writing about this, commentators have spoken of a situation of 'policy limbo' (Lowe 2002), an 'individualized social safety net' (Trudeau 2002: 150), 'idiosyncratic deals' (Rousseau, cited in Florida 2002: 135) and the 'individualization of risk' (Fudge and Cossman 2002; Beck 1992).

A snapshot of the current situation of many self-employed workers and small business owners can be gleaned from Table 6.3 which outlines their eligibility for various forms of employment-related benefits.

This summary is selective and based on a extensive policy scan prepared by Bell (2003b). As we can see, the self-employed are not eligible for employment insurance benefits, unless their self-employment can be proven to be minor in extent.[1] The exceptions to this are self-employed fishers who have been eligible for benefits since 1956 (HRSDC nd; Schrank 1998), as well a handful of other groups, such as barbers, hairdressers, manicurists, and taxi drivers (Rooney et al. 2003: 4). Self-employed workers are also not eligible for paid maternity leave, parental leave, compassionate care leave, and sick leave benefits – though there is the exception of Quebec, where the current provincial Liberal government passed legislation in 2001 (Bill 140), that would allow the self-employed in Quebec to access maternity and parental leave (Bell 2003b; Rooney et al. 2003: 52–7). Though initially challenged by Ottawa, the Quebec and federal governments have now reached an agreement that will allow this program to come into effect on January 1 2006 (Séguin 2004: A12). Finally, while the self-employed participate in the Canadian and Quebec Pension Plans (CPP/QPP) – which provide pension, disability, and survivor benefits – they must make a 'double contribution' on behalf of the worker and employer. For workers' compensation, they are not automatically eligible for benefits, but can purchase additional personal coverage to attain benefits.

Compared to the typical employee, then, the average self-employed workers lacks a basic level of social protection and is left instead to cobble together a 'do it yourself safety net' that draws on family resources, friends, and existing savings and assets. In this respect, they are left out of many programs designed in the postwar period with the express purpose of socializing risk. Understandably, this lack of coverage is a concern for many. As Chapter 5 demonstrated, a good portion of self-employed women earn relatively low incomes and lack the resources to purchase private benefits to provide insurance against unemployment and business failure, maternity benefits, medical benefits, sick leave, pensions, and the like. While some women may be able to access benefits through their family partners, or through private providers if resources allow, many simply do not have access to this type of support. Relying on partners for support also places great social, psychological, and economic stress on families (Lowe 2002: 97). Moreover, support from a partner typically provides only medical, dental, and retirement benefits, but does not provide for other types of benefits, such as maternity, parental, compassionate care or sick leave.

Concern over the lack of adequate social protection was also highlighted in the Prime Minister's Task Force on Women Entrepreneurs. As the task force notes, this issue was repeatedly raised in the submissions they received and the consultations they held with women entrepreneurs in more than twenty-four Canadian cities from December 2002 to June 2003 (see Appendix G, Canada 2003 for details of these consultations). Speaking to this in their final report, the task force observed:

> Self-employed individuals, including women entrepreneurs, face a unique dilemma. As employers, they contribute financially to the Employment Insurance (EI) program and the Canada Pension Plan (CPP) on behalf of their employees. However if the self-employed individual, the employer, becomes ill or disabled, has a child, or suffers a business disaster, there is no protection for that individual or his/her family in existing federal social safety net programs.

Outside of Canada, the lack of adequate social protection has also been highlighted by organizations such as the International Labour Organization and the European Commission. The ILO has emphasized the need to improve social protection for workers as economies restructure and transfer greater risk onto the individual. It is included as one of the four key objectives under the 'Decent Work' program, which focuses on the promotion of rights at work; employment; social protection; and social dialogue (ILO 1999). Likewise, the European Commission has placed significant emphasis recently on improving social protection. In 2000 it established the Social Protection Committee which monitors and exchanges information between member states in the hopes of strengthening existing social protection systems.

In Canada, there is a pressing need to address the issue of social protection more fully, as can be seen by looking at some of its key components in more detail. In concluding this Chapter I focus on three area of policy where there are clearly emerging gaps: employment and income insurance; work-family leave; and retirement savings programs. I have selected these as key examples to illustrate the range of concerns and challenges facing policy-makers. While space precludes me from addressing the full range of policy issues, there are many others, both in relation to policy (for example, sick leave, disability, health and safety) as well as labour law and regulation (see Fudge et al. 2002, 2003 for a valuable discussion on collective bargaining and employment standards).

Employment and Income Insurance

For many, the idea that small business owners and self-employed workers should have access to employment insurance or some form of income insurance program is illogical – after all, they are supposed to be risk-takers, comfortable with the idea of flying high without a safety net. In this respect, they represent the model neoliberal citizen who makes minimal demands on the state (Fudge and Cossman 2002; Abu-Laban and Gabriel 2002). But, as we have seen, there is considerable diversity among the self-employed. Recent estimates suggest at least one in ten are 'disguised employees' or 'dependent contractors,' who actually works in an employee-employer relationship as defined by standard tests of control, ownership of tools, integration, and risk of profit/loss (Lowe and Schellenberg 2001; Revenue Canada 1998). Moreover, as the study of Alberta women shows, even where the self-employed are truly independent, many head relatively small businesses where survival is difficult, either working alone or as employers of a very small number of people.

Existing research clearly shows how volatile the SE/SBO sector is. Each year there are significant flows in and out of self-employment, and the long-term viability of many businesses is far from certain. According to the Global Entrepreneurship Monitor, just half of small businesses in Canada survive the first four years. By eight years the survival rate is down to just one-fifth (Peterson 1999: 6). Even when successful, the self-employed are more vulnerable than employees to income fluctuation, irregular work patterns, and economic cycles and shifts in demand (HRDC 2002). The SSE indicates one-third of women and four in ten men have experienced personal difficulties as a result of being self-employed. In lieu of any form of income insurance, the most common ways of dealing with financial difficulties were to reduce personal and family expenditures (51.3%), borrow money (37.2%), use savings (26.5%), rely on other sources of income (15.3%), and cash in RRSPs (11.6%).

While self-employed individuals are generally excluded from employment insurance, it is interesting to note that there are exceptions – most notably self-employed fishers.[2] They have been eligible for benefits since 1956, despite many amendments and changes to the program over the years, and repeated discussions about their inclusion.[3] But most groups of self-employed workers have never been included, despite attempts in the 1970s to make the unemployment program universal. In explaining this, the *History of Unemployment Insurance* (HRSDC nd) notes that while the 1971 Unemployment Insurance Act (Bill C-229) attempted to extend coverage broadly to create universal access to the program, there were 'minor exceptions' to this, including the self-employed.

Today it would be difficult to describe the self-employed as a minor exception, accounting as they do for almost one in six Canadian workers. For some commentators, sheer numbers alone are a compelling reason for inclusion within an employment or income insurance program. Certainly there is some precedent for inclusion on this basis. Throughout its history, the groups deemed worth of inclusion in unemployment/employment insurance have shifted to reflect major shifts and transitions in the economy. This is also true of social protection programs in other countries such as the United States (Osterman 1999: 125). In Canada, for example, when the 1940 unemployment insurance Act was introduced, it excluded workers in many sectors – teaching, professional nursing, federal government, agriculture, forestry, fishing, hospitals, charitable institutions among others – that were subsequently included. In the 1970s coverage was again extended to new groups of workers with the push for universality in program reforms. But overhauls in the 1990s had the opposite effect, tightening eligibility rules and reducing coverage for workers. Some of these changes – most notably the hours threshold – have been widely criticized as discriminating against non-standard workers, and particularly women (Porter 2003; Townson 2003: 61–2).

Rising levels of self-employment certainly provide one reason to rethink the issue of employment and income insurance. The growing flexibility and fluidity between different types of work over the life course also suggest a need to make employment and income insurance programs more flexible – a point made by commentators in Canada (Lowe 2002; Trudeau 2000), the United States (Osterman 1999), and Europe (Wilthagen 2002). Discussions in Europe, for example, have focused on the concept of 'flexicurity'[4] – 'a policy strategy that attempts synchronically, and in a coordinated way, to enhance the flexibility of labour markets, the work organisation and labour relations on the one hand, and to enhance security – employment security and social security – notably for weaker groups in and outside the labour market on the other hand' (Wilthagen and Rogowski 2002: 250; Wilthagen 2002: 4). While these reforms are motivated by traditions of social-liberal citizenship, a neoliberal concept of citizenship would also support changes in employment insurance on the basis of 'getting one's money worth out of the state' (Voet 1998: 9-10). For example, many self-employed individuals have at earlier points in their career worked as employees and have already made contributions to employment insurance and other social insurance programs. As the *SSE* shows, 86.0% of self-employed women have worked at some point as a paid employee (unpublished data), and nearly half worked for an employer the year before they became self-employed (HRDC 2000: 25). In this light, they might argue, it is difficult to see why a woman who is laid off from her job by a large private sector organization, after working full-time for them for ten years and contributing to EI should be entitled to protection against unemployment, while her former colleague who has also contributed for ten years but who, fearing lay-off, leaves a year earlier to set up a business that subsequently fails, should not.

Reflecting concerns over the lack of a social safety net, the Prime Minister's Task Force on Women Entrepreneurs recommended that HRDC (now HRSDC) and their standing committee 'undertake further study on extending employment insurance benefits and other social safety net programs to the self-employed.' In addition, they emphasized the value in exploring diverse views and key issues such as mandatory versus voluntary coverage (Canada 2003: 82). Likewise, in her review of policy for contingent workers, Townson (2003) recommends that HRDC re-examine the extension of regular benefits and special benefits (such as sickness, maternity, and parental leave) available under employment insurance to self-employed workers, noting that the House of Commons Standing Committee on Human Resources Development and the Status of Persons with Disability had already made these same recommendations in their 2001 report. Recently the minister of human resources and skills development has acknowledged the need to include self-employed workers in employment insurance, training, and other programs (Thompson 2005).

While attention to this issue is clearly needed, existing research does suggest potential roadblocks to reforms. According to the *SSE*, for example, just 39.9% of the self-employed express interest in an income insurance program, though interest is higher among the involuntarily self-employed (55.2%), and those self-employed less than two years (47.6%) (HRDC 2000: 45–9; 97–9). While a large majority of the women (85.1%) and men (79.2%) interested in such a program felt it would help them feel more secure and less stressed, only a minority felt they would use it or find it helpful. Key reasons for a lack of interest was a low probability of using the program (38.7%), a belief that there should not be income insurance program for the self-employed (24.3%), having other income to rely on (21.2%), and a feeling that the program would not do enough to help (13.9%). Research by Rooney et al. (2003) finds similar concerns about such a program.

While the *SSE* indicates that women and men have the same level of interest in an income insurance program, there are important variations. As we might expect, those most interested are more likely to be solo workers, recent entrants, young, single, with experience of financial difficulties. Interest is also highest for those in the middle income groups, suggesting that those earning low incomes may be concerned about paying premiums while those with high incomes deem such programs as unnecessary. These differences reflect major fault lines between the high and low end of the SE/SBO sector and suggest significant hurdles to policy reform. This polarization is itself a double edged sword, sparking the need for policy reform, especially for low-income workers, but posing challenges for fashioning uniform policy and identifying shared concerns (Rooney et al. 2003; Lero et al. 2004).

Work-Family Leave: Maternity, Parental, and Compassionate Leave

Work-family issues represent a second important policy area. Despite the widespread belief that self-employment is a way for women to juggle work and family responsibilities successfully, women business owners in fact encounter many of the same problems as other women in raising their children, as well as some unique problems of their own. Like other women, the self-employed risk losing clients and visibility, as well as skills and contacts, during maternity leave. But they also face substantial costs, paying for a replacement, keeping the business operating, and covering their expenses while on leave. In addition, they may also face other critical hurdles on return to work, such as finding suitable childcare for their long hours and hectic working schedules (see, for example, Hall-Hoffarth 2003; Rooney et al. 2003: 26–31). Illustrating these difficulties, Rooney et al. report that over one-third of the Canadian women they interviewed had been unable to take leave for family or health-related reasons because of these types of constraints (2003: 28).

Recognizing some of the work-family difficulties faced by new mothers and fathers, the federal government introduced Bill C-32 in

2000 which extended combined leave from twenty-five to fifty weeks in total (Marshall 2003: 15). Greeted with great fanfare, and certainly benefiting many new mothers and some fathers in the country, this change did little for self-employed women, as they remain ineligible for these benefits which are provided through the employment insurance act. This is well documented in research by Marshall (1999, 2003) which shows that self-employed women continue to return work quickly, irregardless of the policy changes that have taken place. Prior to 2000, self-employed women took just one month of leave on average, compared to six months for women working for an employer. With the extension of benefits under Bill C-32, the average time away for female employees increased to ten months, while for self-employed women it remained exactly the same at just one month.

These disparities in maternity and parental leave have been the focus of growing public attention. A recent special report in the *National Post*, for example, highlighted the problems of self-employed and other contingent workers, noting that '40% Get Nothing for Maternity Leave' (Sokoloff 2004). Likewise, the task force placed strong emphasis on this issue, criticizing arguments that self-employed workers are not interested in such benefits. As they state in their report:

> Human Resources Development Canada claims that the majority of the self-employed are not interested in parental leave of other temporary income support and that voluntary coverage is preferred. The Task Force found this is not to be the case and instead repeatedly heard that women entrepreneurs would gladly pay into Employment Insurance (EI) if it meant that they would have access to benefits. Many women are forced to choose between motherhood and their businesses because self-employed women and women who own more than a certain percentage of their own companies cannot receive EI or maternity benefits. Some women have been forced to reduce their equity in their companies in order to qualify for maternity benefits. Many work full time until the baby is born and return to work almost immediately after the birth of the child because they cannot afford to employ someone to take their place and cannot afford to live without the income their business provides. (Canada 2003: 81–2)

On the basis of its research and country-wide consultations, the task force recommended that maternity benefits be extended to self-employed women. While they did not specify how this should be done, they did recommend that the government look at examples in other countries where self-employed women do have access to maternity/parental benefits. As one of the submissions points out, drawing on earlier research from the ILO (1997: 29), countries such as the Bahamas, Costa Rica, Finland, the Philippines, Portugal, Slovakia, and Tunisia include self-employed women under existing maternity programs, providing the same level of benefits and payments. Other countries, such as France, Luxembourg, and Spain, have set up special systems to provide benefits to such workers (2003: 78–9). While not noted in the task force's report, the ILO report, *Maternity Protection at Work*, which reviewed existing provisions internationally, also recommended the extension of maternity leave to the self-employed and other workers:

> Priority consideration should be given, as appropriate to national circumstances, to the gradual extension of maternity protection to women in all sectors of activity and enterprises of all sizes, including women who are casual, temporary, part-time, sub-contract and home-based workers, as well as self-employed and family workers. (1997: 29)

At present we do not have nationally representative data that indicate the level of interest in such benefits. Unlike the topics of income insurance and retirement, for example, the *SSE* did not ask about this issue. However, research for HRDC in 2000 by Compas Research on the possibility of extending maternity/parental and sickness insurance did survey 802 self-employed individuals, finding that 44% of the self-employed were interested in the extension of maternity/parental leave (with 26% being very interested) and that 37% were willing to pay premiums for such benefits. When asked to identify their biggest priority, however, maternity leave was last (identified by 3% of respondents), following benefits for sickness (40%), retirement (21%), disability (16%), and training and education (15%) (2000: iii, 23). While the report emphasizes that the majority of respondents were not interested in maternity/parental benefits, there are significant gender and age differences as we might expect. In particular, women were much more likely to be very interested in these benefits than men, and interest declined steadily with age (Compas 2000: 29–30).

One of the limitations of the Compas Research data is the use of a general sample to address issues that pertain to a specific subset of the population, such as women of childbearing age. Given this, it is hardly surprising that maternity/parental leave would be less of a priority than sickness, retirement, and other benefits which have the potential to affect many more respondents. More targeted research of self-employed women by Rooney et al. (2003) in fact suggests very high levels of interest in extending maternity/parental benefits to self-employed women. Based on a mixture of interviews and surveys with 160 self-employed women from diverse backgrounds, and 60 stakeholders, they found that 52% of women were personally interested (very or moderately interested) in having such benefits extended, and that 90% felt that it was very important that such benefits be extended regardless of their own personal interest and circumstances. Especially interesting, there was a high level of support from stakeholder groups (86% agreeing it was important to extend benefits), which included representatives from self-employment organizations, financial planners, insurance providers, owners of daycare agencies that contract self-employed childcare providers, and government representatives at provincial and federal levels. Also of interest, maternity/parental benefits were identified as the top priority, with 92% of women indicating these were benefits they would like to see. Other benefits also had high level of support, with 90% of women interested in sickness benefits, 69% in disability, and 77% dependent care (Rooney et al. 2003: 35–6).

In addition to maternity/parental leave, it needs to be noted that the self-employed are also excluded from the compassionate care policy which was introduced by the federal government in January 2004 and operates through employment insurance in a similar way to maternity/parental leave. It provides six weeks of paid leave from work to provide care or support to a child, parent, spouse or common-law partner who has a serious medical condition with a significant risk of death within six months (HRSDC 2004). Again, this exclusion is a source of concern, particularly in the context of a growing 'care deficit' in families and an aging society where care-giving demands are set only to increase (Hochschild 2002: Jenson and Sineau 2001; Neufeld et al. 2002).

Finally, beyond family-related leave, other work-family issues have been highlighted by the task force, particularly around issues of childcare. Central among their recommendations are an increase in the child care expense deduction, so that self-employed women can deduct the full cost of childcare rather than the current limit of $7,000 a year (a suggestion also made by Rooney et al. 2002: 88). In the view of the task force this change would recognize that this cost, like many others, 'is an expense for the purpose of producing income under the Income Tax Act' (Canada 2003: 78). In addition, the task force recommends that the federal government, in conjunction with provincial and territorial counterparts, expand its support under the new multilateral framework on early learning and childcare. Other commentators have also emphasized the need for enhanced childcare to support self-employed women and help their businesses grow (Rooney et al. 2003: 88; Hall-Hoffarth 2003).

Retirement Savings

A final area of policy concern relates to self-employed women's long-term economic security and their potential to save adequately for a secure retirement. As we saw in Chapter 5, ability to save for retirement was one of the areas where women have the lowest levels of satisfaction. Just one-third of Alberta women were satisfied with their savings, with key differences between solo workers (26.7%) and employers (41.4%). While some felt they were adequately prepared, either through their own savings or their spouse/partner's savings, others were not able to save because of low incomes, or because they had used existing retirement savings to finance their business.

This concern over retirement is also reflected in other studies. In the Compas Research study, retirement was identified as one of the top three priority areas, along with sickness and disability coverage, where government support for the self-employed would be welcome (HRDC 2000: iii, 11). Likewise, while the *SSE* found that 90% of the self-employed had begun saving for retirement (though the amount of savings is unknown), it also found that one in ten workers had no retirement savings whatsoever.

Current policy requires the self-employed to contribute to the Canada Pension Plan. As Townson notes, everyone in the workforce, whether part-time or full-time, employee or self-employed, must contribute to CPP/QPP as long as they earn more than $3,500 a year. But, unlike employees, self-employed persons contribute both the employee and employer share. In 2002, this means that while employees contributed 4.7% of their earnings between the yearly basic exemption and the yearly maximum pensionable earnings, self-employed workers contributed 9.4% of earnings (Townson 2003: 53). For a female employee earning $35,000 a year this represents a contribution of $1,645, compared to $3,290 for her self-employed peer. In recognition that double contributions may be onerous for self-employed workers, the government recently allowed them to claim the employer share as a business expense. As well, individuals can claim a tax credit for contributions to CPP.

While the task force did not make recommendations concerning retirement savings, it did note the difficulties faced by many women in their retirement planning:

> As more women become business-owners, the topic of participation in insurance and pension plans is a constantly recurring theme ... The majority of women small-business owners earn $30,000 per year or less and have no access to low-cost health care, no protection for disability, no employment insurance or maternity benefits, and cannot afford private sector insurance and pensions plans. They are paying both the 'employer's' and 'employee's' contribution to their Canada Pension Plan. On top of this, at $30,000 per year or less, it is virtually impossible to invest in RRSPs for retirement. With no participation in private pension and insurance plans, entrepreneurs are handicapped in their ability to secure a financially independent retirement, thus making it more likely that they will depend solely on government funded programs in old age. (2003: 79)

Estimates from Townson (2003) show that benefits for women relying solely on government-funded retirement programs are very low. In 2002, the maximum CPP pension was $788.75 a month, but the average pension for a woman was just $312.92. In addition to CPP, a woman may be eligible for old age security (OAS) of $442.66 a month, and the guaranteed income supplement (GIS) of $369.62 a month (Townson 2003: 54-55). Together these programs would give her a total income of $1,125.20 per month, or $13,502.40 annually. As Townson points out, this falls far below Statistics Canada's before-tax low-income cut off (LICO) for a single woman living in a major urban area. Moreover, even if a woman earned the maximum CPP, with corresponding adjustment to GIS and OAS, her annual income ($16,357) would still fall below the low-income cut off (Townson 2003: 55).

It has been just a few decades since as many as 70% of older women survived on incomes that fell below Statistics Canada low-income cut off (Benoit 2000: 99). Through the recommendations of the Royal Commission on the Status of Women, the growing labour force participation of women, particularly in full-time employment, and policy initiatives including OAS, GIS, and CPP/QPP, the poverty rate of senior women has dropped dramatically, though women are still about twice as likely as men to be poor in their senior years (Statistics Canada 2000: 279; Benoit 2000: 99). While women's movement into self-employment and small business ownership has often been heralded as a sign of growing economic autonomy and success, and certainly it is for some, there are also reasons for concern over how some women will fare over the long term. Currently we do not have adequate information to know how women's (or men's) greater participation in the SE/SBO sector – particularly solo work – will affect their economic security in later years. Even existing data such as the *SSE* offer no information on existing savings.

Given the level of benefits currently paid from public pension plans, the burden of double contributions and rising levels of contribution, and the limited ability of self-employed women to contribute to private plans such concerns over future outcomes seem warranted, certainly for self-employed women earning low incomes. This is especially the case given debate over the sustainability of public pensions and the potential for further reduced benefits in the future (Townson 2003; Condon 2002). While private pensions are playing a far greater role in the retirement futures of Canadians, the ability of many self-employed women to contribute to private pensions is severely limited (Statistic Canada 2003c). Equally worrisome, the self-employed are far more likely to draw on accumulated RRSPs to provide financial support during times of economic downturns (Condon 2002: 155) – a trend that the *SSE* also observes. In this respect, the policy links come full circle, illustrating how a lack of social protection in the short term can adversely affect the ability to prepare for long-term economic security in the future.

Conclusions

In this chapter I have explored some of the key policy issues that are emerging as a result of women's growing participation in self-employment and small business ownership. Central to my argument has been the critical role that government plays in shaping the SE/SBO sector. Both federal and provincial governments have taken an increasingly active role in attempting to build an entrepreneurial economy in Canada, especially by promoting entrance into self-employment and small business ownership, and trying to encourage its growth. At the same time as they have pushed this policy agenda forward, however, they have shown little appetite for policy reforms that would better respond to the growing diversity within the SE/SBO sector. Nor have they shown much inclination to engage in policy reforms that would better respond to the growing number of independent workers in the economy, who do not fit the profile of a traditional small business owner.

In sketching out some of the key policy issues, I have tried to illustrate how start-up and training programs need to be modified to suit the diverse needs of women in the SE/SBO sector better, particularly in relation to growth. I have also tried to show how a failure to attend to broader areas of labour policy and programs has lead to a growing individualization of risk, and to consider in some detail what the future consequences of this may be. Employment insurance, work-family issues, and retirement policy were used as key examples of how self-employed workers are excluded from existing programs that socialize risks, and to consider what the incentives and barriers to change might be.

On this issue, one outstanding question concerns the appropriate platform for delivering various benefits and social protection. As several writers have noted, there are various approaches to this issue (see for example, Lowe 2002; Fudge et al. forthcoming; Rooney et al. 2003). Benefits can be delivered through national programs that include all citizens, as is currently the case with health care or with other quasi-universal benefits such as old age security. Alternatively, they can be tied to employment or labour market status, as is the case currently with unemployment insurance, maternity/parental leave, and CPP/QPP. A final option is to provide them through special schemes targeted at the self-employed, as is the case currently for the self-employment assistance benefit, as well as some training programs. Each approach has strengths and weaknesses, and there are significant challenges to addressing emerging policy gaps, given the diversity within the SE/SBO sector. But whatever approach is taken, the need to address these issues is pressing.

7 Conclusions

You put everything on the line. Your time, your money, your house, your everything and if that fails there is no one standing on the sidelines ready to cry with you.

(Interview B23)

Oh, there's huge risk. The financial risk for one thing. But my philosophy is this ... What's the worst that can happen? Do you want to be an old lady talking with your friends at Starbucks saying, 'You know, I had an opportunity but I didn't take it'? Or do you want to say, 'You know what? Maybe I screwed up a few times but look where I am now.'

(Interview B17)

Just a few short decades ago less than one million Canadians were self-employed. Today the number hovers around 2.4 million and is expected to grow. Canadian women have been at the centre of this change, entering self-employment and small business ownership in dramatic numbers, and in ways that depart notably from traditional patterns. Once relegated to small unincorporated home-based businesses in traditional sectors such as retail and personal services, they have now considerably diversified their activity, working in a wide range of industries, traditional and non-traditional, as bosses, business moms, and one-woman shows.

Understanding this social and economic phenomenon, and its consequences for women, has been the goal of this study. In particular, it has sought to deepen our understanding of the reasons for women's growing involvement in self-employment and small business, coinciding as it has with deep-seated economic, political, and social change that has rippled through and transformed economies in Canada and many other countries. It has also tried to illuminate and enrich our knowledge about self-employed women's job quality and satisfaction, exploring their daily work and hours, their opportunities for learning and developing skills, and the scope they have to engage in, and actively create, meaningful and challenging work. Importantly, it has sought to shed light on the economic rewards and risks women face, and to consider from a policy perspective some of the responses that women's small business and self-employment requires.

A central question posed in this study is whether women are engaged in 'risky business.' The question is one that can be read at two levels. First, does women's self-employment and small business ownership offer a genuine opportunity for greater economic autonomy and independence, or it is a risky undertaking, offering only meagre rewards? Second, do the activities women engage in conform to or depart from conventional understandings of business, and what does this mean for the future entrepreneurial economy that many Canadian policy-makers and politicians envision?

For some of those watching the self-employment boom over the last decade or more, women are indeed engaged in risky business, but it is a smart risk, a good move, a risk well worth taking. In their view, SE/SBO offers women far greater opportunities than they have traditionally been afforded in the labour market, boosting incomes and economic prospects, enhancing control over work time and schedules, and creating challenging, exciting work. Others, less convinced of the merits of a growing SE/SBO sector, see women's self-employment as part of a broader trend within industrialized societies towards the development of a risk society, where women face eroding opportunities for secure, well-paying jobs, along with the dismantling of safety nets and social protection, and the individualization of risk. In their view, self-employment offers women with few real economic opportunities, serving instead to entrench their position at the economic margins.

In tackling this debate, my main interest has been to explore these competing visions by fleshing out the experiences of Canadian women in a concrete, empirical manner. Working between Canadian survey and labour force data, and a rich set of in-depth interviews with Alberta women, I have sought to contribute new knowledge and insights to the valuable academic research and policy discussion that already exists. I have drawn on debates over economic polarization and restructuring, risk and precarious work, and the enterprise culture to make sense of the larger economic, social, and political context shaping women's SE/SBO. In addition I have drawn from a rich literature on women's work, and entrepreneurship in particular, to help make sense of the everyday experiences of women, and the similarities and differences between them.

Contrary to these two competing visions, what emerges from this study is a more measured reading than either suggest. Women's experiences cannot be understood through the lens of good and bad jobs, with a simple conflation of SE/SBO at one end, or the other. Instead, there is a wide range of job quality and satisfaction. For some women, working solo or as employers, self-employment has been a hands-down success, bringing economic rewards and a welcome opportunity to do work that is personally fulfilling and satisfying. For others, self-employment has been a way to earn an income while raising a family, or to engage in meaningful work that they really love. Others have far less positive experiences, perhaps enjoying the work but facing significant financial hurdles and insecurity. Those forced into SE/SBO by job loss or eroding work conditions typically face the most difficult situations. Taken together, these diverse experiences and situations form a composite picture that is far more complex than simply good or bad. Rather than fuelling growth at the bottom end of the labour market (the marginalization thesis) as some suggest, or at the top (the emancipation thesis) as more popular, optimistic accounts would have it, self-employment is itself highly polarized, dividing women in a number of different ways.

A key axis dividing women's experiences revolves around their reasons for entering this sector – in particular whether they enter voluntarily or are forced by economic circumstance. What the analysis here suggests is that women have for the most part entered into such work voluntarily, driven in particular by a desire for more challenge and independence in their work, a more positive work environment, and the opportunity to do work that is personally meaningful. But alongside those seeking self-employment for positive reasons, there is a significant group who have been directly forced, or at the very least nudged, into such work by downturns in economic circumstances and fortune. Job loss and a lack of work opportunities were very important for nearly one-fifth of women in the Alberta study, a finding mirrored in national data for Canadian women. Probing more deeply, it appears that up to one-third of Alberta women in fact faced some type of economic constraints that at the very least fed into their decision to become self-employed.

Decisions to become self-employed are of course highly complex, as the analysis shows. Indeed, one of the contributions of this study is not simply to contribute to substantive debates, but to show how existing methodological approaches fail to capture the complex social processes that are occurring. On this point, two key insights emerge. One relates to the difficulties of parcelling out, and neatly delineating, decisions into clear-cut push and pull explanations. For many women, a range of factors lay behind the decision to become self-employed, often in ways that are not always readily apparent or articulated. Second, factors that are often seen as attractions, or pulls, into self-employment – such as a desire for independence or a positive work environment – may operate as push factors. Negative work environments, the bad boss syndrome, low morale were all cited as reasons why some women left the security of traditional employment in order to strike out on their own. All of this points to a need for a more comprehensive approach that can get at the nuances and interrelation of diverse personal and family motivations. It also indicates some of the personal, organizational, and economic costs of the restructuring and downsizing that have taken place in both the private and public sectors in Canada over the past decade or more, with women compelled to leave well-paid, secure jobs, in search of healthier, more supportive, work environments.

How and why women enter SE/SBO has significant implications for their job quality. Here again the contrast between forced and voluntary entrepreneurs reveals a striking divide. But equally important is the finding that, in general, women who work for themselves are highly satisfied with the nature of the work they do on a daily basis, and have much higher job satisfaction and intrinsic job quality than most paid employees. New and comprehensive survey data from the 2000 CPRN-Ekos *Changing Employment Relationships Survey* make these patterns clear, revealing a 20% gap in job satisfaction between women who are self-employed and paid employees. Satisfaction is higher on a wide range of indicators, from control, independence, and self-direction, positive work environment, to interesting work, creativity, and personal fulfilment. These findings are reinforced and mirrored in the in-depth interviews with Alberta women, who highlight a range of features, from creativity to meaningful work, that they highly value. In short, if judged solely on the basis of creating healthy workplaces and engaging, challenging work, women in SE/SBO are achieving great success.

But this is not to say that all women are satisfied, or that they all value the same thing about SE/SBO. One clear line of division is between solo workers and employers. Though both are highly satisfied with their work, employers gain much more satisfaction from the project of building a business, whereas solo women place far more value on their ability to control their work environment and engage in creative, meaningful work. In some ways the data suggest an ambivalence among some (though not all) solo women towards building a business in the traditional sense – a finding that has implications for the kind of entrepreneurial economy that may emerge. Perhaps the most important differences we see in intrinsic job satisfaction and quality, however, is between women who are forced into self-employment, and those who enter it willingly. Of all differences, whether socio-demographic or business related, this is the most crucial. Forced entrepreneurs, though quite satisfied with their work, report far lower satisfaction with nearly every job feature: day-to-day work, independence, creativity, authority, personal fulfilment, and work-family balance. The only area where they are more satisfied is with time for themselves.

Given the ongoing struggle North Americans face in balancing work and family, it is important to note that, compared to other intrinsic features of their work, self-employed women are far less satisfied with their work-family balance and in particular the time they have for themselves. This runs contrary to popular accounts of self-employment as a way to better balance and integrate work and family, especially by working in the home. Employers in particular are dissatisfied with work and family, and their lack of personal time. Solo women fare better but only because they appear to gain satisfaction with work-family balance at the cost of personal time for themselves. Significantly those with children, those working part-time and from home, all report higher levels of work-family balance – suggesting that for those who adopt self-employment specifically to accommodate family needs, it may be a successful strategy. But for other women self-employment clearly puts pressure on the work-family equation, a fact that is not surprising given the long hours many full-time women work.

It is in turning to the economic rewards and risks of self-employment, however, that we see the most mixed picture, with some women doing very well financially, while others fare poorly. Here, more than anywhere, the diversity and polarization within women's self-employment and small business ownership becomes clear. As in the labour market generally, factors such as education, occupation, industry, tenure, and work experience all shape income and security. Professional free agents, knowledge workers, and long-established employers, for example, all do very well. In contrast, women in small, home-based businesses in traditional sectors, such as retail or personal and other services, typically struggle, constrained by the low earning potential that has traditionally been part of female-dominated, labour-intensive sectors. In addition to low income, the collected impact of unexpected expenses, a lack of benefits, and business fluctuations further fuel insecurity and dissatisfaction with the financial aspects of SE/SBO.

As with intrinsic job quality, there are key dividing lines in women's economic success and security. Family circumstances – in particular women's responsibility as mothers – clearly shapes financial rewards and satisfaction, with many business moms working part time and trading off income, in exchange for a better balance of work and family life. But the most critical dividing line, as with intrinsic rewards, is again between the forced and voluntary, with the latter being far less satisfied with their income, job security, and ability to save for retirement.

Without doubt one of the great surprises of the study concerns job security. Contrary to analysts of the risk society who highlight growing insecurity, precariousness, and discontinuity, many self-employed women feel secure in their work. In some cases, this is because risk is buffered by family and household support – for example, women have partners whose earnings, savings, benefits or other assets provide financial backup. But other women have made significant financial investments and sacrifices, raising questions about why they should feel so secure. Listening to these women, what stands out is how they evaluate their security against the background of an economy that to them seems to have become riskier in recent years. Ironically, then, while holding similar views as those writing about the risk society, women seem to exempt themselves from the picture, regarding their own work as relatively secure. By taking control of their work and future, women seem to gain a sense of security, even when they face significant difficulties or obstacles in running their business. Certainly this is not the case for all women, but the degree to which women talk about 'making their own security,' and 'being more secure with many bosses rather than one,' is striking. In this respect, their views align with Smith's arguments about risk and opportunity in the new economy, illustrating how individuals may take on risk in order to improve their economic prospects or security. They also illustrate how risk ranges in degree of magnitude and how it is buffered, or sharpened, by the context in which it is taken.

Though self-employed women have taken control of their working lives in significant ways, there is still a role for government policy in helping to ensure their economic success and security. To the extent that Canadian governments, both federal, provincial, and local, have pushed an 'enterprise agenda' in recent years, they have clearly recognized the important role that SE/SBO is playing in the Canadian economy, and will continue to play for many years. An aging population, an expanding knowledge sector, new technologies, and network organizational approaches will all continue to feed the growth of the entrepreneurial economy. But much current policy thinking seems to be bounded by fairly conventional thinking about the nature of small business, business growth, and needed support, with little sense of appreciation for the growing diversity within the SE/SBO sector.

This study suggests that, while some women conform to a classic growth model, others are not interested in large-scale growth, but prefer what Daniel Pink has termed a free agent model – working solo, networking with others, or possible expanding into a very small micro business. All of this suggests that existing training and support programs should be diversified to cover a broader range of business models, especially those that may become more predominant as we move from an old to new knowledge-based economy. In addition, existing gaps within policy force us to think about whether, and how, independent workers might be better included in existing systems of social protection designed to assist and support Canadian workers. While this challenges existing ideas about the risk inherent in entrepreneurship, and may not be a preferred route for all self-employed women, there is a distinct group within this population who are interested in such programs and would be willing to contribute to, and benefit from, existing labour market supports.

Recognizing the diversity among self-employed women and business owners is a significant challenge, both for policy-makers and academics alike, requiring new approaches and ways of thinking. But it is diversity that most characterizes the female face of enterprise in Canada today. Whether forced or voluntary, high income or low, self-employment and small business ownership is significantly reshaping women's economic lives and prospects. In the process it is also challenging us to think about the entrepreneurial economy in new ways.

Appendix 1: Interview Schedule

A. Work and Education History

1. To begin, could you tell me a bit about your work and education history prior to starting this business – I'm interested in knowing about your education, and other types of self-employment or paid employment you were involved in prior to this business. Check:

   - self-employment in other businesses? If yes, type of business? How long?
   - paid employment for someone else? If yes, type of job? How long?
   - periods of unemployment? If yes, for how long?
   - periods of time to raise family/or for education? If yes, how long?

B. Current Business

In terms of your current business ...

2. Can you tell me how you became involved in it?

3. Can you tell me about the business in terms of

   - the services or products you provide
   - who your clients/customers are
   - how diverse your client base is (number, type-individuals, orgs)
   - approximate annual sales last year

4. In terms of your involvement in this business is it *your main source of work*, or are you involved in other jobs or business as well?

- if other work:
  - what are the other jobs or businesses you are involved in?
  - approximately how many hours/week worked in these?

5. In terms of *this* business, could you tell me about the main types of work you do – the kinds of activities you are involved in on a *daily basis* (e.g., managing, selling, production)?

6. Approximately how many hours per week do you work in your business?

7. Do you have employees working for you?

  - if employees
    - how many?
    - what sorts of jobs do they do?
    - are they permanent or casual staff?
    - do they work part-time/full-time hours?
    - do they receive wages and benefits, or wages only?

C. Reasons for Being Self-employed

I've already asked you to indicate some reasons why you are self-employed (on information sheet) and I'd like to discuss this more with you now.

8. Of the reasons that are very important to you ...

  - could you tell me more about why they are important to you?

D. Satisfaction with Self-employment

I also asked you about your satisfaction with a number of different aspects of self-employment (on sheet) and would like to discuss these more

9. Could you tell me what you indicated as most satisfying, and explain why? (probes: could you give an example, what do you find satisfying about that?)

10. Could you tell me what you feel is least satisfying, and explain why? (probes: could you give an example, why do you find it dissatisfying?)

E. Challenges and Experiences in Self-employment

I'm also interested in the challenges and opportunities women face in their businesses ...

11. Can you tell me about the current challenges and opportunities that you are facing?

I'm also interested in how you've dealt with several specific issues:

12. In terms of *support* ...

- what kind of support has been most important to you in self-employment?
  - eg. family, friends, organizations, mentors
- are there any self-employment organizations that have been particularly helpful?
- are there certain kind of support you don't have, that you wish you did?
  - eg. training for self, or employees

13. In terms of the *risks* involved in self-employment ...

- do you find it stressful or exciting? (probe for examples)
- why?
- if stressful, do you have particular ways of dealing with it?

14. In terms of your *approach to business* ...

- do you feel you have a particular ethical approach or philosophy that distinguishes you from other businesses?
  - e.g., a code of ethics, relationship to employees, customers, community
- if yes, could you briefly describe it to me?

15. In terms of *your success* ...

- how do you evaluate your success? What does success mean to you?
- do you feel you've been successful?

16. In terms of *being a women in self-employment* ...

- do you think gender makes any difference to being successfully self-employed?
- is being a women an advantage, disadvantage, or is it largely irrelevant?

F. Future

17. Finally, looking to the future, can you tell what your plans are for the next 2-3 years in terms of self-employment?

- if yes SE
    - what are your future plans for your business?
    - if you had to, would you be willing to work for someone else?
    - what type of work would you be doing?
- if no SE
    - what type of work would you like to be doing in the future?
    - would you consider being self-employed again at some point in the future?

Conclusion

Thank you very much for sharing your time and experiences.
Is there anything you would like to add that you think is important?

Appendix 2: Summary Sheet

To start, we would appreciate getting your responses to the following two questions. There will be an opportunity to discuss these questions in more detail in the interview.

1. In terms of your reasons for being self-employed, could you indicate how important each of these are to you (circle):

	Very important	Somewhat important	Not at all important
Desire for independence	1	2	3
Challenging work	1	2	3
Having responsibility	1	2	3
Better income	1	2	3
Flexible schedule	1	2	3
Ability to work from home	1	2	3
Work-family balance	1	2	3
No other job opportunities	1	2	3
Job loss	1	2	3
Contracting out by past employer	1	2	3
Family business	1	2	3
Positive work environment	1	2	3
Desire for meaningful work	1	2	3
Other	1	2	3

2. How satisfied are you with the following aspects of self-employment (circle):

	Very satisfied				Very dissatisfied
Nature of your day to day work	1	2	3	4	5
Independence	1	2	3	4	5
Opportunity for creativity	1	2	3	4	5
Authority to make decisions	1	2	3	4	5
Financial responsibility	1	2	3	4	5
Level of personal income	1	2	3	4	5
Job security	1	2	3	4	5
Work and family balance	1	2	3	4	5
Time for self	1	2	3	4	5
Ability to save for retirement	1	2	3	4	5
Personal fulfillment	1	2	3	4	5
Managing employees (if applicable)	1	2	3	4	5
Working from home (if applicable)	1	2	3	4	5
Other	1	2	3	4	5

In order to provide summary statistics for our study, we would also appreciate it if you could provide a few details about yourself and your business. This information will be used for summary purposes only and will be kept strictly confidential.

About Yourself:

1. Year of birth: _____

2. Country of birth: _____

3. Highest level of education (check one):
   Grade 9 or lower _____   College diploma _____
   Grades 10–12 non-graduate _____   University degree (Bachelor) _____
   High School graduate _____   University degree (Professional) _____
   Some post-secondary _____   University degree (Master) _____
   Trade certificate or diploma _____   University degree (Doctoral) _____

4. Marital status (check one):
   Single ___   Married / Cohabiting ___   Sep / Divorced ___   Widowed ___

   If you are married / cohabiting, what is your partner's work status:
   Paid Employee ___   Self-Employed ___   Unemployed ___   Retired ___

5. Do you have any children?   Yes ____   No ____
   If you have children, how many? _____
   What ages? _____

   Do you belong to any of the following equity groups?

   Visible minority ____   Disabled ____   Aboriginal ____   None of these ____

About Your Current Business:

1. How long have you been self-employed in your *current* business? _____
   years

2. Is your *current* business (check one):
   a new business you created   _____
   an existing business you purchased   _____
   a family business   _____
   other _____   _____

3. Is your *current* business (check one):
   incorporated _____   unincorporated _____

4. Could you indicate your approximate before-tax income for last year
   (check):

$	Your Own Income	Total Family Income	$	Your Own Income	Total Family Income
1 – 4,999	_____	_____	30,000 – 39,999	_____	_____
5,000 – 9,999	_____	_____	40,000 – 49,999	_____	_____
10,000 – 14,999	_____	_____	50,000 – 59,999	_____	_____
15,000 – 19,999	_____	_____	60,000 – 69,999	_____	_____
20,000 – 24,999	_____	_____	70,000 – 79,999	_____	_____
25,000 – 29,999	_____	_____	80,000 plus	_____	_____

4. Approximately what percentage of your *own income* comes from your *current* business? _____%

5. Have you used any of the following to finance your *current* business
   (check):

a commercial bank loan   _____
a community loan fund   _____
a government loan fund   _____
personal credit (eg. VISA) _____
none of these   _____

Thank you very much for providing this information.

Appendix 3: Interview Participants and Individuals/Organizations Assisting with Recruitment*

Janet Adenken
Alberta Women's Economic
   Enterprise Initiative
   Association (AWEIA)
Lynda A. Arial
Phyllis Arnold
Cynthia Bahnuik
Joanna Bartley
Susan Barylo
Brenda Belokrinicev
Winnie Bogosoff
Lorraine Brokelsby
Leonard Buckles
Scarlett Wilson-Campbell
Tina Chang
Changing Together: A Centre for
   Immigrant Women
Connecting Women
Jean Crozier
Barbara Dale
Charlene Davis
Lynda Doll
Edmonton Community Loan Fund
Lucie Ewanchuk
Maureen Ford
Dr. Margaret Fulford
Wendy Grahl

Diana Halverson
Judy Harcourt
Elnora A. Hibbert
Jill Hilderman
Karen Hobson
Jennifer Hughes
Mary Lynn Ilnitsky
Geri Iwanciw
Susan James
Ksenia Kopystynska
Dr Janet Lockington
Debra MacDonald
Kathleen Marshall
Linda Martin
Linda Maul
Tanis Moland
Linda Nider
Laura O'Neill
Tina Park
Pam Pettie
Rosemary Pon
Salma Rajwani
Louise Reinich
Beverly Rink
Dr Carole E. Ross
Nancy Rubilak
Carolyn Saganski

Shusila Samy

Monica Santiago

Maureen Seebaran

Sandi Stetson

Dr Jennifer Strong

Sharlene Thomas

Julie Trachuk

Women Business Owners of Canada
(WBOC)

*A small number of participants preferred not to be named.

Notes

1. Introduction

1 There has been much debate over how to define self-employment, small business ownership, and entrepreneurship. Here the terms 'self-employed,' 'small business owner,' and 'entrepreneur' are used interchangeably, and refer both to self-employed workers who work alone (also known as *own account workers* but what I call *solo workers*) and those who employ others (often called *employers*). I discuss definitional issues further in Chapter 2.

2 For some examples of these differing views, see Allen and Truman (1993a), Beck (2000), Burrows (1991), MacDonald (1996), and Smeaton (2003). For a more positive, popular account in the United States, see Daniel Pink, *Free Agent Nation* (2001).

3 In Canada, see Cohen (1996) and Industry Canada (1998). In the United States, see Carr (1996, 2000), Clark and James (1992), Loscocco and Robinson (1991), and Moore and Buttner (1997). In Britain, see Carter and Cannon (1992) and Green and Cohen (1995). For an interesting international comparison of Canada, United States, Australia, Mexico, Ireland, Russia, and Argentina, see Weeks (2000).

4 There is a vast literature addressing the polarization debate that I will not attempt to catalogue here. For particularly influential contributions, see, in Canada (ECC 1990, 1991), in the United States (Harrison and Bluestone 1988; Kuttner 1983; Smith 2001), and in Britain (Burchell et al. 2002; Westergaard 1995).

5 This shift is perhaps most striking in the British context where, as Allen and Truman (1993b) note, entrepreneurs moved from being the subject of mild abuse to being seen as key to regenerating a declining economy (Allen and Truman 1993a; see also Hobbs 1991).

6 In Canada, see also Rubin *Bulldog: Spirit of the New Entrepreneur* (1999). In the United States, see books such as *Spare Room Tycoon* and Daniel Pink's manifesto *Free Agent Nation: How America's New Independent Workers are Transforming the Way We Live* (2001).

7 The Entrepeneurial Motivation Index (EMI) was created by asking key informants in each country to respond to five statements concerning attitudes towards enterprise. A sample question was: 'In my country, people consider becoming an entrepreneur a desirable career option.' A high correlation (0.93) exists between the EMI and business start-up activity (see Peterson 1999: 13 for fuller details).

8 Dennis (1996) cites: first, a survey of three thousand small business owners in the mid- to late-1980s that found just 8% were self-employed due to a lack of alternatives; and second, a 1995 survey of independent contractors by the Bureau of Labor Statistics (BLS) which found that 82.5% preferred their existing work arrangements, and only 9.8% preferred a more traditional one (648–9, 654–5).

9 In 1995, full-time, full-year self-employed women earned 64% of their male peers, compared to 73% for paid employees (Statistics Canada 1997: 26). Underlying lower earnings are a variety of factors: the tendency for more self-employed women to work part-time, to be concentrated in 'low return' industries, and to be own account workers rather than employers (Cohen 1996: 26–7).

10 The SEA program is discussed further in Chapter 6. For details, see Industry Canada (1997). For evaluations and overview, see Graves and Gauthier (1996), Orser and Hoggarth-Scott (1998) and Wong et al. (1998).

11 See Haynes (1998); McGilly (1998); Osberg et al. (1995). Fishers are the one group of self-employed covered by employment insurance (McGilly 1998: 57). This issue is discussed further in Chapter 6.

2. Researching Women in the Entrepreneurial Economy

1 I appreciate the suggestions given to me by Dallas Cullen, Andrea Doucet, Margaret Harrison, Kiran Mirchandani, Anne Neufeld, and Denise Spitzer on strategies for increasing the diversity of women participating in this study.

2 I use the term 'business' here even though some of the women may not see themselves, or be legally established, as a business owner.

3 The level of original start-ups is higher than the national average. According to the Canadian Federation of Independent Business, approximately 50% of business owners start their business from scratch (2002: 5).

4 For example, results from the *CPRN-Ekos Changing Employment Relation-ships Survey* indicate that up to 12% of the self-employed may be 'disguised employees' based on tests of ownership of tools and equipment, and control over tasks and working conditions (Lowe 2002: 96; Lowe and Schellenberg 2001: 13–16).

5 For example, EU countries define small and medium enterprises (SMEs) as ranging in size from 200 to 250 employees, compared to the United States, which defines them as having less than 500 employees (OECD 2000c, 2000d). Some argue that an embedded notion of size relative to industry standard should be used (Dale 1991).

3. Women's Paths into Self-Employment and Small Business

1 Lin et al. (1999a; 1999b) suggest that both push and pull factors are involved, citing potential factors such as demographic shifts, public and private sector restructuring/downsizing, shifting industrial composition, contracting out, taxation policy, self-employment assistance programs, growing entrepreneurial spirit, and growing uncertainty in paid employment.

2 A fall of 1.0% in the quarterly rate of growth of paid employment was associated with an increase of 1.5% in the quarterly rate of growth of self-employment (Chambers 1998: 5).

3 Additional reasons included the desire to make more money (9.6%), to have a flexible schedule (6.0%), to work from home (5.6%), and the nature of the work (3.5%).

4 Where gender differences are notable is on work-family issues. Just 2% of men cited working at home as a reason for self-employment, compared to 12.6% of women. Flexible schedules were important for 9.2% of women, but just 4.4% of men (Statistics Canada 1997: 35).

5 Of the remainder, 25% entered self-employment voluntarily and the other 56% noted both push and pull factors.

6 Women discussed their work, education, and family background at the start of the interview in a format that suited their own life history. Later the excerpts from the transcripts were coded to indicate whether their education and work experience were directly relevant, somewhat relevant, and not at all relevant to their business. Each interview was coded separately by myself and one other interviewer, and compared to ensure reliability.

7 Respondents were asked: 'In terms of your reasons for becoming self-employed, could you indicate how important each of these is to you?'

Responses included 'very important,' 'somewhat important,' and 'not at all important.'

8 At the time of the study, the *Survey of Self-Employment in Canada (SSE)* had not yet been conducted. However, the response categories in the *SSE* draw on many of the same items in the *Survey of Work Arrangements*.

4. 'I Love What I Do'

1 This measure was developed in research carried out with colleagues Grant Schellenberg and Graham Lowe for Canadian Policy Research Networks. The research is published in a report, *Men and Women's Quality of Work in the New Economy*, available through CPRN's website at www.cprn.org.

5. Players or Paupers?

1 My thanks to Jody Ciufo at the Canadian Federation for Humanities and Social Sciences for suggesting this title.

2 Debate exists over the reliability of earnings data for self-employed workers, with some researchers arguing that there is significant under-reporting (for example, due to cash payments or business deductions), and others finding little discrepancy between actual and reported earnings. For example, Devlin (2001) notes that net revenue or net profit may understate income due to the generous use of deductions (see also Hamilton 2000). Given the lack of conclusive evidence, and the inability to make reliable adjustments, however, we rely on reported figures in the discussion that follows.

3 It bears noting that the estimated earnings differentials understate the differences in compensation, as fringe benefits are not included in the measure (Hamilton 2000).

4 It is important to note that these statistics exclude negative earnings and earnings for those in self-employment less than sixteen months, which slightly inflates income levels.

5 Because income data in the *SSE* were collected in ranges, it is not possible to provide figures on average income. As with previous Statistics Canada research, income figures exclude those making net losses, which may produce a more positive picture than exists. HRDC (2002) notes that prudence is advised in using the *SSE* data as results vary from other data. However, it is unclear whether this is a statistical artefact, or instead represents real changes in the labour market.

6 There are some exceptions to this which are discussed in Chapter 6.

7 It bears noting, as HRDC (2002: 59) points out, that the business cycle may make it difficult for the self-employed to retire when they want. A recent *Survey of Financial Security* found that one-third of assets are tied up in businesses and are illiquid.

8 This question allowed multiple answers. Responses also included 'received government assistance' and 'bankruptcy' but the numbers are too small to provide reliable estimates.

9 It is possible that women may be more likely to express dissatisfaction with income due to feelings of 'self-referenced relative deprivation' – that is, comparing their own current situation to their past (see Krahn and Harrison 1992). Many of these women worked previously as paid employees, where incomes were typically higher, and they have likely experienced a drop in earnings, at least initially, on entrance into self-employment. By relative standards, then, they may feel less satisfied. As one employer said, 'You go from making $50,000 a year, to making nothing. There's a big, big gap' (interview A02). Another employer noted: 'When we started, I saw the potential in the organization, but my take-home pay was much less than what I was making at my previous job. But it was a sacrifice that I made a conscious decision to make' (interview A12).

10 This is not to suggest that all paid employees have access to benefits, as there is typically a marked divide between standard and non-standard employees (for example, part-time, temporary). Notwithstanding this variance, on average paid employees are more likely to have benefits than self-employed workers and small business owners (Lowe and Schellenberg 2001).

11 The notion of a potential business draws on Hochschild's discussion of the potential self in *The Time Bind* (1997: 235–8). She suggests that time-poor parents created dreams of the potential self and potential family life as a way to cope with the time bind they faced. In the same way, the dream of the potential business may keep some women going through periods of adversity.

6. Building an Entrepreneurial Economy

1 The extent to which self-employment is considered to be minor in extent is determined by the time spent, nature and amount of the capital and resources invested, financial success or failure of the business, continuity of the business, nature of the business, and the intention and willingness to seek immediately acceptable alternative employment (Bell 2003a: 2).

2 See Schrank (1998) for a very interesting account of the inclusion of fishers into UI/EI. My thanks to Judy Fudge for mentioning this article.

3 UI/EI has a history of discriminating against women, from its treatment of married women in the 1950s to the hourly thresholds established with EI reforms in the 1990s (see Porter 2003 for an excellent account). Given this, we might reasonably question whether and how gender, as well as region, has historically shaped the selective inclusion of some self-employed workers. Why were self-employed fishers (predominantly male) included in this program, for example, when other types of self-employed workers such as those employed in childcare (predominantly women) were not?

4 I am grateful to Graham Lowe for bringing this debate to my attention.

References

Abu-Laban, Yasmeen, and Christine Gabriel. 2002. *Selling Diversity. Immigration, Multiculturalism, Employment Equity and Globalization*. Peterborough, ON: Broadview Press.

Adams, Barbara. 1995. *Timewatch: The Social Analysis of Time*. Cambridge: Polity Press.

Aglietta, Michel. 1979. *A Theory of Capitalist Regulation: The U.S. Experience*. London: New Left Books.

Akyeampong, Ernest B., and Deborah Sussman. 2003. 'Health Related Benefits for the Self-Employed.' *Perspectives in Labour and Income* 15(2): 41–6.

Aldrich, Howard E. 1999. *Organizations Evolving*. London: Sage Publications.

Allen, Sheila, and Truman, Carole. 1992. 'Women, Business and Self-Employment: A Conceptual Minefield.' Pp. 162–74 in *Women and Working Lives: Divisions and Change*, edited by Sara Arber and Nigel Gilbert. London: Macmillan.

– 1993a. *Women in Business: Perspectives on Women Entrepreneurs*. London and New York: Routledge.

– 1993b. 'Women and Men Entrepreneurs: Life Strategies, Business Strategies.' Pp. 1–13 in *Women in Business: Perspectives on Women Entrepreneurs*, edited by Sheila Allen and Carole Truman. London and New York: Routledge.

Angus Reid Group Inc. 1998a. 'Half (47%) of Canadians Not Already Self-Employed Interested in Running Their Own Business,' Released 14 September 1998. Retrieved 1 December 2001 (http://www.ipsos-na.com/news/pressrelease.cfm?id=756).

– 1998b. 'The Public's Esteem for Selected Professions', Released 10 November 1998. Retrieved 1 December 2001 (http://www.ipsos-na.com/news/pressrelease.cfm?id=805).

Appelbaum, Eileen. 2001. 'Transformation of Work and Employment and New

Insecurities.' Paper presented to the ILO Conference on the Future of Work, Employment and Social Protection. Geneva: ILO. Retrieved 14 November 2003 (http://www.ilo.org/public/english/bureau/inst/papers/confrnce/annecy2001/docs.htm).

Arai, A.B. 1997. 'The Road Not Taken: The Transition from Unemployment to Self-Employment in Canada.' *Canadian Journal of Sociology* 22(3): 365–82.

– 2000. 'Self-Employment as a Response to the Double Day for Women and Men in Canada.' *Canadian Review of Sociology and Anthropology* 37(2): 125–42.

Armstrong, Pat. 1996. 'The Feminization of the Labour Force; Harmonizing Down in a Global Economy.' Pp. 29–54 in *Rethinking Restructuring: Gender and Change in Canada*, edited by Isabella Bakker. Toronto: University of Toronto Press.

– 1997. 'Restructuring Public and Private: Women's Paid and Unpaid Work.' Pp. 37–61 in *Challenging the Public/Private Divide: Feminism, Law, and Public Policy*, edited by Susan B. Boyd. Toronto: University of Toronto Press.

– and Hugh Armstrong. 1994. *The Double Ghetto: Canadian Women and their Segregated Work*, 3rd ed. Toronto: McClelland and Stewart.

Aronson, Robert L. 1991. *Self-Employment: A Labor Market Perspective*. Ithaca, NY: ILR Press.

Arthur, M.B. and D.M. Rousseau, eds. 1996. *The Boundaryless Career: New Employment Principles for a New Organisational Era*. New York: Oxford University Press.

Atkinson, J. 1984. *Flexibility, Uncertainty and Manpower Management*. Brighton: Institute of Manpower Studies Report No. 89.

Audretsch, David S. and A. Roy Thurik. 2001. 'What's New about the New Economy? Sources of Growth in the Managed and Entrepreneurial Economies.' *Industrial and Corporate Change* 10(1): 267–315.

Baines, Susan, and Jane Wheelock. 1998. 'Reinventing Traditional Solutions: Job Creation, Gender and the Micro-Business Household.' *Work, Employment and Society* 12(4): 579–601.

– 2000. 'Work and Employment in Small Businesses: Perpetuating and Challenging Gender Solutions.' *Gender, Work and Organization* 7(1): 45–56.

Baines, Susan, Jane Wheelock, and Alison Abrams. 1997. 'Microbusiness Owner-Managers in Social Context: Household, Family, and Growth or Non-Growth.' Pp. 47–60 in *Small Firms: Entrepreneurship in the Nineties*, edited by David Deakins, Peter Jennings, and Colin Mason. London: Paul Chapman Publishers.

Bakker, Isabella, ed. 1996. *Rethinking Restructuring: Gender and Change in Canada*. Toronto: University of Toronto Press.

Baldwin, John R., and James Chowhan. 2003. *The Impact of Self-Employment on*

Labour-Productivity Growth: A Canada and United States Comparison. Ottawa: Statistics Canada. Catalogue No. 11F0027MIE No. 016.

Baldwin, John R., and Garnett Picot. 1994. *Employment Generation by Small Producers in the Canadian Manufacturing Sector*. Ottawa: Statistics Canada. Catalogue No. 11F0019MPE No. 70.

Bank of Montreal. 1996. *Myths and Realities: The Economic Power of Women-Led Firms*. An independent study supported by Bank of Montreal's Institute for Small Business.

Beck, Nuala. 1995. *Excelerate: Growing in the New Economy*. Toronto: HarperCollins.

Beck, Ulrich. 1992. *Risk Society: Towards a New Modernity*. London: Sage Publications.

– 2000. *The Brave New World of Work*. Cambridge: Polity Press.

Belcourt, Monica. 1988. 'The Family Incubator Model of Female Entrepreneurship.' *Journal of Small Business and Entrepreneurship* 5(3): 34–44.

– 1991. 'From the Frying Pan into the Fire: Exploring Entrepreneurship as a Solution to the Glass Ceiling.' *Journal of Small Business and Entrepreneurship* 8(3): 49–55.

Belcourt, Monica, Ronald Burke, and Helen Lee-Gosselin. 1991. *The Glass Box: Women Business Owners in Canada*. Ottawa: Status of Women Canada.

Bell, Daniel. 1973. *The Coming of the Post-Industrial Society*. New York: Basic Books.

Bell, Tricia. 2003a. 'Financing and Business Services Available to Self-Employed Workers: A Background Report.' Unpublished paper for C-WISE Project. Montreal.

– 2003b. 'Self-Employment Workers and Labour Market Benefits: A Background Report.' Unpublished paper for C-WISE Project. Montreal.

Benoit, Cecilia M. 2000. *Women, Work and Social Rights: Canada in Historical and Comparative Perspective*. Scarborough: Prentice Hall Allyn and Bacon.

Betcherman, Gordon, and Graham S. Lowe. 1997. *The Future of Work in Canada: A Synthesis Report*. Ottawa: Canadian Policy Research Networks.

Betcherman, Gordon, Kathryn McMullen, and Katie Davidman. 1998. *Training for the New Economy: A Synthesis Report*. Ottawa: Canadian Policy Research Networks.

Beutel, Ann M., and Margaret Mooney Marini. 1995. 'Gender and Values.' *American Sociological Review* 60 (June): 436–48.

Birch, David. 1987. *Job Generation in America: How Our Smallest Companies Put the Most People to Work*. New York: Free Press.

Bird, Sharon, and Stephen Sapp. 2004. 'Understanding the Gender Gap in Small Business Success.' *Gender and Society* 18(1): 5–28.

Birley, Sue. 1989. 'Female Entrepreneurs: Are They Really Any Different?' *Journal of Small Business Management* 2(2): 32–46.

Blanchflower, D., and A. Oswald. 1999. 'Well-Being, Insecurity and the Decline of American Job Satisfaction.' Unpublished paper. Retrieved August 5, 2003 (http://www.dartmouth.edu/~blnchflr/papers/)

Blanchflower, David, Andrew Oswald, and Alois Stuatzer. 2001. 'Latent Entrepreneurship across Nations.' *European Economic Review* 45(4–6): 680–91.

Bluestone, Barry and Bennett Harrison. 1982. *The Deindustrialization of America*. New York: Basic Books.

Blumer, H. 1954. 'What's Wrong with Social Theory?' *American Sociological Review* 19(1): 3–10.

Bogenhold, D., and U. Staber. 1991. 'The Decline and Rise of Self-Employment.' *Work, Employment and Society* 5(2): 223–39.

Bradbury, Bettina.1993. *Working Families: Age, Gender and Daily Survival in Industrializing Montreal*. Toronto: McClelland and Stewart.

Brisbois, Richard. 2003. *How Canada Stacks Up: The Quality of Work – An International Perspective*. Ottawa: Canadian Policy Research Networks. Research Paper W23.

Brodie, Janine, ed. 1996. *Women and Canadian Public Policy*. Toronto: Harcourt Brace.

Bruni, Attila, et al. 2004. 'Doing Gender, Doing Entrepreneurship: An Ethnographic Account of Intertwined Practices.' *Gender, Work and Organization* 11(4): 406–29.

Bryman, A. 1988. *Quantity and Quality in Social Research*. London: Unwin Hyman.

Burchell, Brendan, David Ladipo, and Frank Wilkinson, eds. 2002. *Job Insecurity and Work Intensification*. London: Routledge.

Burrows, R. 1991a. *Deciphering the Enterprise Culture: Entrepreneurship, Petty Capitalism, and the Restructuring of Britain*. London and New York: Routledge.

Burrows, Roger. 1991b. 'Introduction.' Pp. 1–16 in *Deciphering the Enterprise Culture: Entrepreneurship, Petty Capitalism and the Restructuring of Britain*, edited by Roger Burrows. London and New York: Routledge.

Business Development Bank of Canada. 1997. *Canadian Women Entrepreneurs in Growth Sectors: A Survey*. Ottawa: Business Development Bank of Canada.

Buttner, E. Holly, and Dorothy P. Moore. 1997. 'Women's Organizational Exodus to Entrepreneurship: Self-Reported Motivations and Correlates with Success.' *Journal of Small Business Management* 35(1): 34–46.

Calmeadow. 1997. *Directory of Micro-Loan Funds in Canada*. Prepared by Jennifer Harold. Toronto: Calmeadow.

- 1998. *15 Years of Microenterprise: Calmeadow Annual Report for the Year Ending March 31, 1998*. Toronto: Calmeadow.

Canada. 2003. *Prime Minister's Task Force on Women Entrepreneurs*. Ottawa: Canada. Retrieved 30 October 2003 (http://www.liberal.parl.gc.ca/entrepreneur/documents/031029_final_report_en.pdf).

Canada. Privy Council Office. 2002. 'Prime Minister Announces the Creation of a Task Force on Women Entrepreneurs.' Press release, 19 November.

Canadian Federation of Independent Business (CFIB). 1999. *Study on Workplace Satisfaction in Private, Public Sectors*. Available on-line at www.cfib.ca

- 2000. 'Alberta Small Business Primer.' Available on-line at www.cfib.ca

- 2002. 'Small Business Primer.' Available on-line at www.cfib.ca

Canadian Labour Congress. 1997. *From McJobs to 'My Own Job': The Growth of Self-Employment*. Ottawa: Canadian Labour Congress.

Canadian Policy Research Networks. *Job Quality Indicators Website*. Retrieved 12 September 2003 (http://www.jobquality.ca/indicator e/default.stm)

Capelli, Peter, et al. 1997. *Change at Work*. New York: Oxford University Press.

Carr, Deborah. 1996. 'Two Paths to Self-Employment? Women's and Men's Self-Employment in the United States, 1980.' *Work and Occupations* 23(1): 26–53.

- 2000. 'The Entrepreneurial Alternative.' Pp. 208–29 in *Women at Work: Leadership for the Next Century*, edited by Dayle M. Smith. Englewood Cliffs, NJ: Prentice Hall.

Carter, Sara, and Tom Cannon. 1992. *Women as Entrepreneurs: A Study of Female Business Owners, Their Motivations, Experiences and Strategies for Success*. London: Academic Press, Harcourt Brace Jovanovich.

Chambers, Ted. 1998. *Alberta's Human Resources: Changing Profiles over the Last Quarter Century of Who We Are and What We Do*, Bulletin No. 51. Edmonton: University of Alberta, Western Centre for Economic Research.

Chambers, Ted, and Nataliya L. Rylska. 2001. *A Portrait of Small Business Growth and Employment in Western Canada*. Edmonton: University of Alberta, Western Centre for Economic Research.

Chan, James. 2000. *Spare Room Tycoon*. London: Nicholas Brealey Publishing.

Clark, Thomas, and Franklin J. James. 1992. 'Women-Owned Businesses: Dimensions and Policy Issues.' *Economic Development Quarterly* 6(1): 25–40.

Church, Elizabeth. 1998. 'The Dirty Secret of Female Owners,' *Globe and Mail*, 10 August 1998: B11.

Cliff, Jennifer E., 1998. 'Does One Size Fit All? Exploring the Relationship between Attitudes towards Growth, Gender and Business Size.' *Journal of Business Venturing* 13: 523–42.

Cliff, Jennifer E., and Michelle Provorny Cash. 2005. 'Women's Entrepreneurship in Canada: Progress, Puzzles, and Priorities.' In *Growth Oriented Women*

Entrepreneurs and Their Businesses: A Global Research Perspective, edited by C.G. Brush, N. Carter, E.J. Gatewood, P.G. Greene, and M. Hart. London: Edward Elgar (forthcoming).

Cohen, Gary. 1996. 'Women Entrepreneurs.' *Perspectives on Labour and Income* 8(1): 23–8.

Cohen, Laurie, and Mary Mallon. 1999. 'The Transition from Organisational Employment to Portfolio Working: Perceptions of Boundarylessness.' *Work, Employment and Society* 13(2): 329–52.

Condon, Mary. 2002. 'Privatizing Pension Risk: Gender, Law and Financial Markets.' Pp. 128–65 in *Privatization, Law, and the Challenge to Feminism*, edited by Brenda Cossman and Judy Fudge. Toronto: University of Toronto Press.

Connelly, M. Patricia. 1996. 'Gender Matters: Global Restructuring and Adjustment.' *Social Politics* 3(1): 12–31.

Connelly, Rachel. 1992. 'Self-Employment and Providing Child Care.' *Demography* 29(1): 17–29.

Cossman, Brenda, and Judy Fudge, eds. 2002. *Privatization, Law, and the Challenge to Feminism*. Toronto: University of Toronto Press.

Coughlin, Jeanne Halladay, with Andrew R. Thomas. 2002. *The Rise of Women Entrepreneurs: People, Processes and Global Trends*. Westport, CT: Quorum Books.

Cranford, Cynthia, Leah F. Vosko, and Nancy Zukewich. 2003. 'Precarious Employment in the Canadian Labour Market: A Statistical Portrait.' *Just Labour: A Canadian Journal of Work and Society* 3: 6–22.

Dale, Angela. 1991. 'Self-Employment and Entrepreneurship: Notes on Two Problematic Concepts.' Pp. 35–52 in *Deciphering the Enterprise Culture: Entrepreneurship, Petty Capitalism and the Restructuring of Britain*, edited by Roger Burrows. London and New York: Routledge.

Danziger, Sheldon, and Peter Gottschalk, eds. 1993. *Uneven Tides: Rising Inequality in America*. New York: Russell Sage Foundation.

Das Gupta, Tania. 1996. *Racism and Paid Work*. Toronto: Garamond Press.

Dennis, William J. Jr. 1996. 'Self-Employment: When Nothing Else Is Available?' *Journal of Labor Research* 17(4): 645–61.

Department of Foreign Affairs and International Trade (DFAIT) and the Trade Research Coalition. 1999. *Beyond Borders: Canadian Women in International Trade*. Prepared by Barbara Orser (principal investigator), Eileen Fisher, Sue Hopper, Rebecca Reuber, and Allan Riding. Ottawa: DFAIT.

DeVault, Marjorie. 1999. *Liberating Method: Feminism and Social Research*. Philadelphia: Temple University Press.

Devine, Theresa J. 1994a. 'Characteristics of Self-Employed Women in the United States.' *Monthly Labor Review* 117(3): 20–34.

Devine, Theresa J. 1994b. 'Changes in Wage-and-Salary Returns to Skill and the Recent Rise in Female Self-Employment.' *Economic Issues for Work and Family* 84(2): 108–13.

Devlin, Rose Ann. 2001. *The Determinants of Earnings and Training for the Self-Employed in Canada: Some Preliminary Finding from the Survey of Self-Employment.* Working Paper W-01-12-2E. Ottawa: Human Resources and Development Canada, Applied Research Branch, Strategic Policy.

Doogan, Kevin. 2001. 'Insecurity and Long-Term Employment.' *Work, Employment and Society* 15(3): 419–41.

Du Gay, Paul. 1996. *Consumption and Identity at Work.* London: Sage Publications.

Du Gay, Paul, and Graeme Salaman. 1992. 'The Cult[ure] of the Customer.' *Journal of Management Studies* 29(5): 615–33.

Du Plessis, Valier. 2004. 'Self-Employment Activity in Rural Canada.' *Rural and Small Town Canada Analysis Bulletin* 5(5): 1–21. Ottawa: Statistics Canada. Catalogue 21–006–XIE.

Duffy, Ann, Daniel Glenday, and Norene Pupo, eds. 1997. *Good Jobs, Bad Jobs, No Jobs: The Transformation of Work in the 21st Century.* Toronto: Harcourt Brace.

Duffy, Ann, and Norene Pupo. 1992. *Part-Time Paradox: Connecting Gender, Work and Family.* Toronto: McClelland and Stewart.

Duxbury, Linda, and Christopher Higgins. 1999. *Human Resource and Work-Life Practices in Canadian Small Businesses: Managing People and Managing Growth.* London, ON: Richard Ivey School of Business, University of Western Ontario.

– 2001. *Work-Life Balance in the New Millennium: Where Are We? Where Do We Need to Go?* CPRN Discussion Paper No. W12. Ottawa: Canadian Policy Research Networks.

Economic Council of Canada. 1990. *Good Jobs, Bad Jobs: Employment in the Service Economy.* Ottawa: Supply and Services Canada.

– 1991. *Employment in the Service Economy.* Ottawa: Supply and Services Canada.

Economic Development Edmonton, 2000. *Economic Outlook.* Edmonton.

Ehlers, Tracy B., and Karen Main. 1998. 'Women and the False Promise of Microenterprise.' *Gender and Society* 12(4): 424–40.

European Commission. *The Social Protection Committee.* Retrieved 24 April 2004 (http://europa.eu.int/comm/employment_social/social_protection_commitee/index en.htm)

European Foundation for the Improvement of Living and Working Conditions. 2000. *Self-Employment: Choice or Necessity?* Retrieved 7 November 2003 (http://www.eurofound.eu.int/publications/EF0022.htm).

Fenwick, Tara. 2002. 'Transgressive Desires: New Enterprising Selves in the New Capitalism.' *Work, Employment and Society* 16(4): 703–23.

Frenette, Marc. 2002. *Do the Falling Earnings of Immigrants Apply to Self-Employed Immigrants?* Research Paper No. 195. Ottawa: Statistics Canada. Catalogue 11F0019MIE.

Finnie, Ross, Christine Laport, and Maud-Catherine Rivard. 2002. *Setting Up Shop: Self-Employment amongst Canadian College and University Graduates.* Ottawa: Statistics Canada, Business and Labour Market Analysis Division. Catalogue No. 11F0010MIE – No. 183.

Finlayson, Jock. 2003. 'Where the Jobs Aren't,' *Financial Post*, 8 November FP11.

Fischer, E. 1992. 'Sex Differences and Small-Business Performance among Canadian Retailers and Service Providers.' *Journal of Small Business and Entrepreneurship* 9(4): 2–13.

Fischer, E., A. Rebecca Reuber, and Lorraine S. Dyke. 1993. 'A Theoretical Overview and Extension of Research on Sex, Gender, and Entrepreneurship.' *Journal of Business Venturing* 8: 151–68.

Florida, Richard. 2002. *The Rise of the Creative Class.* New York: Basic Books.

Fowlie, Laura. 1998. 'Why Don't Female Entrepreneurs Earn as Much as Men?' *National Post*, 7 December, D9.

Fudge, Judy. 1996. 'Fragmentation and Feminization: The Challenge of Equity for Labour-Relations Policy.' Pp. 57–88 in *Women and Canadian Public Policy*, edited by Janine Brodie. Toronto: Harcourt Brace.

– 2003. 'Labour Protection for Self-Employed Workers.' *Just Labour: A Canadian Journal of Work and Society* 3 (Fall): 36–45.

Fudge, Judy, and Brenda Cossman. 2002. 'Introduction: Privatization, Law, and the Challenge to Feminism.' Pp. 3–37 in *Privatization, Law, and the Challenge to Feminism,* edited by Brenda Cossman and Judy Fudge. Toronto: University of Toronto Press.

Fudge, Judy, Eric Tucker, and Leah F. Vosko. 2002. *The Legal Concept of Employment: Marginalizing Workers.* Ottawa: Law Commission of Canada. Retrieved 10 November 2003 (http://www.lcc.gc.ca/en/themes/er/tvw/fudge/fudge_toc.asp).

– 2003. 'Employee or Independent Contractor? Charting the Legal Significance of the Distinction in Canada. *Canadian Journal of Labour and Employment Law* 10(2): 193–230.

– Forthcoming. 'Changing Boundaries in Employment: Developing a New Platform for Labour Law.' *Canada Labour and Employment Law Journal.*

Gauthier, James, and Richard, Roy. 1997. *Diverging Trends in Self-Employment in Canada.* Ottawa: Applied Research Branch, Human Resources Development Canada.

Gee, P., G. Hull, and C. Lackshear. 1996. *The New Work Order: Behind the Language of the New Capitalism*. Boulder, CO: Westview Press.

Goffee, Robert and Richard Scase. 1999. 'Business Ownership and Women's Subordination: A Preliminary Study of Female Proprietors.' Pp. 649–72 in *Women in Business*, edited by Mary A. Yeager. Northampton, MA: Edward Elgar Publishers.

Gottschalk, Peter, and Timothy M. Smeeding. 1997. 'Cross-national Comparisons of Earnings and Income Inequality.' *Journal of Economic Literature* 35 (June): 633–87.

Graham, Nancy. 2004. 'The Federal Perspective on Women Owned Firms.' Presentation to *Sustaining the Momentum: An Economic Forum on Women Entrepreneurs*, Ottawa, 27–9 October. Conference CD. Ottawa: Industry Canada.

Grameen Bank. 2001. *Annual Report*. Retrieved 7 January 2004 (http://www.grameen-info.org/annualreport/2001/foreword.htm).

Granger, Bill, John Stanworth, and Celia Stanworth. 1995. 'Self-Employment Career Dynamics: The Case of "Unemployment Push" in U. K. Book Publishing.' *Work, Employment and Society* 9(3): 499–516.

Grasmuck, Sherri, and Rosario Espinal. 2000. 'Market Success or Female Autonomy? Income, Ideology, and Empowerment amongst Microentrepreneurs in the Dominican Republic.' *Gender and Society* 14(2): 231–55.

Graves, Frank, and Benoit Gauthier. 1996. *Evaluation of the Self-Employment Assistance Program: MacroEvaluation*. Ottawa: Human Resources Development Canada.

Green, Eileen, and Laurie Cohen. 1995. 'Women's Business: Are Women Entrepreneurs Breaking New Ground or Simply Balancing the Demands of Women's Work in a New Way?' *Journal of Gender Studies* 4(3): 297–314.

Greenhaus, Jeffrey H., and Saroj Parasuraman. 1999. 'Research on Work, Family and Gender.' Pp. 391–412 in *Handbook of Gender and Work*, edited by Gary N. Powell. Thousand Oaks, CA: Sage Publications.

Grubb, W. Norton, and Robert H. Wilson. 1989. 'Sources of Increasing Inequality in Wages and Salaries, 1960–80.' *Monthly Labor Review* 112(April): 3–13.

Gunderson, Morley. 2002. 'Ten Key Ingredients of Labour Policy for the New World of Work.' *Canadian Public Policy* 28(1): 117–31.

Hall-Hoffarth, Deana. 2003. 'Self-Employment and Family Life: Adaptive Work-Family Balance Strategies.' Ph.D dissertation, University of Alberta.

Hamilton, Barton H. 2000. 'Does Entrepreneurship Pay? An Empirical Analysis of the Returns to Self-Employment.' *Journal of Political Economy* 108(3): 604–31.

Handy, Charles. 1994. *The Empty Raincoat: Making Sense of the Future*. London: Hutchinson.

Harding, Sandra, ed. 1987. *Feminism and Methodology*. Bloomington Indiana University Press and Open University Press.

Harrison, Bennett, and Barry Bluestone. 1988. *The Great U-Turn: Corporate Restructuring and the Polarizing of America*. New York: Basic Books.

Harvey, David. 1990. *The Conditions of Postmodernity: An Enquiry into the Conditions of Cultural Change*. Oxford: Basil Blackwell.

Haynes, Paulette S. 1998. *Human Resources Guide to Non-Standard Employment*. Aurora, ON: Aurora Professional Press.

Heinzl, John. 1998. 'Canada Shows its Entrepreneurial Colours,' *Globe and Mail*, 22 June, B11.

Hobbs, Dick. 1991. 'Business as a Master Metaphor: Working Class Entrepreneurship and Business-Like Policing.' Pp. 107–25 in *Deciphering the Enterprise Culture: Entrepreneurship, Petty Capitalism, and the Restructuring of Britain*, edited by Roger Burrows. London and New York: Routledge.

Hochschild, Arlie. 1997. *Time Bind: When Work Becomes Home and Home Becomes Work*. New York: Metropolitan Books, Henry Holt and Company.

– 2002. 'Love and Gold.' Pp. 15–20 in *Global Women: Nannies, Maids, and Sex Workers in the New Economy*, edited by Barbara Ehrenreich and Arlie Hochschild. New York: Metropolitan Books.

– 2003. *The Commercialization of Intimate Life: Notes from Home and Work*. Berkeley: University of California Press.

Howell, David. 1999. 'Small Business a Big Deal to Economy.' *Edmonton Journal*, 22 October, G1.

Hughes, Karen D. 1990. 'Trading Places: Men and Women in Non-Traditional Occupations, 1971–1986.' *Perspectives on Labour and Income* 2(2): 58–68.

– 1995. 'Women in Non-Traditional Occupations.' *Perspectives on Labour and Income* 7(3): 14–19.

– 1999. *Gender and Self-Employment in Canada: Assessing Trends and Policy Implications*. CPRN Study No. W04. Ottawa: Canadian Policy Research Networks.

– 2001. *Self-Employment, Skill Development and Training in Canada*. Ottawa: Human Resources Development Canada

– 2003a. 'Pushed or Pulled? Women's Entry into Self-Employment and Small Business Ownership.' *Gender, Work and Organization* 10(4): 433–54.

– 2003b. 'How Are Women Faring in the Entrepreneurial Economy?' Presentation to the 'Breakfast on the Hill,' Canadian Federation of the Humanities and Social Science, 1 May 2003. Ottawa.

Hughes, Karen D., and Tricia Bell. 2000. *Canadian Women in Self-Employment: A Summary Report (Project Newsletter)*. Edmonton: University of Alberta.

Hughes, Karen D., Graham S. Lowe and Allison L. McKinnon. 1996. 'Public Attitudes toward Budget Cuts in Alberta: Biting the Bullet or Feeling the Pain?' *Canadian Public Policy* 22 (3): 268–84.

Hughes, Karen D., Graham S. Lowe, and Grant Schellenberg. 2003. *Men's and Women's Quality of Work in the New Canadian Economy*. CPRN Study No. W19. Ottawa: Canadian Policy Research Networks.

Human Resources Development Canada (HRDC). 1998. *Lessons Learned: Own-Account Self-Employment in Canada*. SP-AH044E-02-98. Ottawa: Evaluation and Data Development, Strategic Policy, Human Resources Development Canada.

– 2000. *Perceptions of Self-Employed Regarding Possible Extension of Maternity, Parental and Sickness Benefits*. Ottawa: Compas Inc.

– 2002. *Results From the Survey of Self-Employment in Canada*. SP-465-01-02E. Ottawa: Applied Research Branch, Human Resources Development Canada.

– *History of Unemployment Insurance*. Retrieved 24 April 2004 (http:// www.hrsdc.gc.ca/en/ei/history/unemployment_insurance.shtml).

Human Resources and Skills Development Canada (HRSDC). 2004. *Compassionate Care Benefits*. Retrieved 24 April 2004. (http://www.hrsdc.gc.ca/asp/ gateway.asp?hr=en/ei/types/compassionate_care.shtml&hs=tyt).

Industry Canada. 1994a. *Building a More Innovative Economy*. Ottawa: Industry Canada.

– 1994b. *Growing Small Businesses*. Ottawa: Industry Canada.

– 1997. *Guide to Government of Canada Services and Support for Small Business, 1998–99*. Ottawa: Industry Canada.

– 1998. 'Shattering the Glass Box? Women Entrepreneurs and the Knowledge Based Economy.' *Micro-Economic Monitor*, third quarter (special report).

– 2001. *Business Service Centres, Annual Report 2000–01*. Ottawa: Industry Canada (available on-line at: www.cbsc.org/annual_report).

– 2004a. *Key Small Business Statistics*. Ottawa: Industry Canada. Catalogue IU4–32/2004E.

– 2004b. *Sustaining the Momentum: An Economic Forum on Women Entrepreneurs*, Ottawa, 27–9 October. Conference CD. Ottawa: Industry Canada.

– 2005. *Final Report and Recommendations: Sustaining the Momentum: An Economic Forum on Women Entrepreneurs*. Ottawa: Industry Canada.

International Labour Office (ILO). 1997. *Maternity Protection at Work*. Geneva: ILO.

–1998. 'Maternity Protection at Work.' *World of Work*, no. 24 (April). Geneva: ILO. Retrieved 23 April 2004 (http://www.ilo.org/public/english/bureau/ inf/magazine/24/matern.htm).

– 1999. *Decent Work: Report of the Director General*. Retrieved 23 April 2004: (http://www.ilo.org/public/english/standards/relm/ilc/ilc87/rep-i.htm).

Jacoby, Stanford M. 2001. 'Risk and the Labor Market.' Pp. 31–60 in *Sourcebook of Labor Markets: Evolving Structures and Processes*, edited by Ivar Berg and Arne L. Kalleberg. New York: Kluwer Academic/Plenum Publishers.

Jayaratne, Tony Epstein. 1983. 'The Value of Quantitative Methodology for Feminist Research.' Pp. 140–61 in *Theories of Women's Studies*, edited by Gloria Bowles and Renate Duelli Klein. Boston: Routledge and Kegan Paul.

Jenson, Jane. 1989. 'The Talents of Women, The Skills of Men: Flexible Specialization and Women.' Pp 141–55 in *The Transformation of Work? Skill, Flexibility and the Labour Process*, edited by Stephen Wood. London: Unwin Hyman.

Jenson, Jane, and Mariette Sineau. 2001. *Who Cares? Women's Work, Childcare, and Welfare State Redesign*. Toronto: University of Toronto Press.

Jessop, Bob. 1990. 'Regulation Theories in Retrospect and Prospect.' *Economy and Society* 19(2): 153–216.

Johnson, Steve and David Storey. 1993. 'Male and Female Entrepreneurs and Their Businesses: A Comparative Study.' Pp. 70–85 in *Women in Business: Perspectives on Women Entrepreneurs*, edited by Sheila Allen and Carole Truman. London and New York: Routledge.

Jungbauer-Gans, Monika. 1994. 'Chances of Survival and Success of Male and Female Businesses.' Pp. 249–69 in *Gender and Organizations: Changing Perspectives*, edited by Jean deBruijn and Eva Cyba. Amsterdam: VU University Press.

Jurik, Nancy. 1998. 'Getting Away and Getting By.' *Work and Occupations* 25(1): 7–35.

Kalleberg, Arne L. 2000. 'Nonstandard Employment Relations: Part-Time, Temporary, and Contract Work.' *Annual Review of Sociology* 26: 341–65.

– 2003. 'Flexible Firms and Labour Market Segmentation: Effects of Workplace Restructuring on Jobs and Workers.' *Work and Occupations* 30(2): 154–75.

Kalleberg, Arne L., and K. Leicht. 1991. 'Gender and Organizational Performance: Determinants of Small Business Survival and Success.' *Academy of Management Journal* 34(1): 136–61.

Kalleberg, Arne. L., Barbara F. Reskin, and Ken Hudson. 2000. 'Bad Jobs in America: Standard and Nonstandard Employment Relations and Job Quality in the United States.' *American Sociological Review* 65 (April): 256–78.

Kemp, Alice Abel. 1994. *Women's Work: Degraded and Devalued*. Englewood, Cliffs, NJ: Prentice-Hall.

Kohn, Melvin. L. 1990. 'Unresolved Issues in the Relationship between Work and Personality.' Pp. 36–68 in *The Nature of Work: Sociological Perspectives*, edited by Kai Erickson and Steven Peter Vallas. New Haven, CT: American Sociological Association and Yale University Press.

Kohn, Melvin L., and Carmi Schooler. 1983. *Work and Personality: An Inquiry into the Impact of Social Stratification*. Norwood, NJ: Ablex.

Krahn, Harvey. 1991. 'Non-Standard Work Arrangements.' *Perspectives on Labour and Income* 3(4): 35–45.

– 1995. 'Non-Standard Work on the Rise.' *Perspectives on Labour and Income* 7(4): 35–42.

Krahn, Harvey, and Trevor Harrison. 1992. 'Self-Referenced Relative Deprivation and Economic Beliefs: The Effect of Recession in Alberta.' *Canadian Review of Sociology and Anthropology* 29(2): 91–209.

Krahn, Harvey, and Graham S. Lowe. 2002. *Work, Industry and Canadian Society*. 4th ed. Scarborough, ON: Nelson Canada.

Kuhn, Peter J., and Herb J. Schuetze. 2001. 'Self-employment Dynamics and Self-Employment Trends: A Study of Canadian Men and Women, 1982– 1998.' *Canadian Journal of Economics* 34(3): 760–84.

Kuttner, Robert. 1983. 'The Declining Middle.' *Atlantic Monthly* (July): 60–72.

Lavoie, Dina. 1988. *Women Entrepreneurs: Building a Stronger Canadian Economy*. Ottawa: Canadian Advisory Council on the Status of Women.

Lazar, Harvey. 2002. *Shifting Roles: Active Labour Market Policy in Canada under the Labour Market Development Agreement*. Ottawa: Canadian Policy Research Networks.

Leadbeater, Charles. 2000. *Living on Thin Air: The New Economy*. London: Penguin.

Lee-Gosselin, H., and J. Grise. 1990. 'Are Women Owner-Managers Challenging our Definitions of Entrepreneurship?' *Journal of Business Ethics* 9 (4/5): 423–33.

Lero, Donna, et al. 'Self-Employed Women: Policy Options that Promote Equality and Economic Opportunities,' *Canadian Woman Studies* 23(3/4): 184–91.

Levy, Frank, and Richard J. Murnane. 1992. 'U.S. Earnings Levels and Earnings Inequality: A Review of Recent Trends and Proposed Explanations.' *Journal of Economic Literature* 30(3): 1333–81.

Li, Peter. 2000. 'Economic Returns of Immigrants' Self-Employment.' *Canadian Journal of Sociology* 25(1): 1–34.

Lin, Zhengxi, Garnett Picot, and Janice Yates. 1999a. *The Entry and Exit Dynamics of Self-Employment in Canada*. Paper No. 134. Ottawa: Statistics Canada, Analytic Studies Branch.

Lin, Zhengxi, Janice Yates, and Garnett Picot. 1999b. *Rising Self-Employment in the Midst of High Unemployment: An Empirical Analysis of Recent Developments in Canada*. Paper No. 133. Ottawa: Statistics Canada, Analytic Studies Branch.

Little, Bruce. 1994. 'Small Firms Big Job Creators,' *Globe and Mail*, 22 November, B1.

Littlejohn, Virginia. 2004. 'Best Practices: Communications, Knowledge-Sharing, Networking, and Advocacy.' Presentation to *Sustaining the Momentum:*

An Economic Forum on Women Entrepreneurs, Ottawa, 27–9 October. Conference CD. Ottawa: Industry Canada.

Littler, Craig R., and Peter Innes. 2003. 'Downsizing and Deknowledging the Firm.' *Work, Employment and Society* 17(1): 73–100.

Loscocco, Karyn A., and Joyce Robinson. 1991. 'Barriers to Women's Small-Business Success in the United States.' *Gender and Society* 5(4): 511–32.

Lowe, Graham S. 2000. *The Quality of Work: A People-Centred Agenda.* Don Mills, ON: Oxford University Press.

– 2002. 'Employment Relationships as the Centrepiece of a New Labour Policy Paradigm.' *Canadian Public Policy* 28(1): 93–104.

Lowe, Graham, and Kathryn McMullen. 2000. *Barriers and Incentives to Training.* Ottawa: Industry Canada (Advisory Council on Science and Technology).

Lowe, Graham S., and Grant Schellenberg. 2001. *What's a Good Job? The Importance of Employment Relationships.* Ottawa: Canadian Policy Research Networks.

Luxton, Meg, and June Corman. 2001. *Getting by in Hard Times: Gendered Labour at Home and on the Job.* Toronto: University of Toronto Press.

MacDonald, Martha. 1991. 'Post-Fordism and the Flexibility Debate.' *Studies in Political Economy* 36(Fall): 177–201.

MacDonald, Robert. 1996. 'Welfare Dependency, the Enterprise Culture and Self-Employed Survival.' *Work, Employment and Society* 10(3): 431–47.

Mahon, Rianne, and Susan Phillips. 2002. 'Dual-Earner Families Caught in a Liberal Welfare Regime? The Politics of Child Care Policy in Canada.' Pp. 191–218 in *Childcare Policy at the Crossroads: Gender and Welfare State Restructuring,* edited by Sonya Michel and Rianne Mahon. New York and London: Routledge.

Manser, Marilyn E., and Garnett Picot. 1999a. 'The Role of Self-Employment in U.S. and Canada.' *Monthly Labor Review* 122: 10–25.

– 1999b. 'Self-Employment in Canada and the United States.' *Perspectives on Labour and Income* 11(3): 37–44.

Marlow, Sue, and Adam Strange. 1994. 'Female Entrepreneurs – Success by Whose Standards?' Pp. 172–84 in *Women in Management: A Developing Presence,* edited by Morgan Tanton. London and New York: Routledge.

Marshall, Katherine. 1999. 'Employment after Childbirth.' *Perspectives on Labour and Income* 11(3): 18–25.

– 1999. 'Working Together – Self-Employed Couples,' *Perspectives on Labour and Income* 11(4): 9–13.

– 2003. 'Benefiting from Extended Parental Leave.' *Perspectives on Labour and Income* 15(2): 15–21.

Mauthner, Natasha, and Andrea Doucet. 2003. 'Reflexive Accounts and Accounts of Reflexivity in Qualitative Data Analysis.' *Sociology* 37(3): 413–31.

Maxwell, Judith. 2001. *Towards a Common Citizenship: Canada's Social and Economic Choices*. Ottawa: Canadian Policy Research Networks.

– 2003. 'Transformations and Visions.' *Network News* (Summer). Ottawa: Canadian Policy Research Networks.

McDaniel, Susan. 1997. 'Serial Employment and Skinny Government: Reforming Caring and Sharing among Generations.' *Canadian Journal of Aging* 16(3).

McGilly, Frank. 1998. *An Introduction to Canada's Public Social Services*. Toronto: Oxford University Press.

McGregor, Judy, and David Tweed. 2002. 'Profiling a New Generation of Female Business Owners in New Zealand: Networking, Mentoring and Growth.' *Gender, Work and Organization* 9(4): 420–38.

McManus, Patricia A. 1994. 'Autonomy, Dependency, and Mobility: Self-Employed Women in the United States and the Federal Republic of Germany.' Presented to the Research Committee on Social Stratification of the International Sociological Association at the 13th Work Congress of Sociology, Bielefeld, Germany.

McMichael, Philip. 2000. *Development and Social Change: A Global Perspective*. Thousand Oaks, CA: Pine Forge.

McRobbie, Angela. 1997. 'A New Kind of Rag Trade?' Pp. 275–89 in *No Sweat: Fashion, Free Trade, and the Rights of Garment Workers*, edited by Andrew Ross. New York: London.

Meager, N. 1992. 'The Fall and Rise of Self-Employment (Again): A Comment on Bogenhold and Staber.' *Work, Employment and Society* 6(1): 127–34.

Mirchandani, Kiran. 1998. 'Protecting the Boundary: Teleworker Insights on the Expansive Concept of 'Work.' *Gender and Society* 12(2): 167–86.

– 1999. 'Feminist Insight on Gendered Work: New Directions in Research on Women and Entrepreneurship.' *Gender, Work and Organization* 6(4): 224–35.

Moore, Carol S., and Richard E. Mueller. 2002. 'The Transition from Paid to Self-Employment in Canada: The Importance of Push Factors.' *Applied Economics* 34(6): 791–801.

Moore, Dorothy P. 1999. 'Women Entrepreneurs: Approaching a New Millennium.' Pp. 371–89 in *Handbook of Gender and Work*, edited by Gary Powell. Thousand Oaks, CA: Sage Publications.

Moore, Dorothy P., and E. Holly Buttner. 1997. *Women Entrepreneurs: Moving Beyond the Glass Ceiling*. Thousand Oaks, CA: Sage Publications.

Morse, J. 1995. 'Designing Funded Qualitative Research.' Pp. 220–35 in *The Handbook of Qualitative Research*, edited by Norman Denzin and Yvonna Lincoln. Thousand Oaks, CA: Sage Publications.

Morse, J., and P.A. Field. 1995. *Qualitative Research Methods for Health Professionals*. 2nd ed. Thousand Oaks, CA: Sage Publications.

Myles, John, and Adnan Turgeun. 1994. 'Comparative Studies in Class Structure.' *Annual Review of Sociology* 20: 103–24.

Neufeld, Anne, Margaret Harrison, Miriam Stewart, Karen D. Hughes, and Denise Spitzer. 2002. 'Immigrant Women: Making Connections to Community Resources for Support in Family Caregiving.' *Qualitative Health Research* 12(6): 751–68.

Nippert-Eng, Christena E. 1996. *Home and Work: Negotiating Boundaries through Everyday Life.* Chicago: University of Chicago Press.

O'Connor, Julia S., Ann Shola Orloff, and Sheila Shaver. 1999. *States, Markets, Families: Gender, Liberalism and Social Policy in Australia, Canada, Great Britain and the United States.* Cambridge: Cambridge University Press.

OECD. 1994. *Women and Structural Change: New Perspectives.* Paris: OECD

– 1996. *SMEs: Employment, Innovation and Growth.* Paris: OECD.

– 1997. *Women Entrepreneurs in Small and Medium Enterprises: A Major Force in Innovation and Job Creation: Synthesis.* Paris: OECD. Retrieved 12 January 2004 (http://www.oecd.org/document).

– 2000a. 'The Partial Renaissance of Self-Employment.' OECD Employment Outlook. Paris: OECD.

– 2000b. *Is There a New Economy?: First Report on the OECD Growth Project.* Paris: OECD.

– 2000c. *Small and Medium Enterprise Outlook.* Paris: OECD.

– 2000d. 'Small and Medium-Sized Enterprises: Local Strength, Global Reach.' *OECD Observer* (June).

– 2000e. 2nd OECD Conference on Women Entrepreneurs in SMEs: Realising the Benefits of Globalisation and the Knowledge-Based Economy: Conference Recommendations. Paris: OECD. Retrieve 12 January 2004 (http://www.oecd.org/document).

Orser, Barbara. 1999. 'Growing Pains: Why Do Men's Businesses Outpace Women's? *Chatelaine* (November).

– 2003. *A Pilot Study about Federal SME Policies to Support Women Business Owners and Trade.* Ottawa: Department of Foreign Affairs and International Trade and Status of Women Canada.

– 2004. 'Perceptions of Success and Public Policy.' Presentation to *Sustaining the Momentum: An Economic Forum on Women Entrepreneurs,* Ottawa, 27–9 October. Conference CD. Ottawa: Industry Canada.

Orser, Barbara, and Sandy Hoggarth-Scott. 1998. 'Case Analysis of Canadian Self-Employment Assistance Programming.' *Entrepreneurship and Regional Development,* 10: 51–69.

– 2002. 'Opting for Growth: Gender Dimensions of Choosing Enterprise Development.' *Canadian Journal of Administrative Sciences,* 19(3): 284–300.

Orser, Barbara, and Allan Riding. 2003. 'Estimating the Impact of a Gender-Based Training Program,' Unpublished paper.

Osberg, Lars, Fred Wien, and Jan Grude. 1995. *Vanishing Jobs: Canada's Changing Workplaces*. Toronto: Lorimer.

Osterman, Paul, ed. 1996. *Broken Ladders: Managerial Careers in the New Economy*. New York and Oxford: Oxford University Press.

– 1999. *Securing Prosperity: The American Labor Market: How It Changed and What to Do about It*. Princeton, NJ: Princeton University Press.

Parker, Rachel. 2001. 'The Myth of the Entrepreneurial Economy: Employment and Innovation in Small Firms.' *Work, Employment and Society* 15(2): 373–84.

Perlow, Leslie. 1998. 'Boundary Control: The Social Ordering of Work and Control in a High Tech Corporation.' *Administrative Science Quarterly* 43 (June): 328–57.

Perrons, Diane. 2003. 'The New Economy and Work-Life Balance: Conceptual Explorations and a Case Study of New Media.' *Gender, Work and Organization* 10(1): 65–93.

Peters, Joseph. 1999. *An Era of Change: Government Employment Trends in the 1980s and 1990s*. Ottawa: Canadian Policy Research Networks.

Peterson, Rein. 1999. *Global Entrepreneurship Monitor: 1999 Canadian National Executive Report*. Retrieved 14 November 2003 (www.gemconsortium.org/document.asp?id=278).

– 2001. *Global Entrepreneurship Monitor: 2001 Canadian National Executive Report*. Retrieved 14 November 2003 (www.gemconsortium.org/document.asp?id=278).

Picot, Garnett, and Andrew Heisz. 2000. 'The Performance of the 1990s Canadian Labour Market.' *Canadian Public Policy* 26, supp. 1: 7–25.

Pink, Daniel. 2001. *Free Agent Nation: How America's New Independent Workers Are Transforming the Way We Live*. New York: Warner Books.

Piore, Michael J., and Charles F. Sabel. 1984. *The Second Industrial Divide: Possibilities for Prosperity*. New York: Basic Books.

Porter, Ann. 2003. *Gendered States: Women, Unemployment Insurance, and the Political Economy of the Welfare State in Canada, 1945–1997*. Toronto: University of Toronto Press.

Poster, Winifred, and Zakia Salime. 2002. 'The Limits of Microcredit: Transnational Feminism and USAID Activities in the United States and Morocco.' Pp. 189–219 in *Women's Activism and Globalization*, edited by Nancy A. Naples and Manish Desai. New York and London: Routledge.

Project Tsunami. 2004. *Project Tsunami*. Retrieved 24 May 2004 (http://www.projecttsunami.org/).

Raheim, Salome, and Jacquelyn Bolden. 1995. 'Economic Empowerment of

Low-Income Women through Self-Employment Programs.' *Affilia* 10(2): 138–54.

Reed, Kimberly A. 2001. *Managing Our Margins: Women Entrepreneurs in Suburbia*. New York and London: Routledge.

Reich, Robert. 2001. *The Future of Success*. New York: Alfred A. Knopf.

Reinharz, Shulamit. 1992. *Feminist Methods in Social Research*. Oxford: Oxford University Press.

Reskin, Barbara F., and Irene Padavic. 2002. *Women and Men at Work*. 2nd ed. Thousand Oaks, CA: Pine Forge Press.

Revenue Canada.1998. *Employee or Self-Employed?* Catalogue RC4110(E) 1219. Ottawa: CCRA.

Reynolds, Paul D., Michael Hay, and S. Michael Camp. 1999. *Global Entrepreneurship Monitor, 1999 Executive Report*. Retrieved 5 August 2003 (http://www.gemconsortium.org/download/1068315283406/WebGlobalGEMReport11.12_1.pdf).

Reynolds, Paul D., William D. Bygrave, Erkko Autio, Larry W. Cox, and Michael Hay. 2002. *Global Entrepreneurship Monitor, 2002 Executive Report*. Retrieved 5 August 2003 (http://www.gemconsortium.org/download/1068315283406/WebGlobalGEMReport11.12_1.pdf).

Richards, Thomas J., and Lynn Richards, 1995. 'Using Computers in Qualitative Research.' Pp. 445–62 in *The Handbook of Qualitative Research*, edited by Norman Denzin and Yvonna Lincoln. Thousand Oaks, CA: Sage Publications.

Robertson, Heather. 1997. *Taking Care of Business: Stories of Canadian Women Entrepreneurs*. Bolton, ON: Fenn Publishing Company.

Rooney, Jennifer, Donna Lero, Karen Korabik and Denise L. Whitehead with Mona Abbondanza, Jocelyne Tougar, Jane Boyd, and Lise Bourque. 2003. *Self-Employment for Women: Policy Options that Promote Equality and Economic Opportunities*. Ottawa: Status of Women Canada.

Rose, Michael. 2003. 'Good Deal, Bad Deal: Job Satisfaction in Occupations.' *Work, Employment and Society* 17(3): 503–30.

Rowe, Reba, and William E. Snizek. 2003. 'Gender Differences in Work Values.' Pp. 134–40 in *Workplace/Women's Place: An Anthology*, edited by Paula J. Dubeck and Dana Dunn. 2nd ed. Los Angeles: Roxbury Publishing.

Rubin, Ellie. 1999. *Bulldog: Spirit of the New Entrepreneur*. Toronto: HarperCollins.

Rubin, Irene B., and Herbert Rubin. 1995. *Qualitative Interviewing: The Art of Hearing Data*. Thousand Oaks, CA: Sage Publications.

Ryscavage, Paul. 1995. 'A Surge in Growing Income Inequality?' *Monthly Labor Review* 118 (August): 51–61.

Sassen, Saskia. 2002. 'Global Cities and Survival Circuits.' Pp. 254–74 in *Global*

Women: Nannies, Maids, and Sex Workers in the New Economy, edited by Barbara Ehrenreich and Arlie Hochschild. New York: Metropolitan Books.

Saunders, Ron. 2003. *Defining Vulnerablity in the Labour Market*. Research Paper W/21. Ottawa: Canadian Policy Research Networks.

Schrank, W.E. 1998. 'Benefiting Fishermen: Origins of Fishermen's Unemployment Insurance in Canada, 1935–57.' *Journal of Canadian Studies* 33(1): 61–85.

Schuetze, Herb J. 2002. 'Profiles of Tax Non-Compliance among the Self-Employed in Canada: 1969 to 1992.' *Canadian Public Policy* 28(2): 219–38.

Schwartz, Joe. 1992. 'Low-wage Workers Growing Rapidly.' *American Demographics* (July): 12, 17.

Séguin, Rhéal. 2004. 'Quebec to Assume Control of Parental-Leave Program.' *Globe and Mail*, 20 May, A12.

Sennett, Richard. 1998. *The Corrosion of Character: The Personal Consequences of Work in the New Capitalism*. New York: W.W. Norton and Company.

Sexton, Donald. 1989. 'Growth Decisions and Growth Patterns of Women-owned Enterprise.' Pp. 135–49 in *Women-Owned Businesses*, edited by Oliver Hagan. New York: Praeger.

Sherman, Barrie, and Phil Judkins. 1995. *Licensed to Work*. London: Cassell.

Shirk, Martha, and Ann S. Wadia. 2004. *Kitchen Table Entrepreneurs: How Eleven Women Escaped Poverty and Became Their Own Bosses*. Boulder, CO: Westview Press.

Siltanen, Janet. 1994. *Locating Gender: Occupational Segregation, Wages and Domestic Responsibilties*. London: University College London Press.

Simpson, Sandra M. 1991. 'Women Entrepreneurs.' Pp. 113–30 in *Women at Work: Psychological and Organizational Perspectives*, edited by Jerry Firth-Cozens and Michael West. Milton Keynes: Open University Press.

Smeaton, Deborah. 2003. 'Self-Employed Workers: Calling the Shots or Hesitant Independents? A Consideration of the Trends.' *Work, Employment and Society* 17(2): 379–91.

Smith, Vicki. 2001. *Crossing the Great Divide: Worker Risk and Opportunity in the New Economy*. Ithaca, NY: Cornell University Press.

Sokoloff, Heather. 2004. '40% Get Nothing for Maternity Leave,' *National Post*, A1, A10.

Spector, Paul. 1997. *Job Satisfaction: Application, Assessment, Causes and Consequences*. Thousand Oaks, CA: Sage Publications.

Standing, Guy. 1989. 'Global Feminization through Flexible Labour.' *World Development* 17(7): 1077–95.

– 1999. *Global Labour Flexibility: Seeking Distributive Justice*. London: Macmillan.

Statistics Canada. 1997. *Labour Force Update: The Self-Employed*. Ottawa: Statistics Canada.

– 1998a. *Labour Force Update: Canada–US Labour Market Comparison*. Ottawa: Statistics Canada

– 1998b. *Work Arrangements in the 1990s*. Ottawa: Statistics Canada, Analytic Report No. 8. Catalogue 71–535–MPB.

– 2000. *Women in Canada 2000: A Gender-Based Statistical Report*. Ottawa: Statistics Canada.

– 2003. *Guide to the Labour Force Survey*. Ottawa: Statistics Canada. Available on-line at: http://www.statcan.ca/english/freepub/71-543-GIE/71-543-GIE03001.pdf (accessed April 10/2003).

– 2003a. 'Working Hours in Canada and the United States,' *The Daily*, 11 September.

– 2003b. 'General Social Survey: Social Support and Aging.' *The Daily*, 2 September.

– 2003c. *Canada's Retirement Income Programs: A Statistical Overview, 1990–2000*. Ottawa: Statistics Canada. Catalogue 74–507–XIE.

– 2003d. *Income of Canadian Families. 2001 Census Analysis*. Ottawa: Statistics Canada. Catalogue 96–F0030XIE2001014.

Statistics Canada and Human Resources Development Canada. 2000. *Survey of Self-Employment in Canada: Microdata User Guide*. Ottawa: Statistics Canada and HRDC.

Stevenson, Lois. 1986. 'Against All Odds: The Entrepreneurship of Women.' Journal of Small Business Management 24(4): 30–6.

– 1990. 'Some Methodological Problems Associated with Research Women Entrepreneurs.' *Journal of Business Ethics* 9: 439–46.

– 2004. 'Multi-country Perspectives on Women Entrepreneurs: Where Does Canada Fit?' Presentation to *Sustaining the Momentum: An Economic Forum on Women Entrepreneurs*, Ottawa, 27–9 October. Conference CD. Ottawa: Industry Canada.

Storey, John. 1994. *Understanding the Small Business Sector*. London and New York: Routledge.

Swift, Catherine. 2001. 'Small Business Really Fires Our Economy.' *Edmonton Journal*, 15 August, A11.

Tabi, Martin, and Stephanie Langlois. 2003. 'Quality of Jobs Added in 2002.' *Perspectives on Labour and Income* 15(1): 34–9.

Tal, Benjamin. 2000. *Self-Employment in Canada: Trends and Prospects*. Toronto: Canadian Imperial Bank of Commerce.

Taniguchi, Hiromi. 2002. 'Determinants of Women's Entry into Self-Employment.' *Social Science Quarterly* 83(3): 875–93.

Taylor, Mark. 1997. *The Changing Picture of Self-Employment in Britain*. Colchester: Institute for Labour Research, University of Essex.

Terkel, Studs. 1972. *Working*. New York: The New York Press.

Thompson, Elizabeth. 2005. 'Minister Wants EI Programs Expanded,' *Edmonton Journal*, 28 January, A5.

Thorne, S. 2000. 'Civil Servants Burning Out as Work Piles Up.' *Edmonton Journal*, 21 April, A3.

Thrasher, Barbara, and Madelon Smid. 1998. *Smart Women: Canadian Entrepreneurs Talk about Making Money, Leadership, Management and Self-Development*. Toronto: Macmillan.

Torjman, Sherri. 2000. *Survival of the Fittest Employment Policy*. Ottawa: Caledon Institute of Social Policy.

Townson, Monica. 2000. *Reducing Poverty among Older Women: The Potential of Retirement Income Policies*. Ottawa: Status of Women Canada.

– 2003. *Women in Non-Standard Jobs: The Public Policy Challenge*. Ottawa: Status of Women Canada.

Trudeau, Gilles. 2002. 'Changing Employment Relationships and the Unintentional Evolution of Canadian Labour Relations Policy.' *Canadian Public Policy* 28(1): 149–52.

United Kingdom, Department of Trade and Industry. 2003. *A Strategic Framework for Women's Enterprise*. U.K. Department of Trade and Industry. DTI/5000l/04/03. URN 03/867.

Vannoy, Dana and Paula J. Dubeck., eds. 1998. *Challenges for Work and Family in the Twenty-First Century*. Hawthorne, NY: Aldine de Gruyter.

Voet, Rian. 1998. *Feminism and Citizenship*. Thousand Oaks, CA: Sage Publications.

Vosko, Leah. 2000. *Temporary Work: The Gendered Rise of a Precarious Employment Relationship*. Toronto: University of Toronto Press.

– 2002. 'The Pasts and (Futures) of Feminism and Political Economy in Canada: Reviving the Debate.' *Studies in Political Economy* 68: 55–85.

Vosko, Leah F., and Nancy Zukewich. 2003. 'Challenging "Choice": Gender and Precarious Self-Employment.' Presented at Workshop on Precarious Employment in the Canadian Labour Market, York University, 26–7 September.

Vosko, Leah F., Nancy Zukewich, and Cynthia Cranford. 2003. 'Precarious Jobs: A New Typology of Employment.' *Perspectives on Labour and Income* 15 (Fall): 16–26.

Walby, Sylvia. 1997. *Gender Transformations*. London and New York: Routledge.

Wallace, M. 1998. 'Downsizing the American Dream: Work and Family at Century's End.' Pp. 23–38 in *Challenges for Work and Family in the Twenty-First Century*, edited by Dana Vannoy and Paula J. Dubeck. Hawthorne, NY: Aldine de Gruyter.

Walsh, Mark. 1999. 'Working Past Age 65.' *Perspectives on Labour and Income* 11(2): 16–20.

Ward, Thomas B. 2004. 'Cognition, Creativity, and Entrepreneurship.' *Journal of Business Venturing* 19(2): 173–88.

Weeks, Julie. 2000. 'The Face of Women Entrepreneurs: What We Know Today,' Panel 1 in Workshop 4: Improving Knowledge about Women's Entrepreneurship. Presented at The 2nd OECD Conference on Women Entrepreneurs in SMEs: Realising the Benefits of Globalisation and the Knowledge-Based Economy, 29–30 November, Paris 2000.

– 2004. 'Best Practices in Women's Enterprise Development in the United States: Lessons Learned.' Presentation to Sustaining the Momentum: An Economic Forum on Women Entrepreneurs, Ottawa, 27–9 October. Conference CD. Ottawa: Industry Canada

Westergaard, John. 1995. *Who Gets What? The Hardening of Class Inequality in the Late Twentieth Century.* Cambridge: Polity Press.

Wilthagen, Ton. 2002. 'The Flexibility-Security Nexus: New Approaches to Regulating Employment and Labour Markets.' Presented to the British Journal of Industrial Relations *The Politics of Employment Relations* Conference, 16–17 September, Windsor, U.K.

Wilthagen, Ton, and R. Rogowski. 2002. 'Legal Regulation of Transitional Labour Markets.' Pp. 233–73 in *The Dynamics of Full Employment: Social Integration through Transitional Labour Markets,* edited by G. Schmid and B. Gazier. Cheltenham: Edward Elgar.

Williams, Cara. 2003. 'Sources of Workplace Stress.' *Perspectives on Labour and Income* 15(3): 23–30.

Williams, Toni. 2003. 'Requiem for Microcredit? The Demise of a Romantic Ideal.' *Banking and Finance Law Review* 19: 145–98.

Winson, Anthony, and Belinda Leach. 2002. *Contingent Work, Disrupted Lives: Labour and Community in the New Rural Economy.* Toronto: University of Toronto Press.

Wong, Ging, Harold Henson, and Chris Riddell.1998. 'Earnings Impact of Self-Employment Assistance for the Canadian Unemployed, 1987–1996.' Ottawa: Human Resources Development Canada, Strategic Evaluation and Monitoring.

Wood, Stephen, ed. 1989. *The Transformation of Work? Skill, Flexibility and the Labour Process.* London: Unwin Hyman.

Yaccato, Joanne T., with Paula Jubinville. 1998. *Raising Your Business: A Canadian Women's Guide to Entrepreneurship.* Scarborough, ON: Prentice Hall.

Yeager, Mary A. 1999. 'Will There Ever Be a Feminist Business History?'

Pp. 3–43 in *Women in Business*, edited by Mary A. Yeager. Northampton, MA: Edward Elgar.

Zeytinoglu, Isik U., and Jacinta K. Muteshi. 2000. 'A Critical Review of Flexible Labour: Gender, Race, and Class Dimensions of Economic Restructuring.' *Resources for Feminist Research* 27(3/4): 97–120.

Index

DATE DUE

GAYLORD

PRINTED IN U.S.A.